WELCOME ABOARD!

HERE'S WHAT PEOPLE WHO HAVE FLOWN WITH HEATHER McKEOWN HAVE TO SAY ABOUT "ABOVE AND BEYOND"

"Heather is personable, passionate, and committed to bringing positivity and kindness to everyone she comes in contact with. She is the ultimate optimistic, positive thinker!" **—DEBRA,** *former flight attendant*

"Flying with Heather is a breath of fresh air in any stuffy airplane cabin!!" **—JIM,** *flight attendant, Mexico City, Mexico*

"I've been a passenger on a flight with Heather, and observing how she responds to cranky, nervous, and impatient passengers is a joy to behold. She is an angel in the sky with an EQ (Emotional Intelligence) that is off the charts. I've also been privileged to read Heather's stories. Wow! This lady can write!" **—JOEL BLOCK, PH.D.,** *Clinical Faculty, Einstein College of Medicine*

"Being up in the air with Heather is something that no airfare booking site, nor any safety card, nor any boarding pass, nor any airport monitor can ever attempt to describe… Actually, being on the ground with her actually makes one feel they are soaring through cloudless skies headed towards a runway paved with platinum!" **—JAY LESLIE,** *member of vocal group The Tokens ("The Lion Sleeps Tonight")*

"Heather McKeown's stories are worth reading because she has a deep understanding of the human condition and how and why we relate to each other the way we do. You'll walk away from this experience with a love for life, a lust for learning, and a big ol' smile on your face." **—ETHAN DEZOTELLE,** *Director, Rural Partnerships*

"Working on the operational side of SkyNation for me has always been more of a passion than a job. I love being outside and working around 'things.' They either work or they don't. The people outside also are just EASY to deal with. You ask a question you get an answer, and since we're in a deadline-oriented atmosphere (the ramp at the airport) there's not too much discussion…You say it, you do it, you move on to the next issue. Heather provides me with a refreshing sense of what it means to be human and her writing captures it all beautifully within another realm of my airline and our industry. She brings a humanness (and all the complications that go along with that) to a world that I'm in. What I see in black and white Heather brings forward in vivid color. Her writing does EXACTLY the same thing, which is why I love to read what she writes." **—MARC,** *Operations Manager, cargo*

"I had the pleasure of meeting Heather in january of 2004... She was a passenger on the aircraft I was working to Burlington, VT... You immediately noticed her, her personality was on the aircraft before she was... I had the pleasure of talking to her during the flight... She told me she was too short to be a flight attendant... And I told her that was so not true... that she should apply. And I knew in my gut that the next time I saw Heather... she would be in a SkyNation uniform... And guess what!!! Heather belongs on an airplane... She is fabulous,,. Approachable... Makes you feel welcome and at ease, which is so important to be good at your job... And a great sense of humor. She gets complimentary letters, from customers on a monthly basis, which is difficult to do... I'm so glad she is here, and SkyNation is very lucky to have her." **—LUCINDA,** *flight attendant*

"The ultimate optimist goes through the darkness to realize it was, in the end, worthwhile. Heather McKeown's project allows us the light on the other side." **—COLUM McCANN,** *author of Let the Great World Spin*

"Since our first meeting, and through the stories she has written, Heather's charm, wit, and sincere kindness have warmed my heart. I've never met anyone with so much love to offer. Heather is a wonderful example of how more people should be. She is my best friend and the love of my life!" **—RICK BUSHEY**

"As a friend and coworker, I marvel at Heather McKeown's ability to make profound connections with anyone who crosses her path. *Above and Beyond* vividly describes these serendipitous encounters. Heather's openness reminds us that life-enhancing moments or life-long friends may be found anywhere, even on the shortest flight." **—HEATHER,** *flight attendant*

"I have known Heather since I was a child. She was a contemporary of my older brother Frank, who is ten years my senior. Heather is someone I have always had great respect for. Indeed, in many ways, she has been a role model for me personally. The attributes I admire most about her? Her positive spirit, even during times of great personal strain. Her wonderful sense of humor — and fun. Her boundless energy. Her love and her dedication to her children. Her determination to achieve her personal goals, but never at the expense of her beliefs and integrity. Her open-mindedness. Her love of people (as opposed to material things). And her love of life in general." **—MATTHEW FARFAN,** *Historian / Writer / Editor, Author, The Vermont-Quebec Border: Life on the Line*

"Being vulnerable, available, and never missing an opportunity to connect with someone in the air is Heathers mission! Being compassionate, understanding, and listening to her customers is how she completes the mission. These stories of Heather's travels are touching and eye-opening.

As Heather's Inflight Supervisor I have been reading her stories for the past three years. In that time I have been deeply touched and moved by her ability to connect to her customers! Heather never misses an opportunity to make a connection! I know that you too will enjoy reading about her journeys and the impact Heather has had on people's lives. Also the impact that her customers have had on her life." **—SHAUN,** *Supervisor, Inflight Service*

"Through all the years I've worked with Heather, it has always been an honor and a privilege. Heather has a connection with people that I have never seen before. Not only is she caring and compassionate, she is an amazing person who has a very special gift." **—ROGER,** *flight attendant, Buffalo, NY*

"Heather has the gift of translating words, like poetry, into visual and emotional scenes. I always look forward to her next correspondence." **—LYNDA,** *flight attendant*

ABOVE

AND

BEYOND

ABOVE AND BEYOND

INSPIRING ADVENTURES INTO THE BLUE

HEATHER McKEOWN

This work remains faithful to actual events and real people, although some details have been altered to protect the privacy of individuals, corporations, and the sanctity of locations.

FIRST EDITION: November 2011

Published by VANTAGE POINT BOOKS
Vantage Press, Inc.
419 Park Avenue South
New York, NY 10016
www.vantagepointbooks.com

Manufactured in the United States of America
ISBN: 978-1-936467-12-9

Library of Congress Cataloging-in-Publication data are on file.

0 9 8 7 6 5 4 3 2 1

Cover design by Victor Mingovits

Thank you, Dad

CONTENTS

PART TWO: TAKEOFF

PART THREE: CRUISING ALTITUDE

PART FOUR: A BIT OF TURBULENCE

PART FIVE: INITIAL DESCENT

PART SIX: LANDING

INTRODUCTION

ANYONE WORKING IN the service industry can allow a callous sensibility to build between the customer and himself. The demands of the public can injure the thin skin of people who usually enter service because of the simple desire to serve, save, entertain, and enjoy customers. Becoming part of the decor on a plane, for instance, is the fate accepted by some of us. Anonymity may become destination, because even as we deliver drinks, snacks, safety, and smiles, so many of us are ignored. Yet we can overcome this natural reaction to being dismissed and classified as nonentities while we provide whatever the customer needs or desires. Fatigue and burnout are two by-products of service to the public. The schedule is subject to unexpected changes that can alter not only our sleep patterns but the private lives we cherish.

Overcoming all the problems inherent to our chosen job takes a bit of effort, but it certainly can be done. Finding a purpose to be the best we can be to folks we meet once and may never see again works for me. How? I look only for the positive in each person as they board any flight I'm working. Everyone comes aboard with a clean slate, and even if they're having a really bad day or terrible life, I know that it's my personal challenge to give them a bit of unconditional love during the time they spend in my little home away from home. My plane. I don't always get an equal return on my investment. Sometimes I get less, but most of the time I get much more than I bargained for. You see, people like to be heard; listening to what they wouldn't tell anyone else or letting them vent or express themselves, one-on-one, leaves me feeling informed, and the speaker usually feels relieved. Getting personal, holding a hand, touching an arm, giving a hug, or kneeling beside someone just because it seems like a good idea at the time is my way.

Fatigue and burnout are overcome by giving some positive energy to a lot of people from boarding to landing. It's a very easy mathematical equation. Here's my proven formula:

Energy to the power of one multiplied by however many people I'm hosting on my plane equals what I get in return. I'm surprised the concentrated return of positivity doesn't short out all my circuits, but it doesn't. It simply charges my batteries, and I store the energy for the next flight.

When working with the public we need a full spectrum of frequencies and pitch-perfect ear to receive every mood brought aboard. Meeting up to six hundred individuals daily has me turning the dial on my internal receiver just about that many times. Yet to bring everyone into a harmonious melding of souls, I try to reach a vibration that resonates universally. Most flights hum along in perfect synchronicity. Start with an open mind and a loving heart, and you'll make no mistake. The subtle shift in the energies of the collected group will be palpable before takeoff if you give of yourself and remain totally open at first sight. This I promise.

Whenever I hear complaints about how hard done by folks are who serve, I suggest they try to find a deeper purpose than the topical and transient chores we do by rote. Look into the eyes and hearts of the people you're meeting. Look into their minds. Feel the love pouring out of you, and they'll send some back. Guaranteed. Sometimes they'll just tell you a bit about themselves, and that will be enough.

That's what I do. I listen and I learn.

We all do.

Welcome to my plane.

Shall we board?

PART ONE

BOARDING

ARRIVING HOME

THE FIRST THING I saw upon my arrival home were the two long-stemmed yellow roses surrounded by ferns and perched in a bud vase on the kitchen table. As I bent to appreciate the floral essence, my immediate thought was, "I knew he'd do something like this." At the base of the display were two of those tiny cards that accompany bouquets from the florist's.

8/23/04
My dearest Heather,
Congratulations for never having to wonder what might have been. I admire your courage.
With love, Rick

Courage? I have courage? I always figured it takes a brave person to accept a life without questions, without the sleeplessness caused by unquenchable curiosity. So I've never considered myself brave in that way. Au contraire, claustrophobia would overcome me within seconds if I were sentenced to forever live a life without that adrenalin rush brought on by changes and new people, problems and challenges. That's why I live in Vermont, for heaven's sake. Nothing's guaranteed or totally secure—except our granite-solid love of this Green Mountain State.

What would it be like to hold back and never step off the cliff of supposed security into the abyss of personally uncharted thin air? Would breathing stop, eyes go blind, ears turn deaf, and complete physical numbness ensue? For some, normal life functions depend on external stimuli, with adventures and question marks ending almost every thought. These are the individuals who die little deaths every time they see a dog chained to someone's back porch, and empathetically feel the pains suffered by everyone from the misunderstood or the unjustly accused to the dominated wife of an insecure man. The sort of person who jumps into the unknown, unsure, and unexpected realms that surround us isn't the type who looks back as the final tally of life is posted for their perusal, before some final curtain descends, and says, "Damn. I woulda', coulda', shoulda'." It's more likely that they smile with every checkmark on the "I Tried" side of the list, and frown, shake their head, and utter an "Ah, shoot" as checks are made in the "Played It Safe" column. After flying to my part-time partnership in Manhattan for a year, I'd become aware of the joys of being on a SkyNation plane. I found, even though I was loving my work at the Muscular Therapy Center of New York, the flights between Burlington and New York were something I enjoyed even more than massaging the masses.

On August 23, 2004, I was submerged in a melee of people who were, at first glance, ordinary in their demeanor. We were all in one place at the same time to compete for a chance to work for the only company that's turned me on since I stored all my corporate trappings and went into the wonderful world of the self-employed many decades ago. Vowing never to darken the doorstep of another place of normal working conditions, I've become spoiled by my ability to access leisure time when needed and jaded further by the depressions, failing physical health, and frustrations of all my friends who've steadily climbed the corporate ladders to great heights with immense financial gains but at greater costs to mind, body, and soul.

There were about forty of us ready to toss whatever we'd become used to aside for the chance to be a part of a family.

"I'm an only child, and I'd love an extended family."

"I've been a flight attendant for two other airlines. I've lived your dream."

"I'll go the extra mile."

"I love learning about new cultures."

The question "Why should SkyNation hire you?" was answered in so many ways, spanning the entire spectrum of human emotions. Yet, in all the responses, one theme resonated:

"I'll change my life for SkyNation if you'll just give me the chance. I'll jump off this cliff for you if you'll catch me. I'll risk my security because I believe in SkyNation, and I believe in myself."

You see, most of us have been jumping all of our lives, hoping to be picked up by a passing airliner.

After interacting from 9 a.m. until late afternoon with this eclectic group I was hoping at least thirty-five of us would be chosen because I wanted to see these incredible people again and know them even better—and I wanted them to succeed. They touched me with their biographical vignettes, uncensored frustrations with their present or past employers, and the rawness of their hunger for this new chapter in their lives.

Always, after scholarship pageants, we hear the same worn-out cliché from every competitor: "All the girls were so nice, I wanted *all* of us to win." I never bought that for a minute. I figured it was just some expected rhetoric from the typical beauty queen wannabe. That's all changed now. The candidates vying for a flight attendant title that day were from all walks of life with every conceivable talent and educational profile. I was totally inspired by every one of these people! What a deep pool of talent filled that room! Everything from a woman working on her PhD, to a single mom finishing a master's degree and a fellow who rides canoes down snowy mountain slopes, to me, a massage therapist, editor/publisher of a subtle counter-suicide prevention newspaper for teens, mediator, and granny, fifty-five going steady. Everyone trying out for an in-flight job has lived life with a certain flair, a definite spark, and with a bit of JP-1 jet fuel, this spark will ignite and become a beacon when this group moves as one into the SkyNation family. We became a team on the day we met. Gosh, I hope we all get a chance to see each other for years to come while we strive to make this family work and grow.

Unlike the naysayers and pooh-poohers dotting our lifetime landscape, we understood each other. Life begins anew daily for those of us who forsake the expected, the mundane, and the minutiae of a dull existence to work for something larger, be it a philosophical ideal, emotional satisfaction, or spiritual fulfillment. Nobody can get any of this by passively accepting a status quo existence. If it takes jumping off the peak of an already secure mountain to see if the updraft will further elevate one's being, then there were about three dozen leapers in that room that day. For once, I felt like I belonged.

The second card from my beloved, Rick, waiting for me at home read:

> Congratulations and Welcome Home.
> Love, Rick

I was "home" all day, too. I think, after the initial nerves and jitters had subsided, most of us at the review melted into each other, and the SkyNation team vibration resonated and touched us at a cellular level. If that's not being home, what is? If it's considered courageous to find home at the place where the intonation of that universally accepted mantra, *om*, is happening, then "om is where the brave heart is."

THE FIRST STEP

THE ADVENTURE THAT I'd wanted as a young woman became a reality in the same year I became a granny. Amazing how life happens, isn't it?

Fifty-three rejections based on my inconsequential physical stature between the ages of eighteen and twenty-one. I got over it: I worked; traveled; competed in grueling athletic endeavors; married; bore children; started (and still have) many businesses; divorced; endured postsecondary education in my forties, graduated, and gave the commencement speech a couple of times; married; divorced; and hosted TV talk shows. I haven't been bored for a minute. I absolutely love my previous life, really.

Yet that old song kept playing in my head, the one that was crooned at the turning points of a woman's life when she was strong enough to admit something was missing: "Is that all there is, my friend? If that's all there is, then let's keep dancing."

SkyNation hired me. For a month I attended SkyNation University, which took every second of spare time and the students' ability to breathe through a combination of spitfire teaching techniques and great accommodations. Anything else I've ever tackled in my life has gone down as easy compared to the unbelievable amount of knowledge force-fed to me during that amazing time under the tutelage of the most energetic professors I've ever feared. I didn't thrive; I survived.

Now I understand that the demanding challenges and schedule of SkyNation "Boot Camp and Charm School" was to prepare us, the flight attendants who are a part of this airline's team, for the chaos and adventure, challenges and well-earned gratification that a dream job provides.

I've "slipped the surly bonds of Earth," and I hope to see Cape Cod. John Gillespie Magee, Jr. wrote one of my two favorite poems, *High Flight*, in which 'slipped the surly bonds of Earth and touched the face of God" rings true for me. I've cut out this poem and glued it to a wall in our home in hopes that our grandson, Shea, feels what the author tried to convey.

The first fortnight of in-flight training was in Miami. By the time we were sent upcountry for the final two weeks in New York City, we were well on our way to becoming part of the SkyNation family of crew members. The second half of our education took place within our corporate offices in New York City. Symbolic of the mobility and forced adaptation to the constantly changing landscape/airscape that our new career would demand, the duality of our far-apart campuses did its duty.

Nowadays, new recruits remain at our fabulous Florida

base because the school was built in this location. Whereas the pioneers of our company were taught without the benefit of simulators and reality, today's new hires are brought up to speed with actual mock-ups of aircraft and technologically realistic onboard scenarios. What we learned through dictation and our imaginations, we now review annually in the most modern of teaching facilities. What hasn't changed from the days when I was trained is the overwhelming anticipation of putting our education to use after the wings have been pinned to our uniforms.

I grew up in Quebec, and when I graduated with a junior matriculation, my ambition, according to my yearbook, was "to learn French, Spanish, and German, grow three inches, and become a stewardess."

My mother, Bernice Althea (née Bilton) James, died on September 26, 1970. By the first of 1971, my dad had already decided that he'd never spend another Christmas alone. After reconnecting with Evelyn (née Strathdee) Munro, who had been his first-ever girlfriend, love was in the air. Healing for Dad was complete with the entrance of this healthy woman into his heart.

We were supposed to have healed, too. My brother, Alan, and I were told by all, "You must be glad that your mother's no longer in pain." We were glad. For Mom. In those days, when the world continued to turn at the same rate as always, Alan and I just couldn't jump back onto the planet. We had so much in common: many of the same weaknesses and strengths, funny bones, and energy level were evidence and proof that we were siblings. We could have been twins at certain points during our lives.

After Mom died, life returned to an outward appearance of normalcy for everyone. I was thrilled that Dad had found a kindred spirit for numerous reasons. I'd have two new sisters if they married. I'd be ousted from my position as chief cook and bottle washer at home, which would be awesome. Dad would spend nights laughing with Evelyn instead of visiting my hospitalized mother. Life should have been getting better, right? It should have *felt* better.

Who, at seventeen, understands grieving? The mourning process isn't supposed to follow the requisite dates on a calendar. Mom dies. Wake. Funeral. Lots of single women bring baking to the house. Back to school. Dad and I go for walks in the evenings because he's not going to the hospital anymore. Dad and Evelyn reconnect. Single ladies stop bringing junk food to the house. Why did everything seem so empty? What was wrong with me? I didn't even know Alan was hurting as much as I was because we didn't tell each other. In those days, we just didn't discuss our feelings because we were supposed to be relieved. We were supposed to carry on, have a stiff upper lip, get on with life. Why couldn't we? Alan and I just didn't understand our hearts.

By February 1971, I just wanted to quit school. Who'd ever heard of situational depression in those days? Graduating from one of only two schools that offered a senior matriculation option, which would count as two years of Quebec's compulsory precollege requirements, was an amazing academic opportunity. Jumping into this condensed academic program course load was a great challenge, but it's always been a family trait to take on twice as much as expected by societal norms. However, after losing Mom, I didn't have any passion for anything. I felt like I'd lost half of my heart and all of my ambition.

"Dad, I want to quit school."

"How about staying until your March vacation and then coming on a cross-Canada business trip with me?"

"Okay."

March came. We had a snowy ride to the Montreal International Airport for our predawn takeoff. Dad was a great driver in all weathers, and although I'd been registering an emotional flatline for months, I remember feeling pretty excited about this trip.

I'd grown up with aviation. Dad took us to our first air show when I was three or four. A child can pick up the scent of an adrenalin rush just like most animals can smell fear. I caught Dad's rush of excitement even before we got to that first air show. I was wearing a little pink dress with smocking and little shiny rhinestones on the front. We were outside, and Dad kept me looking up. I felt like I was going to fall backwards but I didn't care.

"Look, a flying boxcar."

Look, at this, at that. Whatever aircraft made its way overhead, Dad knew the name. When I see folks looking up at fireworks, I think of planes. Fireworks could never move me as much as the sight of an airplane on high. No matter how loud, colorful, or choreographed, fireworks will always fail to move me when compared to the thrill of looking up and seeing aerodynamics in action.

Dad caught the flying bug big time when I was about ten. He took flying lessons with heavy ground school courses and, by golly, he started going everywhere in a Cessna. He was making it happen. Best of all, he shared his love of aviation with Alan and me. We both suffered terribly from air sickness, but this didn't dampen my interest. I found that if I sat in the copilot's seat, I would only throw up a few times on the way to our summer cottage. It was worth it. Dad would watch as I turned a lighter shade of green and say, "Heather, take the controls. Keep us straight and level." I'd forget the part about being sick and follow his commands. It worked better than the antinauseant Dramamine!

For years we flew around together. Before I could drive a car, I could land a plane. I still have a tendency to center my car on the painted line on some highways. This isn't safe, but it sure brings back great memories.

Now, to get my mind back into academics, Dad was bribing me with what he knew would have a positive effect: a trip to the airport and my first commercial flight. Air Canada from Montreal, Quebec, to Vancouver, British Columbia.

Mother Nature had a different plan.

Our flight was canceled because of the weather, and we were booked on the next one. It kept snowing. The next one was canceled, and we were put on the later one. The snow continued to pile up. Then the announcement came: "All roads to the airport are closed and this airport is also closed." That was it—the announcement that helped mold my attitude when flights are canceled or I'm delayed from now till next Tuesday. Aah, sweet memories of a youthful adventure.

We were stuck in a jam-packed international airport with others going to even more exciting destinations than ours: Italy, France, Switzerland, England, Portugal, Greece, Spain, Hungary.

Montreal fashion is gorgeous; every woman was perfectly groomed, and each man was impeccably dressed.. We had to in those days, and we were proud to do so. For the entire day, as the population of the airport doubled and quadrupled—all the optimists believing that plows, snowblowers, and the weather would work in perfect harmony so we could take off—I watched people. Dad would say, "She knows how to conduct herself." "He is not being polite." "It's obvious *they* haven't flown before." His favorite line was, "Are you hungry?" We ate a few meals and people-watched. Most importantly, Dad was teaching me what was acceptable etiquette in an airport.

It was evident that we'd have to spend the night in the airport. Dad, the savvy traveler, knew where there were unoccupied gates with clean and comfy seats. I found a ladies room and took a sink bath, donned clean clothes, and fell asleep with the storm raging outside and Dad on guard close by. There was no security back then. (How many of you, dear readers, remember those innocent times?)

Day two in the airport was no different. No roads out or in. No flights in or out. The faces of the stranded were beginning to look familiar to me, and I started talking to people. Dad found other businessmen for companionship, and I began my wandering and chatting. This would become a lifelong habit with me in airports around the globe.

At one point an airline employee raised her hands and called for the attention of everyone nearby.

"Is there anyone here who can sing?" she yelled.

Hands rose. Not mine. I wanted to sing but was holding back. There was a powwow of sorts, and the few who'd volunteered began a pretty good tune. Others joined in.

Bystanders looked up and smiled. The singsong grew. People who'd been in other parts of the airport started coming over. The music got louder. Laughter between songs. A dignified man in a camel hair coat stepped forward. The crowd grew quiet. He assumed the posture of the great Caruso and began an Italian operatic favorite. There were tears. There were gasps. When he finished, he received the ovation of a couple thousand marooned people. At that point, I know I was thrilled to have canceled flights and two days under my belt at the Montreal International Airport YUL. I still love opera to this day. More importantly, I love gathering people during delays and starting impromptu music festivals. Life is what you make it. I began to fill the empty part of my heart with the songs of strangers. I still draw on the energies and talents of others to heal present-day injuries to my soul.

The Canadian ski team had its own set of songs. One was "Put All Your Faith in the Pill" and another was "Cocaine on the Brain." I was transfixed. I still can't ski, yet I would love to be good enough just to join a team that could sing with such conviction and humor. Remember, it was 1971, and I was a naive school girl who knew a Piper from a Mooney from a Cessna, but I couldn't tell you anything about sex and street drugs. Rock 'n' roll I knew, though, and the music in that airport never stopped from the first song to the first takeoff. What a blast.

By the time we finally made it onto a Vancouver-bound jet, I had already, absolutely decided that airport work was what I wanted more than anything else. What drama. What an adventure. What humor. What music. I was surer of my original high school ambition than ever before.

Our pretty and perfectly bilingual flight attendant was lovely and gracious. She answered my questions and never made me feel like I was being pesky. When you're flying cross-country, there's a lot of time for questions, but this patient young lady gave me great answers.

To my delight, when I went down to the Hotel Vancouver's restaurant for breakfast the morning after our flight, that very stewardess, in a red knit turtleneck and tailored black pants, joined me. She was absolutely the most perfect person I'd ever met, and I wanted to be just like her, have her job, and be nice to people. I'll never forget her kindness and indulgence.

On that same business trip, Dad and I flew Pacific Western through the Canadian Rockies. We drove from Banff to Calgary, but that wasn't nearly as thrilling as being on a plane, even though it was on the breathtaking Rogers Pass with the scenery and wild beasts everywhere. From Calgary it was Air Canada to Winnipeg. We finished off with an Air Canada trip home to Montreal.

"Dad, I still want to quit school," I told him on the first morning after our trip.

"The hell you will. Now you get up, get out, get to school, and for God's sake don't be so lazy."

I got my senior matric a few months later.

I perfected French, understand Spanish, and never learned a lick of German. I never grew those three inches, so I had fifty-two or fifty-three rejections from airlines all over hell's half acre and back. The years between 1972 and 1978 were marked with failure after failure in the height department. I never did get to be a stewardess in my youth. Luckily, in this day and age, all the physical requirements of old have been vanquished. Some of you may not know this, but in the early days of aviation, stewardesses had to be rather perfect in the eyes of beholders. Tall, tiny-waisted, perfectly groomed at all times and fully made-up. I wasn't acceptable to the carriers thirty years ago. I was short. I had the build of a thirteen-year-old. I was one hundred per cent naïve, too. Would I have been a good air hostess in my youth?

Nope. Instead I became a flight attendant in my early fifties. I'm not the beautiful young thing that was so nice to me. I'm a bit wrinkled, a granny, and yet I hope, in some small way, I touch lives as that Air Canada air hostess touched mine. I hope I make fun like that ground agent did when she brought a myriad of strangers together to sing.

I know that the flying public touches my heart every single day and makes life for this old granny a lot of fun.

I'm not sure, even now, that I'm able to jump into the normal games people play. Yet, miles above Mother Earth, in the rarified air of an aircraft, I feel steady on my feet, normal, joyous, in touch, in love, and in sync.

Thanks, Dad. I love you.

WE'VE COME A LONG WAY, BABY

THE HISTORY IN our collective memory reverberates with images of misdoing. Every nation, every mortal being has made mistakes, participated in both good and bad peer activity, and moved from point A to some other alphabetic landmark on the road to maturation. People have an average lifespan. Corporations come and go with the tides of consumerism or availability of raw materials or manpower. On average, democracies last about four hundred years. Where are we—as individuals, an airline, or a nation—on this vast yardstick of viability?

My company's vice president of Inflight Service, once said that we're in our adolescence. SkyNation the teenager: open for suggestions, a bit vulnerable, and in need of guidance. We have the energy, curiosity, and physical presence to take on all comers with a smile on our face and the dreams of a fulfilling adulthood. No dotage in sight for us who kick up our heels when school's out as we forge ahead through one growing pain after another. We have dreams unfettered by pessimism, but our reality has given all a bit of accelerated learning. We're a great company!

I prefer to say that SkyNation is spread out from the point of conception to the end game of omniscience. The evolutionary process of an industry, any industry, can be a positive process only if the participants think ahead while working to survive today. Perceptions of present-day onlookers will either benefit or hurt an organization down the road of Time. We have a great obligation to raise each other up socially, economically, physically, spiritually, and professionally right now. The obligation to open uncomfortable channels and launch our ideas to improve the human condition for those who will follow us is also immediate.

Even as airlines are born and then meet their demise, the industry continues to expand beyond the original expectations of those first-in-flight dreamers. When SkyNation is stripped down to raw components, it's all about me. Within each of us lie the seeds of what will be, and of these seeds, dreams are made. First, the full potential of one seed. Second, as a life is created, some cohesive force fueled by common goals, ranging from survival to saving the world, naturally exists. Then there's that incredible glue that holds us together as we surround ourselves with dreams and a shared belief that all is possible. Multiple and irreversible dreams. Not only those embodied by our five SkyNation values, but those we bring into this wonderful melting pot of a family that are products of our own family cultures. In other words, our twelve-thousand-plus crew members have more opportunity to spread good will and peace in this world than many other collectives anywhere! And we can do this, one by one by one, with every interaction with the millions of customers we meet every year in the airports on our system. We, with the power of one word, one touch, one smile, one kind word, or a listening ear can change this world for the better. Yes we can.

CRASH PAD LIFE

Our home away from home, close to our base airport

THE WEEK BEFORE graduation and nowhere to hang my hat. What's a girl to do? My class found itself in the crew lounge at JFK one evening. It must have been obvious to seasoned crew members that we were babes in the wood as we scanned the bulletin board for crash-pad possibilities, because a lovely, soft-spoken woman approached and said that her apartment did, indeed, have a bed or two to offer. "We are an older group and coed. The price is $210 monthly." The price was within my range, and I'm admittedly way past middle age and hoping against hope that our medical insurance eventually subsidizes the Botox patch. Being raised by my father and brother allowed me to render the coed information a nonissue. It's also my belief that estrogen overload in a confined space becomes less hostile when diluted by testosterone. I took my soon-to-be-landlord's number, and we played phone tag for a week, but when I did go for my site visit, I was sure the fit was a good one. Why? Like I stated earlier, I am old, set in my ways, need my rest (not for beauty—gave up on that a decade ago), like to cook my own food for economic and health reasons, and need access to transportation, a gym, the Internet, great running trails, a grocery store, and a Laundromat or dry cleaner. I couldn't live with smoking in my living quarters. The cinemas, quaint shops, ethnic diversity, restaurants, drug store, and terrific roommates were added bonuses in my case.

So, you're looking for a place to recharge your batteries in between shifts? There's a plethora of available places posted in every crew lounge. Online you might find a listing service (i.e., Craigslist). Who ya' gonna' call? Firstly, you probably have about a minute and a half to relocate, right? Secondly, you're paying a mortgage in your hometown and are being transplanted for employment and need temporary or only occasional housing around your base. It's best to be honest at the onset. Ask yourself burning questions and be prepared to share with any prospective landlord your concerns and needs. How important is cleanliness to you? What domestic responsibilities are expected individually or collectively? Will you be able to live with limited, allotted bathroom or kitchen time? Is one of the expectations of the roommate group that you not invite guests to stay? What are the storage limitations for food or personal items? Is linen provided? Are there television options (cable, satellite, or bunny ears with aluminum foil tips, VHS, DVD)? Computer/Internet on premises? Are utilities included? What about air conditioning? How many beds to a room? Can you afford the rent?

On the social side, it's really important to know whether

you'd be a good fit among the other occupants. There are the smoking, drinking, partying, heavy-metal music lovers among us. Then there's the quiet, book-loving, teatotaling, nonswearing, God-fearing extreme to round out our ranks. Would these folks live together in peaceful harmony? Admit your limits before moving in, for the sake of your sanity.

I struck it lucky when I moved into my crash pad—two bedrooms, one living room, and kitchenette—with ten others. My fellow inhabitants are mature, respectful folks from a variety of departments and an incredible array of "past life" professions. The conversations are upbeat, and boundaries are set and respected among us in a very civilized way.

What works for you? You'll be spending quality, if not quantity, time with strangers in a strange land, which could be a wonderful addition to your SkyNation experience. Bottom line? Don't settle for what doesn't suit your own sweet self. There's something out there for everyone.

PAJAMA PARTIES: THEN AND NOW

From Montreal in the 1960s to Fort Lauderdale in 2009

I WAS CHIEF cook and bottle washer at home when I was about nine. My mom was an invalid, and the household chores were split between my brother and myself, but in reality, as Alan did the lawns and such, I really did get most of the cooking. We shared the bottle washing, I guess, so nobody was chief in that department.

There came a time when I was just about fourteen that I made forays into the social world of high school girls. Before the age of diets or aerobics entered into our reality, if our parents gave the go ahead, we could go to a girlfriend's house to spend the night. The mothers at these abodes would have cooked and baked all day for these all-night affairs, and there'd be Orange Crush or ginger ale on hand. We'd spread our sleeping bags on the rec room floor, and the talking would commence. The eating went on all night, too.

The girls knew a lot more than I ever did. Somehow, I was not only the least physically developed of any girl at my school but the most unaware and naive person overall. So when a joke was told, I'd laugh with the rest, but I usually didn't understand the punch line at all. Almost every sentence ended or began with the name of some boy. "He's a hunk." "He's a great kisser." "He did this or that with so-and-so." To me, these sales pitches from the omniscient girls seemed pretty lame. (I told you that I was unworldly, but maybe life at home was so dramatic that these little news flashes from the mouths of my peers just didn't matter much to me.) Even though I knew I was unschooled and kindly being included out of charity more than any desire the girls had to socialize with the runt of the litter, I always felt a little superior to the other attendees. I wanted to understand their subject matter or feel as they did about a certain fellow, but I just couldn't get into it.

In retrospect, I was experiencing an acute case of arrested development. When one's mother is half dead, there's not much girl talk in the family. I took care of my mom: brushed her hair, took her pulse to make sure she was still alive, and fed her tiny bites of food with tea on the side. She was only fifty-five pounds and blind for the last few years of her life, so she didn't school me in the ways of womanhood. Instead, I was "Honey" to her and remained her "good little girl." She didn't mean to keep me on the childlike rung of a social ladder, but we were both sort of stuck in a comfort zone that didn't take growth energy. Mom had only enough strength to live, with none left over to teach, show by example, or share the ways of women. I was okay with this because she loved me, and I her. Yet it was at the pajama parties where I felt the already enormous gap between other girls and myself widening. My feet were encased firmly in the cement of my mother's belief (and hope) that I'd stay innocent forever. After all, she had no inner resources to sustain the anxiety that having a typical teenage girl would generate.

Now I'm fifty-six. A month ago, thanks to the amazing warmth of all the women in my crash pad, I realized that, for the very first time in my life, I'm on par with my peers. How so? I accepted an invitation to a pajama party. Women of our age—or those as wise as women our age should be—attended.

In two cars, we were taken from the Fort Lauderdale airport to the amazing home of a sister-in-Sky, Dee. Her lifelong friends from the International School in the Philippines, my own SkyNation sisters, and Dee's adult children and their families or friends stayed or visited. The hugs and kisses among Dee's lifelong friends were spontaneous and full of gratitude for such enduring relationships.. These hugs and kisses rained upon all of us actually. There was such a feeling of "I get it," "Been there, done that," "I understand, and this is what I've done in that situation," "We just have to help each other through this (or that)." The feeling that each of us was there because of mutual understanding overwhelmed me. The very gratitude we felt for knowing each other, having one another in our adult lives, and being on the same level socially, economically, or spiritually just surprised me.

You see, at some point or another we all "get there," I'm sure, but how do we *know* when we've reached that heretofore elusive mark on the graduated cylinder of life, better known as the right place at the right time?

For me, in all five and a half decades, I've missed the boat. It's always left port without me because I've just never been at the same point on the maturity/experience level as other women to qualify for a berth. I've always been different.

Lucky me. The ship that finally stayed at the pier long enough for me to mosey up the gangplank was moored poolside in Fort Lauderdale. The good ship Dee didn't leave without me. And, you know what? I got all the jokes and understood everything said about men, children, in-laws, broken engagements, career losses, ambitions, and apple orchards.

I love my life. I love my friends. I think I love pajama parties now, too.

UPON A YEAR OF SERVITUDE

November 2005

WHEN I LOOK at my hands I see humble beginnings. Peasant hands. Calloused, short of nail, an absence of vanity, pronounced veins, and a visible thickening at each knuckle. By definition, flight attendants of the past have always exemplified a cookie-cutter, classic look that included tiny waists, long legs, perfect skin, and manicured digits. SkyNation has its own look based on the appreciation of an individual's ability to give. Give service. Give love. Give of oneself. We're not generally a spoiled lot who think we should be at one with conceit, but we must guard against a human's natural reaction to what an upset traveling public might dish out. We must have an exterior made of material that will act as a filter. One that allows for the entry of reality but is impermeable to bad vibes.

Over the past year, I've been reminded of the joys of being absolutely humble and willing to take it, do it, and "yes" it. This isn't to say I'm a pushover or a passive person but rather one who finds a great deal of satisfaction in making the customer feel important, even if it puts me into the role of servant. Not servile and cowering am I, just there for anything a nervous, put-upon, downtrodden-in-life, sick, elderly, lonely, injured, or angry individual might require. I know I'm not the source of their physical or emotional pain, so that depersonalizes any negative attitude that might be delivered my way. If we can deflect the insult from the bull's-eye drawn on our uniform, we can look deeply into the offending one and deliver a solidly positive experience. It's a challenge to transmute a rude comment or insulting, dismissive attitude into one of respect and love, but the satisfaction gleaned from this digestive process is satisfying in the extreme. Employing humor, physical comedy, an understanding nod, or an offer of some sort of treat really breaks down the customer's resistance. It's the sincere offer of positivity even as the customer's negativity hangs in the air between us. A touch on the arm with a comment that suggests that the difficulty being experienced by the traveler is understood, and the assurance that all will be well can turn a six-hour flight from hell into one of peace and gratitude.

Not fighting back takes humility. That touch with peasant hands is the olive branch that might take a hurting, disenfranchised person from an angry world into a warm bath of caring, if only for the time he's with us in the air. Yes, a servant I am. A target to the frustrated masses who travel without joy or under duress. Turning 'em around for the duration of a flight isn't always easy, but it's rarely impossible and always gratifying. This past year has returned me to the roots of "upstairs/downstairs" servitude, yet with a knowing that we all are on an equal footing, although I hold all the cards at cruising altitude. "I've gotcha' where I wantcha' so give in, quit fighting, and accept all I have to give you up here." As Tevye says in *Fiddler on the Roof*, "It's a blessing to give." The disgruntled few have no choice but to accept the love, respect, and understanding freely offered at thirty-five thousand feet. Letting a poor attitude from the masses take away this opportunity hurts both sides. Who bends first? Who gives in first? The one with the most to lose and the most humility. It's incumbent upon the flight attendant to forgive and then give. My old hands have seen lesser chores and more difficult tasks, that's for sure.

BLUE BEACON

Upon the opening of our new terminal

WHEN ONE HEARS the word *terminal*, thoughts race toward hospice care or the end in life. Given the unstable economic times, the only sure lifeline is hope—hope that we'll prevail as an industry and as an individual company.

To paraphrase Maya Angelou, "To survive is noble, but to thrive is divine."

With so many airlines biting the dust since oil prices began their unprecedented climb from sea level to the stratosphere, SkyNation's held its own. And now, we've stepped into the spotlight with the opening of our new facility.

What struck me most on the day of our unveiling was the awe. The visible change in the molecular structure of the air space around each crew member who'd been at the ribbon cutting was radiant. Not that I've ever seen auras as other intuitive people might have, but there it was: the obvious acrylic shield of newfound self-worth encasing each and every person who came back to the old crew lounge within that gleeful encasement known as optimism. I saw no gloating, however, just joy without guile.

Yet with all the hoopla and pride, there was also a sense of humility. There was an opportunity for the superiority complex to emerge, as it will in other competitive endeavors. Raising one's arms as finish-line ribbons are broken beneath a timepiece declaring that new records have been set is an accepted practice in athletics. Sometimes wrapped in his country's flag, a winner is permitted his nationalistic display in full sight of those who fell behind or didn't finish at all. These practices that put individualism in broad view have their charm, given the mind-set that's evolved over the centuries: that egocentric superiority dramatized since *Wide World of Sports* gave unprecedented fame to those who medaled and just as much attention to that "agony of defeat." Our minds have been trained to shine for show, but God forbid we go down in the flames of failure because spotlights will focus on that result as well. The tabloids and cable news feed our conscious minds with the downside of life, and we look on with a smirk of superiority. Well, not always—especially not if we work for a company that has tremendous sensitivity for our fellow man in general and our fellow airlines in particular.

The former TWA folks attended the opening in droves because they were invited with utmost respect and empathy. I was fortunate to be sharing a trip with Angel, a former flight attendant from that fabulous airline. There's no doubt that the opening of our terminal was a ground for mixed emotions. The melancholia fraught from the great memories of what TWA meant to her progeny was evident. However, the emerging sense of survivorship was a lifeline thrown by SkyNation to those who harbor both sentiment and that innate class emblematic of TWA's personality.

As "pride goeth before a fall," we are indeed fortunate to be so empathetic to others whose existence has been erased on the big board of our defined commercial enterprise, the airline industry. We have indeed survived, and the fact that we've achieved goals that don't even enter the collective minds of those airlines still in business proves something. We're winners.

But there was no sense that we were rubbing the noses of others in the symbol of our success. There was, instead, a sense that SkyNation was holding up a beacon of hope for our professional siblings. "If we can do it, you can do it" seemed to be the attitude we were projecting. So although we certainly deserved that showy lap around the track, we didn't take it. I felt we were extending a hand backward to those who were still in the race and complete respect for those who had to drop out. "Take my hand. You can do it. You're nearly there." "Looking good." "Maybe next time."

Those who are struggling to survive as we thrive might be envious, but they shouldn't be. No, my impression of our SkyNation family isn't one of superiority during tough times, but one of quiet strength and willingness to be that guiding light for those who are out of breath but still have legs.

THE CALLING

December 26, 2007, the Syracuse crew hotel

IT'S DECEMBER 26, 2007, as I write this. I'm in a Syracuse, New York, hotel room with a *McHale's Navy* rerun playing on the television, and I've made it! Once again, another working Christmas has passed for my brothers and sisters in Sky. There are all sorts of tricks to our trade, those that put the customer in a better frame of mind. Those who are white-knuckle sorts, alcoholics forced off the bottle for the duration of their flights, neurotic pet owners, stressed-out parental units, the infirm or aging masses unable to fathom the altitudes reached, or the over-the-top fatigued individuals—most are easy to control during the Christmas rush. We can manipulate each with eye contact; sincere, caring questions; a nod; or placing their shaky hands between our confident palms. But who does the same for flight attendants who've maxed out their attitudes at Christmastime? Those who've bid for the day off and are missing the big day with loved ones anyway? Well, we should do it for one another, but most of us could learn to meet our needs through those we're transporting from points A to B (unless we're forced to divert).

There are tricks we can employ on ourselves and each other to get through tough times. Not only are we entitled to do so, but we must. The basic survival instincts during lonely days, when we are totally involved in personal pity parties, are about all we can draw upon to help ourselves over a really tough hump: Christmas Day on duty.

Admitting that it's beyond us, as individuals, to just accept our lot in life isn't easy, but it's possible. We have to play a few mind games, and here are some that, believe it or not, can turn a terrible twenty-four hours into an open arena for miracles. Christmas miracles.

I watched Audrey Hepburn in *The Nun's Story* the other night. Just before donning a novice's habit, each neophyte was asked, "Do you come to this decision of your own free will? You must now bid farewell to all things that hold you to the material world. Anything that has heretofore had sentimental value or symbolizes an attachment to your former life must be put in a basket for removal from your life forever. For the next two years you must agree to release all pride or thoughts of self." There was no hesitation; Hepburn and all of her costars agreed to the terms of engagement. A done deal. They had to clear their minds and free their hearts to allow space for a relationship with their chosen God.

I was raised in Montreal, and nuns were ethereal neighbors of mine. Most were harsh, but there were a few whose inner light radiated from their starched-cloth frames. Sister Anthony.

Sister Margaret-Joseph. How I loved them for their pure and tangible bliss. They had obviously chosen their destinies wisely and wore the strict habit with a gleeful bounciness that was incredibly contagious. And they were so kind to me, even though I wasn't a member of their parish, just a little girl who's mother was in the hospital half of every year. I actually find myself tearing up as I write these words. Sister Anthony and Sister Margaret-Joseph were two nuns among many of like dress, order, location, and profession, yet they stood out, and their faces, attitudes, and sparkle are as fresh in my mind now as if they were part of my present-day life,

I'm sure they missed their families, presents under the tree, freedom to travel to chosen destinations, and familiar traditions on their Savior's birthday, just like I did yesterday as I flew here and there with complete strangers. In the time that they were training for taking vows, they were given time to reflect on trade-offs they'd have in religious life. But I'm sure they had to draw from the positivity of others when they themselves felt low. Was it from knowing that they were in the right place at the right time, even at Yuletide, that gave them the strength to smile for me? Was it the understanding that they had chosen their lives and I was simply a victim of circumstance that obligated them to raise my spirits? Were they faking it for a little girl whose mom might not make it home for Christmas? I'll never know, but it doesn't matter. They helped me. A lot. Did their strength come from their training, community of like minds, or their God? This doesn't matter either.

Now, if you are in any service industry job, you've chosen your life, too. The same one as mine. It's far from being religious, but not that different when it's known to be a *calling*. We're servants, one and all.

Very few of us do it for the riches. Most of us do it because we like people. If we love 'em on a Tuesday in July, we must love 'em on December 25, too. I know this is a challenge.

So how do we rationalize our state of being on days like Christmas?

Step one: know commonality.

When entering the crew lounge, feel lucky. Look around at all the others at the computers, checking their e-mails, sleeping in the La-Z-Boys, partaking in a briefing, watching everyone's favorite Christmas movies; *It's a Wonderful Life* or *Elf* on the flat screen, or chatting. They are on the same wavelength. A collective mood from high to low, so average it out. That's already lifted a mood from "poor me" to "we're all in this together."

Step two: give of yourself.

As long as we have to work, know that we might just be the only sane person in the crazy lives of the travelers. It's true, once on our planes, all the average Joe has to worry about until landing is whether or not his TV works, the snacks and drinks are okay, or if he'll have his seatbelt fastened appropriately. Hey, the time onboard is probably the most irresponsible time of any customer's entire holiday. So allow them that, and the love you'd be giving your granny or parents, significant other, children or friends, bestow instead upon the stressed-out customers. Why not? A smile, a hug, a gentle pat on the shoulder, or an attentive ear are great gifts. Maybe the best ever received by those on our planes.

Step three: believe in projection.

During the hours when we know our families are under a tree, surrounded with torn tissue paper, bows and laughter, how do we survive, let alone thrive? Well, we can either fall back into that pity pit or realize that not being there doesn't mean we're not being thought of and missed. Feel that love coming through the miles and let it fill your heart. It's there. Invisible, intangible, but something that fills a pipeline from them to us. At the time your family is having Christmas dinner, project yourself into the mix with warm knowing. They'll feel your presence, too. This can really cut down on your sense of isolation and disenfranchisement.

Step four: practice assimilation.

When you know they're probably thinking of you, take it in and allow the good vibes to become a part of your being. This will fill those empty holes in your soul and help you feel complete, even in the absence of the tangible.

Step five: rationalize.

Seriously, realizing that others have it worse than we do helps a lot! The fighting peacemakers in Iraq, Afghanistan, Kuwait, or wherever are away for more than a four-day pairing, my friends. People in institutions aren't getting out for turkey either. People on life support, or those undergoing cancer treatments or emergency surgery aren't feeling chipper. People alone with a bottle in a tenement or smoking crack under a bridge in upstate New York are not celebrating. Children being abused, neglected, or in orphanages aren't feeling the joy much either. Maxjet flight attendants aren't jumping up and down because they've been given Christmas '07 off, believe me. 'Nuf said about comparing our lot to that of others.

Step six: fake it till you make it.

Self-explanatory but if you need a parallel think of the tune "I Whistle a Happy Tune," from *The King and I*. Substitute depressed, sad, resentful, or any other natural emotional response to having to work on Christmas, and you'll be amazed at how your mood is transmuted after you start to "whistle a happy tune"! Figuratively or literally, we can talk ourselves onto a different emotional plane.

Step seven: again—give, give, give.

You know all about the movie, *Pay It Forward*, eh? Well, this karmic way of life does work. For as much as we've taken, projected, digested, and assimilated the concentrated love of absent loved ones or rationalized, we can now walk aboard a flight with enough inner peace, strength, and love to pass our good feelings on to others. For the hundreds of weary folks we think we should envy as they head back to Granny's or Mom's hearth and home for replays of Christmases past, there are a few who aren't a bit sad for their very own reasons. It's a tough season even if everything goes as planned. We don't know if these folks are going home because of sincere desire or because they feel obligated. Like lemmings, many just feel driven to jump into the chasm. Quite possibly, a nice flight attendant might be the only good thing on their trip down memory lane.

Like those two nuns were mine.

Think back to the people who've made your Christmases wonderful. If you're lucky, it was family. If you're lucky, it was friends. If you're lucky, it was two members of a convent in Montreal. Maybe, if you're really lucky, it was all of the above.

Another way to feel tremendously lucky is to remember

we're not as pure as nuns, but we are in a position to make a stranger's holy day better. Yeah, we're faking our own happiness a bit, but that's natural. Believe this though: once you give a little of yourself, the true meaning of Christmas will be clarified for you. I promise. The Christmas miracles we see in movies really happen on board once you admit to yourself that you've answered your own personal call to service. That inner light you allow to shine on the faces of strangers isn't for naught. And you'll never be forgotten. Never.

Working on Christmas Day? Not at all what most of us want to do, but maybe it's the best opportunity to really be a part of the true definition of what this season's all about. For each other and for those who are making an annual pilgrimage for love or obligation. Maybe we've never served a higher purpose than to transport folks home for the holidays. That's a gift we can put under our own trees addressed to ourselves, and we can open it another day.

Life doesn't have to be perfect to be wonderful. I mean, this room in Syracuse offers a bland view, but wait a minute! The sun's shining, and I think it's nice enough to go for a long run. I'll bet other folks, who didn't have cold beans and rice, two oranges, and four tablespoons of crunchy peanut butter for Christmas dinner aren't feeling as healthy as I am this morning! Life is good.

WHERE ARE WE?

The evolution of a stereotype

WE'VE EVOLVED BEYOND the old stereotype of the free and easy stewardesses, right? I mean we should have. Even back when my father was zooming all over the world on those now-defunct carriers, he'd come home with sweeping generalizations and his holy opinion of what "those women" did in their spare time. No, he never actually had a conversation with any of those dedicated, beautiful, talented, and gracious ladies, but he should have.

I did. I learned. I admired. I was inspired. Yet I was too short to be hired thirty-some years back. Shooting up to my present height hasn't done me much good in life, really. Somehow a five-footer isn't the one picked for an A team or worshipped as are high fashion models. That's okay. I've managed to do just fine, thank you very much. Enter SkyNation. They hired me, and I've been so proud that I *feel* taller. My dad was even happy for me because he's evolved and feels terrible that his puritanical manner of taxonomy was so terribly narrow, judgmental, and wrong. Even Dad thought that the cookie-cutter stewardesses in the early days of aviation weren't as respectable as women whose feet remained rooted in the terra firma of post-suffrage but pre-women's liberation conformity.

So because our profession is now lauded as one that puts brains and people skills, first aid and firefighting, general aircraft savvy and safety first, those who would have pigeonholed us into the realm of bon vivant swingers have been forced to shut up, sit up, take notice, and reevaluate the myriad positive attributes of us who serve on high. Male and female, from twenty-something to the "great beyond" of flight attendants in their seventies—we rock!

So when fellow flight attendants pass sexist, insulting, or insinuating comments to another crew member, are we not regressing to those days when society as a whole was quick to judge us as morally loose and label us "waitresses in the sky"?

We must not allow or encourage rudeness, disrespect, or any other form of harassment to have fertile ground for perpetuation. If you feel that someone has stepped too far into your comfort zone, please tell the offending crew member that unsolicited remarks are hurtful to those of us who have risen above and proved ourselves to be deserving of respect. To passively allow another to continue in this uncomfortable fashion is sexual harassment at the very least, and a step back in human rights at the very most.

LIFE (SUCH AS IT IS) ON RESERVE

On reserve: that dreaded time between the years we're on call until we have enough seniority to bid for the trips and days off we want as lineholders

---

TO SURVIVE OR to thrive are matters of choice. Rationalizing and bargaining with yourself during the time between graduating from the school of Inflight and becoming a bona fide lineholder may be life-saving and morale-boosting tricks of the trade. (Lineholders can bid monthly for the flights and days off they most desire and, depending on the demand and seniority, are granted same. Lineholders also have the options to drop or pick up trips better suited to personal taste, productivity, and time off after crew services has built and assigned monthly schedules.)

To achieve any goal, there's usually a trade-off of some sort.

Medical doctors have a grueling couple of years in residency programs. No sleep. No life. No time. No perks? There's only the radical training of mind and body to react to a patient's needs without thinking of self. It's a period of humility building in which as much knowledge through exposure is infused as possible. What an opportunity. Considered inhumane by some but totally inspirational to others, this total immersion into the profession provides a fertile proving ground for the neophyte practitioner. Sound like being *on reserve*? You betcha', but there are benefits to our situation, too.

Getting to cities that only extremely senior lineholders see is one terrific bonus: Phoenix, San Jose, San Diego, Salt Lake City, Burlington (just threw this in because it's *my* home city), and others. We also get to fly with folks like Lenny, Patricia, Jamie, and so many other flight attendants who are senior and such gracious teachers.

I've trained and raced everything from half-mile to hundred-kilometer distances. In every way, the training has been beneficial on the day of the competition. Win or lose, my physical strength has increased, and my ability to push through the plethora of reasons to drop out during most races has always given me that "I'm glad I didn't quit" satisfaction. The training was tough. The races, tougher. The finish lines? Gifts to the soul. The payoffs. The brass rings.

The worst part of being on reserve is not knowing what's next. Perhaps a call from crew services at three in the morning saying, "You've got a 5:10 show time and a two-day trip," or "You're sitting airport standby tomorrow from noon until 1800 hours." (Show time is when the in-flight crew meets in the crew lounge for a safety-and-service briefing plus general introductions. This takes place one hour before the initial flight's departure time.) Maybe a reserve might be on home standby for twelve hours on many consecutive days or get a red-eye followed by a daytime sleep break before a double transcontinental trip. Ya' nevah know.

During this gestation period there are a few things that will help the reservist. Eating your vegetables, fruits, low-fat/high-quality protein while avoiding quick-fix, temporary energy boosters like "le junque fude" has the duel benefits of preventing weight gain and helping you stay healthy. Forcing yourself to work out in every gym at every layover hotel will pay tremendous dividends, mentally and physically. Sleeping as regularly as possible is something you should promise yourself. Avoid depressants, be they chemical or negative people. In other words, if you go to have a nightcap and your coworkers start bad mouthing SkyNation, get your sweet self out of that situation before the seeds they've planted germinate. If you're a commuter, get home as much as possible. After three months with the company, start using your paid time off bank. Remember that you're allowed one unpaid time off a month, too. Learn how to use Saber Flight Crew Access Flica to swap days off. What a godsend this is to me. Get to know the folks in crew services and what their very demanding job entails. Learn that it's not a we-they relationship. It's an "us" thing.

Living in airline limbo isn't easy, but what is when the brass ring is so shiny? Be it a medical degree, a first-place finish, or becoming a lineholder, remember that the dues-paying time is always worth the end result. Flip-flop the word *sacrifice* to *investment.*

So being on reserve is no different than the investment of

time for academic, athletic, or professional prowess. It's the ultra marathon of a lifetime. The finish line is illusive, but I know, as sure as I'm writing this story, that it exists. There are no crowds yelling, "You're almost there," or that chronic fib, "Looking good," nor is there a huge salary or noble title for those who survive this time in no man's land. But with every passing month, there's that seductive call to cross your fingers and bid for the moon. What have you got to lose? The sky's the limit.

Bid. You may get a line—next month.

STEPPING OVER THE LINE

A word to the wise about going too far when making unscripted announcements on flights

---

THERE ARE THOSE who have amazing oral talent. They can take a somber, uninvolved crowd and unify them from "We have now closed our main cabin door" to "Welcome to (wherever); the local time is (whatever)," and cause all to bond in shared gales of laughter.

Flying with such vocal geniuses always leaves one a might envious because this is SkyNation. Humor is one of our mainstays, right? I mean, our values are SAFETY, INTEGRITY, CARING, PASSION, and FUN! Fun being in play and in question here.

Most everyone enjoys and loves the side comments that accompany many of the usual compulsory announcements.

The ones who disapprove might have the right amount of carry-on while harboring emotional baggage that won't fit under the seat in front of them. Ya' can please some of the people some of the time, right?

For other in-flight crew members on board these flights of fancy language, the meat has been tenderized from the start with a goodly amount of catchy and well-timed one-liners. How lucky for us, bending toward engaged rather than disenfranchised customers to take drink orders.

One thing a talented on-air personality must avoid, however, is the constant use of the PA system just because the crowd seems receptive. Perform the comedy when appropriate and then let the folks sleep, watch their Direct TV, or have quiet time for their books. Fun is fun, but the appropriateness of the humor must be run through a filter to avoid remarks that might offend the customer (even though it might be hilarious) or a fellow flight attendant who might not like having her legs pointed out as "voted the best in this airline for three years running." Little things like that really do embarrass some of us. Although our senses of humor are well able to hold their own, some remarks made over the PA have the potential for touching a nerve and making one feel objectified. It could happen. . . .

Most of us and our customers are really good sports, but to take this for granted is playing loosey-goosey when it comes to out-of-date classification or labeling of individuals or groups by witticisms or wisecracks.

God forbid that the talented individuals who grace our company with their twinkling eyes and razor-sharp wit should ever be silenced, but remember that tempering the obvious, the subtle, or the obtuse with tact is a professional thing to do. All must be mindful of the feelings of those who might take offense, be embarrassed, or be hurt.

IT'S LONELY AT THE TOP

Dear Heather,

Thank you so, so much for the nice letter you wrote my supervisor. Sometimes when I work a lot I lose sight of myself and kind of just get stuck in a rut. Your letter made me feel like I am not just a nameless face floating around unnoticed. I have struggled with that thought, thinking what difference does it make if I am here today or not; I am easily replaceable. You really made me feel like there was a reason I was there with you; that I was appreciated and not interchangeable with the thousands of other crew members. To say you made my month would be an understatement. Again, I thank you. –C. D.

And this crew member made *my* month when she wrote the above note in response to a compliment she'd received from me.

Being a pilot or flight attendant is work out of the box. We don't have boring schedules, routines, or repetitive, mundane days with zero potential for misadventure or situational stimulation. No brain-cell-sucking pall surrounds our daily lives as we jet around the country and beyond. That's the upside, and this might be enough to rationalize and balance one other basic truth: it's lonely at the top.

We're away from home a lot, and sometimes, five miles above Earth, with 150 strangers and a crew that doesn't gel, even a one-day trip can seem void of emotional nourishment. Then, should we have layovers on longer trips, the sterility that defines most hotel rooms can overwhelm us. The Internet, television, cell phones, good books, magazines, and the omnipresent *USA Today*, awaiting our first foray into a silent corridor, aren't what the heart, mind, or body crave, are they?

The touch of our lover, hugs from our children, chuckles to share or real tears to kiss from the chubby cheeks a grandchild, home cooking, family fun, the acceptance and understanding of best friends back home are conspicuous by their absence during our times away from home.

To avert the desolation that is felt by the young lady who wrote the note that opens this article takes so little, doesn't it? Noticing and showing appreciation for our fellow crew members can make their day, let alone their month. Not only can a little positive reinforcement help build a store of self-worth and pride of place, it usually follows that the laws of karma will revisit kindness in kind.

The faceless anonymity that can give a person such a sense of isolation is a very common by-product of our job descriptions. The feeling that we're all dispensable, on some level, can erode the energy needed to do our best while flying. As my mother would say, "That's the most natural thing in the world." None of us are completely immune to these normal reactions to displacement combined with solitude.

What changed C. D.'s perception of her own importance within the vast scheme of SkyNation was a letter I composed about her. Why? Because there's not one among us who doesn't have some fabulous, innate quality worth noting. When we have a second, we should jot down the good qualities of our fellow crew members or voice our observations to each deserving party. Copying a supervisor is a touch that takes another second before pressing Send, and this helps to strengthen the foundation of what we are: flight attendants and pilots who are alone a lot, away from home much of the time, and trying to give, give, give to a traveling public that takes us for granted more often than not.

If we show appreciation for each other, whether in e-mails, by verbal kudos, or a card in a V file that just says, "Hi, I loved my trip with you" or "Thanks for getting my four-hundred-pound tote bag out of the overhead for me, captain," believe me, you'll make somebody's month. Better yet, it'll come back to you somehow because an appetite grows on what it feeds. If we see the good, give it a bit of our energy by reflecting it, and then stand back and watch, most recipients of well-deserved accolades will live up to them more often. Better yet, the newly appreciated will begin to notice all the good in their peers. Give it a try. None of us should have the sense that we're unimportant or that our absence won't be felt. We're all equally important to each other and the operation. Never forget this.

BURNOUT

It's reversible using energy exchange techniques and empathy.

IN A SPEECH given to a graduating in-flight class, I tried to impress the absolute necessity of recharging one's batteries. Not only on long trips, during extended delays, or when customers aren't feeling the true SkyNation experience is this compulsory, but it's totally doable.

The emotional and physical fatigue that comes from the inconsistent hours, demands of being airborne, or the stresses of being away from loved ones are very natural by-products of airline life. Like most expected reactions in life, we must find something that works as a personal antidote to whatever ails us.

This irritable, dragging, heavy, burdensome weight that defines occasional bouts of burnout is different for everyone. The condition isn't something to be ashamed of; rather, the symptoms might simply indicate that a change is indicated.

Who hasn't reached a breaking point during his or her airline career?

"I've so had it with these people."

"I love the job but can't stand the customers anymore."

"If anyone else asks for three drinks at once, I'll scream."

"What's *wrong* with these people?"

"I used to be a people person; then I got this job."

"I can't believe that my pairing's been modified and I'm being put on reserve for two days."

"Can you believe that my limo from Newark to JFK didn't show up until an hour and a half after we got off the flight?"

Whatever factors bring a flight attendant down to this level are irrelevant, because they are constants in our working environment. However, it's the reaction to the realities of airline life that is being addressed here. I'm not going Pollyanna or anything, but there are techniques that we can adopt and adapt to our lives that will improve our attitudes and affect our overall well-being.

Unfortunately, going negative isn't uncommon, but this doesn't have to be a permanent condition. Did you know that we're all born with a little generator within? One that, if our habitual energy source fails, can be turned on for supplemental power? Knowing *when* to flip the switch is the trick. And each of us has a different kindling point for both flareups and their opposite: that second wind of patience, good humor, and positivity.

OUR DIET

Thanks to brother-in-Sky, Jason for asking me to write about food.

Pack a lunch. The importance of healthy food and its availability can't be overstated. Once real hunger hits, it's really difficult to avoid the temptations of the wrong stuff. You all know that. Investing time to prepare quickly becomes part of the routine. Pack whole wheat bread, peanut butter, cheese, fresh fruit, and anything else that you know you'd enjoy *before* that point of no return—better known as "craving junk," In other words, always have something you enjoy that's good for you close at hand. Don't skip meals, if you can help it.

I cook big time and then divvy up the veggies, lean meat/poultry/fish, brown rice or taters into multiple bags and freeze the lot. It is an ugly mess when it thaws, but it's worth it for the way the food hits the spot and gives me strength.

The usual admonitions apply (but you know these things):

1. Limit alcohol intake.
2. Get plenty of rest.
3. Hydrate.
4. Sleep as much as you can.
5. Laugh a lot.
6. Don't repeat gossip.
7. Always look for the positive in every person and all situations.

OUR PHYSICAL ACTIVITIES

The more you do, the more you *can* do. Try to work in a bit of exercise every day. It doesn't matter what it is, just do it. The fatigue can be overwhelming on trips, but a bit of exercise really gives more than it takes. Making the commitment to a twenty-minute session, six days a week isn't too much to ask of one's aching, tired, overworked, jet-lagged body. As my grandfather used to say, "It pays dividends." Yes, yes, it certainly does.

PACING YOURSELF

What looks amazing when bidding your next schedule, like twenty-two hours in the air over a two-day period or an out-and-back *From Here to Eternity* red-eye trip, might not be possible for us in reality. On paper, all trips look easy, but admit what kills you and avoid it if you can.

If you know that early shows are not for you, do all you can to get later shows and vice versa. Don't recuperate from red-eyes? Drop 'em. Life's too short to suffer, and no job should disqualify you from whatever schedule resonates with you. (Unless you're on reserve, bless your heart.)

There exists the potential to have the kind of schedules that give us a darn good quality of life—providing there are enough reserves—so take advantage of this when bidding. If you possibly can get by with just enough hours to meet financial goals without destroying your mental and physical health, then go that route. Greed breeds burnout.

THE THEORY OF EXCHANGE

When customers are blamed for psychological points of no return, it's a really good trick to take a bit from them. When those near-to-crying jags or urges to tell a customer where to go hit, the suffering flight attendant might employ some of the following tricks.

If you haven't heard of the *theory of exchange*, here it is.

Being interactive with every customer and using your most-active listening skills causes people to open up to you. Really listen, watch their body language, and note their emotional temperature so you can gauge your reactions. How you respond will determine if the customer's story evolves into a complete history or not. As they tell all, you're jacking up your definition of being a flight attendant. You've suddenly become important to the customers as someone who is truly helping, and that loss of anonymity, which our uniform perpetuates, has given way to a beautiful thing: a person-to-person interchange that makes a connection. You're a sounding board and very important to their processing of whatever's on their minds. How cool is that?

From boarding to deplaning, when you're down to the nubs of energy, try to find out more about the travelers on your flight. You needn't be forward, invasive, or intrusive. None of us were hired because we lack social graces. On the contrary, we're hired because we can read a room. If you sense someone's mood, key into that. You'll be amazed how most folks open up and tell you why they're on your plane. By taking in their stories, you're putting our jobs onto a different plateau, and boy, at the end of the day, you'll be energized because you've given of yourself but taken back, too. Taken the trust, the respect, the love of whoever bent your ear. This job of ours can be interesting in the extreme on the planes. Just getting hugs from departing folks at the end of a flight can fill you with enough positive energy to carry you through your next flight and beyond.

PART TWO

TAKEOFF

A LITTLE BOY AGAIN

Tampa to Newark one night in 2010

IT WAS A flight between Tampa and Newark, and there were to be surprises. I'm such a lucky woman to be in the job I have, because I'm always in the perfect position to witness mini-miracles, the synchronicity that comes only when the Universe deems a moment in time to be perfect timing. Perfect timing is a reality, but one must be open for the lessons and willing to hear the messages presented.

The emergency exit rows are usually manned by people who are willing and able to use initiative if the conditions demand. Moreover, they're also willing and able to pay more for these roomier seats. These fliers must be informed of the responsibilities required of them should a situation occur. These Miranda rights of airline travel are supposed to inform the traveler, but the teacher must become the observant student, too. If the passenger is judged unfit to occupy a seat in any way, he must be assigned another place on the aircraft. On the other hand, there are people who seem overqualified, with the mental acuity and physical characteristics of a superhero, the big-man-on-campus sort who exudes personality and leadership potential. Perfectly groomed and the kind that would, as the song says, "walk into a party, like you were walking onto a yacht." The type that, with a wink, would try to convince me that his cell phone could remain on for just a bit longer.

On this flight, in the exit row, was such a man. His persona was big enough to enfold me in its self-serving embrace with the knowledge that he could push any envelope, get more from his fellow man than anyone else, win every bet, come first in every competition, cheat on his wife without her ever suspecting, and—well, he was just that kind of a guy. To top it off, he'd make everything seem like every one of his actions was the expressed desire of those he charmed and victimized. In short, he was a likeable villain who, although not altogether harmless, gave everyone in his path the choice of falling for and accepting him as is, where is, or getting out of his way. I'm sure he left more people smiling in his wake than crying. He could get away with anything. Let the buyer beware. Proceed at your own risk. I told ya' so.

In the middle of our drink service, when we really need to get up and down the narrow center aisle, this man with a monumentally imposing physique placed himself in it. In the fashion I expected from him, he was totally unaware of our need to pass him. He also was bent at the waist with his abdomen and chest between the faces and televisions of the two people separating him from the object of his attention: an elderly man in the window seat.

"Sir, I'm so sorry, but we're serving now. Would you mind stepping out of the aisle until we've finished?" I asked.

As he turned to me, the change in him was evident. The cocky, know-it-all, you'll-bend-to-my needs-and-like-it fellow had been replaced with the demeanor of an innocent. His face, totally transformed, had become the shiny visage of a freshly scrubbed, prepubescent school boy. In his enthusiasm, I wouldn't have been surprised had he grabbed and shook me to make his point even stronger.

"He was my seventh grade teacher. I can't believe it! Look! He was my teacher! Let me get out of your way. I'm sorry. Thank you. He was the best teacher I ever had."

He was beaming, near tears, and a veritable fountain of humility as he gingerly stepped out of my way and scurried back to his seat. He was just being a very good boy, all of a sudden.

As I delivered his drink (a can of beer), he took it and said, "Did you see him? That man I was talking to? He was my seventh grade teacher. It was a Catholic school in upstate New York. Ithaca. I was bigger than the other kids and played football. I think I was a bit ADHD, you know? Well, my grades were just barely passing and on game days, not even that. Well, he's the best man I ever knew. I mean, I'm not taking anything away from my own father, you understand, but he was a teacher who just kicked my ass. Turned me around, you know? He's a great man. The greatest man I ever knew. He taught for forty-six years. *Forty-six years!* He never married. He just gave his whole life to teaching. The greatest man . . . I am what I am today because of him. I know billionaires who want me to kiss their ring and bow down to them and I won't. But I'll kiss that man's ring."

He said this with an eye focused inward. Although speaking to me, he was also judging himself and wondering if, truly, he had really lived up to the great man's expectations or merely stored them for retrieval at a later date. Maybe the day of this reunion would be the day he added the values taught to the life he was living?

This man had regressed in a proverbial New York minute. He'd been forced to return to that role of student in the presence of his most revered mentor. All the ego had been erased in the moment of reunion. The once and former child, who could count on his bulk and athleticism, charm and connivance to supplant other basic ethical requirements of success, had been exposed. The encasing body of the man had birthed the boy who could still be told what to do. That seventh grader, who had been building up, layer upon layer, what the material world not only expects but reveres, was sitting in front of me as I delivered his drink. Such a boy. The boy within the man was nice.

A magic potion that promises a return to youth, a reversal of the aging process, and a rekindling of the flame of innocence had been his first drink of the flight. That elixir was composed of love, respect, and the memory of someone who expected more from the inner being of a boy than what muscle and manipulative methods could bring about. The teacher expected honesty with the self of that young boy. The teacher wanted only that the football player with personality become a good man who could mix hard work and concentration of soul on projects that went beyond the playing fields and locker rooms, overflowing bank accounts, and possessions.

Over the fifty-three-year life span of the youngster before

me, there had been an internal battle of wills and purpose. Which side won out? The one who could get anything by willing it, or the one who knew that honor should be a part of all work. The jury's out on these questions, yet, from what I saw, I was encouraged.

"Don't tell him I'm having a beer, okay?"

"Your secret's safe with me."

Yet, this customer knew that something better had been expected of him. The trappings of success, as defined these days, are of little consequence to those who look deeper than designer outfits and good leather shoes and into hearts and souls.

Sometimes the lessons of a teacher are utilized only after they've had time to germinate and their blossoms are held up to the reflected light of a life only half lived. As that eighty-year-old teacher deplaned, I hugged him fiercely. How many lives had he touched, changed, redirected, or motivated? He'll never know. Chance meetings ages and ages past the point of impact in any classroom aren't guaranteed. This one, though, on this flight, was a pivotal point in a grown man's life and a second chance to learn. He'd boarded with that well-accepted American attitude of superiority and omniscience. After the injection of conscience from a former teacher, that tower of self-importance and Wall Street savvy deplaned a different man. Teachers. Remember the good ones. Remember the one who told you that you could be more than you needed to be. Better than you needed to be.

"He changed my life!" were the last words I heard from my emergency exit customer as he got off the plane.

I think, even though his ass was kicked in seventh grade,

he needed another good, swift kick at the age of fifty-three. Luckily he got it. What will he do in the next few decades of life? Turn off his cell phone when asked? That'll be a start. I believe he left the plane with every intention to return to a path only tangentially followed up until the reunion. He'd been gifted with a refresher course in "do the right thing" by an old-fashioned teacher. Blessed be.

WHAT'S IN A NAME? THE MEANING OF LIFE

Just another meeting at JFK one evening in winter 2010

ALIA. I FORGET what it means in the language spoken by Ethiopians, but I think, in this case, not knowing but imposing my own definition of Alia has served me well this day.

The flight was delayed, so everyone was still at a JFK departure gate. Buffalo was their destination. Usually a quiet group that wears their passions on T-shirts or baseball caps, the Buffalo customers display a quiet facade. Yet scrape the surface of these travelers and you'll find each to have many other things going on in their lives besides the Sabers or Bills, Niagara Falls or academics. These are stalwart family people, and as a rule, they are as honest as the day is long. There aren't many surprises or California quirks, egos, or anyone putting on airs on these flights. I like these people very much. Even those who aren't natives of this city and its environs seem to have the common denominator of self-deprecation and an inner knowledge of just who they are as individuals sharing our planet. The salt of the earth is drawn to Buffalo for some reason.

A woman in loose sweatpants and a bulky sweater came up to me. Her dark blonde hair in a messy ponytail with flyaway remnants that weren't embraced by the cockeyed elastic was evidence of a long trip. Thirty-five hours to be exact. She loosely cradled a tiny blanket in her arms with a face made up of only eyes. There was a question about something, but because I felt compelled to do so, I put out my arms and asked to hold the infant, before she finished the first sentence. I don't always do this. Sure, I adore children, puppies, and kittens, but not always does an irresistible urge to cuddle overcome me. The woman passed the child to me with an easy swooping motion. Featherlight. A blanket, two enormous eyes, and skin. Yet when the tiny head entered the curve of my neck, the warmth and near weightlessness of this living thing became a part of my chest. Part of my heart.

I remember the first time I held my grandson, Shea. He was brand new, weighed eight pounds, four ounces, and was all there. I remember the tears welling up in my eyes as I whispered all the plans I had for doing things together as he grew up. A natural granny thing to do, I suppose; the hoping and dreaming and hugging and kissing goes with the territory. Yet I resisted complete abandon a bit at that first meeting. Not so with Alia. Was it because we wouldn't have a lifetime to share that there was such a rush to feel everything all at once? Or was it because she wouldn't have the time to give all her love to the world since her life might end at any time?

"Her name's Alia. She's five months old. She was found in the streets. Two days ago she nearly died. We're adopting her, but now we're taking her to Hunter Hospital. I'm a social worker and we now have thirteen children from everywhere." The mother was pure and without artifice. She was the real thing, all mother and organization. She was evidently filled with the energy it takes to raise a child, or thirteen. Very likable, too.

As I held this little being, I felt the tears pooling. No, not at all because of what the new mother was saying. No. It was because I felt love for this tinier-than-the-average-American newborn. It was a deep and true love. When you hear about miracles or angels, think of what it must be like to be an abandoned baby, starving on the dirty streets of Addis Ababa, maybe discovered next to the dead body of a starved or murdered mother. Did Alia see her mother die? Did Alia lie beside that corpse and wither from hunger, thirst, and neglect? Perhaps the mother didn't die but chose mobility and survival of self; by leaving this daughter in the streets with the hope that some good person would lay claim to and rescue her child, the birth mother may also live to see another day. Another conception. Maybe only one will survive or ever know what happened. Alia. Too young to intellectualize but old enough to have felt abandonment no matter what really happened.

How could I feel such a strong love for this wisp of a thing? It was an overpowering emotion that seemed to come from my lower abdomen and flare into a full-blown volcanic eruption out of my eyes. Such a physical reaction seemed to come from a person other than myself. How?

A day after this encounter, I got the answer during a jog along the shore of Casco Bay, Maine. The Universe has all the answers if we calmly cast out a question. As I jogged along I wondered how that little one had pulled such strong feelings of sweet love out of me. I really wondered about that. I happened to glance up just after thinking this question for the twentieth time since holding her and saw a graffiti-covered cinder-block hut beside me. There was only one corner that wasn't a disorganized mess of unidentifiable scrawls and ugly paint splatters. In that upper right corner, standing quite alone, was one word: *Alia*.

There are moments in life when, if a person's paying attention, all answers become clear. I suddenly realized that I wasn't crying because I felt my love pouring into that sick child. No. That baby was infusing *me* with *her* love, the sort that is Christly and holy. However forsaken she was, this child was still able to generate everything we should feel for one another every single day. Unconditional love. Just because.

I guess when we say one lives up to one's name, it could be a good thing. In Alia's case, because I have no memory of the meaning of this moniker, I can make something up and it will become my truth. Alia, to me, will always mean "Somebody loves me, therefore, I am," or "Somebody chose me, therefore, I'll always think of myself as worthy of all blessings." Mostly, Alia will always mean "No matter what has happened to a body during life's course, it's possible to give love."

What's in a name? Whatever's in the soul of its owner. Blessed be.

WHO KNOWS WHAT LURKS IN THE MINDS OF MEN?

Tampa to JFK, March 2008

IF MARCH COMES in like a lion, it's due to go out as a lamb. What if youth came in like a lion? Might it be right to hope it departs as something mild-mannered and innocent? It's a poser, that's for sure.

It's not anyone's beeswax what goes on behind closed doors in the homes of America. Certainly opinions can form in the fleeting moments that a flight attendant spends in social discourse with the traveling minions, but there's never anything more concrete to conclude than our own mental pictures as they develop from some point A to another at point B. Folks get on, display their transient colors, some only available "on demand," others pulsating from each pore like true arterial blood. How can an air host ever really know the truth unless the facade is transparent or the wearer volunteers a personal history that matches the outward appearance?

I was walking down the aisle before the closing of the main cabin doors. It was a flight with only a couple of empty seats, and the Tampa crowd was mellow and wholesome. All ages and stages were represented, and the trip to New York would be our last of three East Coast flights that March. My crew, Dave, the Irish wag with the combined spirit of a leprechaun and the devil himself, and Nan, a gentle breeze from Hawaii, had made the three-day trip one of the best in my entire airline career. We felt true affection among ourselves, not to mention our constant laughter and the sharing of thoughts, personal truths, and experiences. This final flight for our group was one we looked forward to, but deep down I knew it would be a frosty Friday before this chemical balance would ever be duplicated.

As I greeted the seated customers and checked on their comfort, all seemed grand. Arriving at row eight, I couldn't help but notice the lad seated between a fiftyish-looking man and a handsome lad of about sixteen. The boy, a well-on-the-way-to-full-development teenager with a healthy head of brown hair cascading over his forehead, looked up at me with expressionless eyes. He was leaning sideways and seemed to have lost skeletal support.

"Are you feeling okay?" I asked, bending over for a closer look.

"Efff-uuuu," came the whispered response.

I reached over and touched his arm saying, "Can I get you

anything to help you feel better?" I thought ginger ale just might ease his flu symptoms.

"Don't touch me," he hissed.

The father didn't respond to any of this but sat there in his aisle seat and had some sort of sick smile on his face. I looked at the angular, stiff but perfectly groomed woman in the opposite aisle seat, and it suddenly hit me that I had misheard the boys original words. He hadn't mumbled "Flu" but had said, "F you."

The mother had the exasperated expression of most moms of teens so I just asked, "Is your son fourteen?"

"Yes. He wanted the window seat."

I continued on, briefed the exit rows, and then returned to the forward galley where I told Dave about the exchange.

As soon as we took off, I saw arms swinging at row eight. "Darren, that boy's beating up his dad."

"I'll go," said my take-charge, serious-at-just-the-right-times number one. When Dave came back up, he said that he'd told that youngster to stop that behavior immediately or the consequences wouldn't be minor, and he ascertained that the offender understood the orders. Again we strapped into the jump seats. Moments later the abusive behavior resumed, and back went Dave to the scene of the crime. Warnings were repeated in the firmest of ways, and the boy was advised of the serious punishment he could expect if he did not employ self-discipline.

During each exchange, the parents did nothing. The mother looked horrified, but the father sat insipid and silent throughout.

The boy then began to bounce his seat back repeatedly until

it nearly hit the woman behind him. This upset the customers in that row, and they asked if there was any way we could stop the teenager before someone got hurt. Yet when asked, the woman directly behind 8B said she felt no immediate danger, but her eldest son (9A) was ready to escalate the war effort in defense of his mom. I advised against such retaliation and received a promise in agreement.

Dave repeated the rules, and the captain was brought into play. Restraining the offender was the next step, and all equipment was readied, just in case. Row 25F (commuting flight attendant Ann) and the customer in 25D were prepared to give up their seats should the boy need restraining and reseating. Another commuter from Crew Services was also prepared to help, should his strength be needed in the restraining process.

It so happened that the customer behaved himself for the rest of the voyage, but everything was in place should there be another outburst of violence.

When we started service, we explained to the patient travelers that we'd had a situation that delayed our food and beverage duties. All understood, and our service, although late, was completed without incident.

Dave took the mother to the back galley to explain that the authorities (Corporate Security) would meet the flight and escort her son from the plane for a chat. By way of explanation, we were informed that her son was jealous of his older brother. "His older brother is really good at school and a good athlete." The younger boy, she explained, wasn't a star like his older brother.

"I don't know what set him off tonight," she added.

I reminded her that the older brother had been awarded the window seat. We all understood, however, that after the bad behavior began, it wouldn't have been prudent to capitulate by rewarding the sought-after seat to the fourteen-year-old.

Yet I wonder: How much favoritism is shown in this family? How many times during his near decade and a half has the "bad" boy heard how much better his older brother is at everything? At what point does a disenfranchised, lesser child just give up, not try at all? What good does being good do if you're not ever going to be good enough? Of course, I'm just theorizing, because I'll never know what goes on in this boy's home, let alone in his head.

Like both the opening gambit of the old radio show *The Shadow* and the title of this piece asks, who knows what lurks in the minds of men? Not a flight attendant who doesn't actually have access to the home life of a customer. Not a once-a-week therapist whose charge is defiant and bitter but without the vocabulary to explain his true feelings of sibling rivalry and hurt. Not a child who, whilst developing, is possibly compared to an older sibling ad nauseam and harbors a resentment that's so toxic it can erupt when just a seemingly innocuous catalyst, like the denial of a window seat, is injected into the test tube of puberty. Maybe that boy had asked nicely to change seats at first. I'll never know.

I hope he's okay. When the security officials took him off the plane, he went like a lamb to slaughter. Nary was a sound uttered. His parents and brother didn't even try to accompany him. They'd washed their hands in their own perfection.

HANK (AKA CHARLES)

JFK to Tampa, circa 2005

HAVE YOU EVER walked through a sea of people only to have one light up the air all around himself? That iridescence beaming out in every direction usually has a human core that's somehow magical in its own way. If you're lucky enough to witness one of these wonders of the world, stop and take a good long look at the source of this energy field. Usually the individual is completely unaware of the radiance around his person.

As I walked through JFK, my view of the anonymous hordes was fairly understimulated. Deadheading to Tampa on December 23, 2007, was about as much of a challenge as spilling ginger ale on a customer (something I manage with incredible élan on a regular basis!). You see, to deadhead is to be paid to fly in a comfy leather seat, in uniform, to the airport where a working flight will originate. Many of us really love these little pockets of relaxing flights.

There seemed to be a parting of the waters ahead, and I registered the separation of airport population somewhere very deep in my subconscious. The reason became clear as a man in a wheelchair, all legs and elation, was wheeled into view. I watched. Stared actually. He was one of the magic ones. He must have been very tall when standing because his legs were obviously the gangly sort seen in cartoons. The knees didn't touch the chin, but if exaggerated or put into the context of the entire man, they could have. His hair was like corn silk, not really colorless but indescribable. It had known perfect grooming but now was a statement in independent thought. And there was an air of excitement about him as he was maneuvered through other people. He really seemed to have his eyes focused on everything, and there was that look of boyish wonder on his face. Interesting, thought I.

I was assigned 3D, an aisle seat. Before sitting there, I worked the boarding of the flight because that's one of my favorite parts of being a flight attendant. Picking up each customer's vibes as they find their seats and settle down for their trip gives me such a rush. Their various moods and behavior patterns clue me in to just about everything anyone would want to know about the way the flight's going to unfold. Socially, that is. And isn't being an air hostess just like welcoming folks into your very own living room? It's one of the fun times. By the time I got back up front to my seat, the middle and window seats were occupied.

The middle seat was filled by an elderly Spanish-speaking woman in a buttoned-to-the-top, brown felt coat. She spoke no English, so our communication was through smiles, nods, head shakes, and hand holding. Of course, at the window, was none other than the ebullient wheelchair-bound man who'd thrilled at his race through JFK earlier!

I looked over and we spoke words of greeting. He seemed happy in the extreme, and his professorial bearing led me to my first interrogatory.

By chance, "Are you a professor or a writer?"

"Well, because I appear to be so to you, maybe I should be so, but I'm not. Far from it." Yet he rose to the bait and feigned an aristocratic and scholarly posture. We both laughed.

"Why are you going to Tampa?"

"I'm going to visit my mother. She's ninety-five and smokes like a fiend. I don't know how she does it. She's a going concern. The doctors are trying to get her to quit. Isn't that silly? Where do you live?"

"On the Canadian border in Vermont."

"Oh! I used to ski. I just loved it! Once you get the hang of it, all the turning and speed, oh, it's the most wonderful thing in the world! I used to do a lot of it."

He was beaming but his eyes were aimed directly into a past that didn't seem far away, but gone forever. "You must ski!" I think he presumed that anyone living in the great north who wasn't in a wheelchair must enjoy catapulting themselves down a slippery slope.

"I spent twenty-five years falling off the T-bar, actually, and I'm petrified of speed. In fact, I'm afraid of the inevitable pain!" I laughed, although the truest words are said in jest, right? He was incredulous and was obviously disgusted that a totally mobile person, living in a gorgeous ski area, didn't take advantage of such gifts.

Time for introductions: "I'm Heather." I figured that

a name, an offered hand for shaking, and a sincere "glad ta' meetcha" smile would help him forgive me for being a scaredy-cat, pantywaist, limp-wristed wuss.

"Hank," he volunteered as he reached across the poor Spanish lady between us. I tried to include her in the conversation by occasionally touching her arm and with a few inquiring looks about her comfort. She was trussed up in that coat like one of those snowsuit-clad boys in the movie *A Christmas Story*. She must have been really warm, not to mention overwhelmed with two chatty people speaking over her ample and felt-bound bosom. Yet she looked stalwartly forward into a dark television screen.

I had looked forward to this flight as a perfect time because I had a story due for a magazine. The assignment was based on two words: *delirium* and *exhilaration*. After a friendly chat, we hit the altitude that allowed laptop use. I extricated myself from conversation by giving a verbal cue, and the gentleman put on his earphones. However, he leaned his long torso as far forward with chest angled to the floor just enough to clue me in to his intention. Assured that he'd caught my attention, he twinkled and smiled an apology, "I'm sorry, this will be my last question, but what are you writing?"

"Well, I don't know where this is going yet, but it's a story with two words as sparkplugs."

"What are the words?"

"Delirium and exhilaration."

"Oh! How are you approaching this?" he asked with a most explosive enthusiasm. His brow furrowed upward to the hairline, and those young, laughing eyes gave me the impression that Hank was about to jump over the immobile one between us and grab my laptop for a quick look. Applying the word *curious* to describe his reaction would grossly misrepresent the word *understatement.*

I admitted that I'd had only a couple of days and a few long runs to work out how I'd introduce these words and somehow marry them into one flowing theme.

"Well, I've kind of been in a state of delirium for about ten years now, and there's been no exhilaration." He said this wistfully but with a deeper look in his eyes and a slight turning away like he was admitting something for the first time. The first time out loud, anyway. It intrigued me, this sudden reticence. His obvious folding inside gave me reason to ask my own tempered-with-tact questions.

"How do you define this state of mind and how it applies to you?"

"Well, I've been sort of hiding for ten years. I haven't been out there, if you know what I mean. It's bad. I mean I just don't get out with people, you know?"

"What were you doing up until ten years ago?"

"Well," and at this juncture he was suddenly alight, and that brilliance I saw out in the terminal was again in play, "I was a motocross racer. I was big time. Then I had the accident, and I just stopped everything. It's not good. I am completely weak on one side since the accident."

The Accident. The two words resonate with me because I had one of those. The Accident is the line of demarcation between one life and another. And it was a gift, really. I'd never have moved to Vermont from Oklahoma had I not been rear-ended by a Monte Carlo going fifty-five miles per hour. I was stopped to turn left at 71st and Lewis at 10:30 on a normal weekday morning. I'd never have been a herdsman on a dairy farm or raised my kids in a tiny village. Without The Accident I'd never have a job in the air. And I'd never have met Hank. For me, these are enough reasons to be grateful for that speeding Monte Carlo on a Tulsa street. Yes. I'm a very fortunate soul to have been flung thirty feet in a new Buick to land in a different Universe. "Wouldn't you really rather fly a Buick?" could have been a great promotional jingle.

Now we were really involved in conversation because in those shiny eyes were a thousand races won, countless women wooed. I could see him at his mightiest, flying over the motocross course, planning his next strategic forward thrust. I could see the wheels of his past escapades turning in his head as he relived the great moments. Winning, losing, passing, leaping, balancing on dead air, and feeling his stomach rise into his throat as the pulse rate maxed out. He took me there with just a facial expression full of memories. Full of breathtaking thrills and glee. Then the shadow fell across his eyes again, and he was a wheelchair-bound shut-in on his way to visit a ninety-five-year-old mother.

"I had a head injury about twenty-one years ago, Hank. I'm different, but I'm all better!" I always throw the last part of this admission in with a chuckle to make the recipient of the news comfortable. Folks get all kinds of uncomfortable if they think they're talking to damaged goods.

"You know, I had a head injury with this accident, too!"

And I knew we'd met for a reason. You see, I'm at over two decades, and Hank's only at ten years. We who've been bopped, dropped, or flopped mark our recoveries by the passage of years. It's a beautiful thing. It's like we're all on different rungs of an infinite ladder up to complete recovery or mastery of adaptation. Each person on a higher rung reaches down to take the hand of one clambering up from another. A very cool chain of encouragement-by-example results. Onward and upward!

Only those who've had a shared condition can really *understand* what it entails. Many can empathize, but rarely is true understanding possible. Not by the layman anyway. Maybe not by the published experts on the subject. As a writer, I'm not able to put it into words because the dimension we live in during the healing process is so completely surreal. At least it was for me. I faked almost everything for a couple of years. I adapted for survival. I perfected compensatory behavior. I healed on my own through routine, exhaustion, and some sort of vague belief that I was still able to get back. Back to what? I don't remember. Oh well, I'm doing everything I want to do now, and have for a long, long time, so I'm 100 percent of whoever I am, right? It's all good.

We talked intensely about how it was at the beginning. Hank admitted that he stopped being who he was and that the anger he harbors makes him feel guilty for even that very natural reaction. I told him my temper developed after The Accident, and that was a huge improvement in my life right there. I ceased to be a passive, acquiescent, nice girl and evolved into someone who didn't feel the least bit of guilt for expression of anger. Being too polite was lovely in society but terrible for one harboring opinions counter to an infused familial culture. Also, the governor on my embarrassment peddle was forever removed. I don't embarrass easily now, and that's a great thing! On the other hand, tears from intentional injuries to my heart, watching sad movies, listening to real gospel music, or watching brides and grooms tie the knot are uncontrollable. The tears that flow like rivers are one of the best residual reminders of the day my car practiced that short takeoff and landing. Did I ever cry before The Accident? I don't think I was allowed. The inhibitions of one raised as a white Anglo-Saxon Protestant need a good whack on the head. An orgasmic release results when the floodgates, born of pent-up waspishness, create rivulets that cascade down one's cheeks. It sure feels fabulous! A knock on the noggin shakes up the old social restraints, and when they settle, there's a whole new gray area just waiting to be mined for previously denied emotional realities. All this, I told Hank, were the benefits possible.

"I don't do anything. I'm by myself too much." Hank was really struggling to solidify and deal with this fact. There was an invisible drawbridge that slammed shut after every word toward his own personal truth. He was having a very tough time transmitting the admission over the stoic woman between us. Once he'd cast it over to me I could grab that bait and he could set the hook . . . if both parties were willing. If the hook sets, then he could cut his line and reel himself back into a tight spool. On the other hand, he could let me run with his line as far as it could go and be left with the catch-of-the-day—a good listener—on the hook. Choices at a time like that must be spontaneous. Backward to darkness? Forward through unchartered waters? Hank chose to let me run out his line, drawing him out of himself with every foot spent.

Another natural fallout from a head injury is the absolute realization that things aren't as easy after The Accident. We learn to pretend we can do things, recognize people, or know where we are and why until it becomes second nature. We live by lists and routine, the art of the familiar and the smallness of one's new world. After we realize that there's a stigma attached to the term *head injury*, we cease to begin every foray into human interactions with, "Hi! I've had a head injury so forgive me for (insert your reason for apology here)."

"I think it's much easier for women because we're allowed to be a bit vulnerable by society. Men, and I don't mean to generalize, but men are supposed to be strong and infallible. When they get knocked off their feet, it's quite possible that they just withdraw instead of allowing friends to help them back onto the horse after they fall off. People reach out to women, and we accept that help because we find it easier to say, 'Hey, I'm not myself today.' People reach out to men, especially champion motocross racers and great downhill skiers, but usually for advice, autographs, or encouragement. You had it made Hank, and the instant swapping of places probably made you feel quite without an identity. After attaining such a lofty position in life maybe it was easier to hide and just hope healing happened. All of a sudden, after ten years, you've realized that you're alone and cut off, right? It's not at all too late to say, 'Okay world, I want to go out and play!' Hank, you've got so much to offer! I noticed you when you were being pushed through JFK, and I had no idea I'd be sitting in your row on a flight. You still have sparkle like you wouldn't believe! If you never see me again, know this, you've still got what it takes."

"Hank's not my real name. It's Charles. They called me Hank when I was young, and it just stuck. I don't like it—I mean, Hank—there just aren't any Hanks, really, are there?

And, as you say, I do look rather academic, so from now on I'm Charles."

I reintroduced myself and we shook hands to make the new baptism official. Charles took on a new posture and said, "I've been in a bit of a state of delirium for ten years. I've withdrawn from everything I did and from everyone I used to know. I think it's time for a change. I still have time!"

"Don't beat yourself up for that. Ten years isn't a long time in the space of an eternity, Charles. Let's say you live in this incarnation for another five or six decades; couldn't they be made into a different, better way of life? I mean, everything would be better than what you have now, even if you put in just a tiny bit of energy, right? You don't have to be a champion motocross racer, the best downhill skier, or anything else you were before. What you could ask yourself is this: why did The Accident happen to you, and then take the changes as gifts that freed you from what you were once. You've got to rebirth yourself into the different, new and improved man. Because you're different, you've got to market yourself as something very special because you've survived. Now you've got to thrive. What have you got to lose? Today's the first day of the rest of your life, as they say. So, what are you going to do with it? You sure aren't happy with your last ten years, but you're young, and you light up a room. There's enthusiasm coming out of your pores. If I see it, others will, but not if you don't get out of your home to show anyone. How old are you?"

"I'm sixty-three. I do have a lot of years left, don't I? My mother's ninety-five, so there's a chance of living that long. I think I'll start doing something." He said this with such verve and a swinging arm. His fist was thrust around with enough speed to make the poor woman in the middle seat give a level-eyed look of as much shock as any totally preoccupied person might. In short, the heavy lids above her eyes just lifted a bit before she realized that the long man who seemed so cultivated had taken on the attitude of a little boy who'd just seen his favorite hockey player score a winning Stanley Cup goal. She hadn't flinched once. She might have been thinking that this man wasn't capable of violence, or maybe her reflexes were numbed by age and body heat. Maybe she was a trained soldier of the Lord or some oppressive political regime. Whatever, she sure could hold her ground.

In the space of a flight, Hank the Shut-In became Charles of Things Yet to Come. Multiple years of possibilities lay ahead for him. And, like myself, life will be different, but there's a good chance that it will also be better. Exhilaration at last.

This is the very first time I've ever written about The Accident. I'm still climbing that infinite ladder to completion. There's always a hand reaching down to help me up, and there's always someone like Charles ready to grasp my own. Blessed be.

LIGHTNING ALL AROUND

Boston to West Palm Beach, summer 2006

ANOTHER DELAY AND another massage chair set up at another departure gate. (I massage delayed folks.)

His name was given. Even though the delay had been hours long and the gate area was humid and dank, this dapper man's long-sleeve, button-down shirt was as crisp as if his laundress had just delivered it and his manservant had just helped this fellow put it on. How do some men keep this professional cool about them? "I have a terrible headache."

"What's causing all your stress?" I asked as he positioned himself in the chair.

"Oh. Work mostly."

Our chat began, but I didn't really get the vibe that work was that terrible for this man. I told him that living simply might be the antidote for his overbooked schedule. Telling him about my Vermont lifestyle and how I raised Holly and David with a make-do or "find a way to earn it" mind-set gave him pause.

"A few years ago, my partner and I started a company and made baby products. We market them. Now it's a billion-dollar concern."

"If it's so profitable, why don't you take your winnings and start a less stressful life? Is it possible?"

He admitted that he didn't take out the maximum stock options at the outset, so he wasn't in a position to actually retire. "Plus, I have three kids." Then the bomb. "My wife was diagnosed with cancer. Leukemia. Two years ago. She went into remission after a year of treatment, but it's back now."

I stopped the massage and knelt down in front of him for some eye-to-eye talk.

"It's really been a blessing in a way. My mother and sister wanted to move in, and I just got them an apartment close by, so I've really been getting to know my children. I mean, I was always working, working, working before my wife got sick. Now I have a relationship with them. My daughter wasn't close to me at all, but now, it's very special."

The prognosis of his wife wasn't discussed at all. The unknown is best left unknown because it's so scary to go down that road. Where there's life, there's hope. Such hope. And love.

The massage continued and so did the conversation. He laid the history of his empire and the rearrangement of priorities on the table, and this young but mature-in-the-extreme pragmatist was counting his blessings out loud. He'll be alright no matter what, and his headaches will be few as more of his true strengths are revealed to him.

When he got up, I gave him a big hug and said, "You're a great man." Here's a man who's juggling so much. He's got so many balls in the air. He'll be fine. His children will be fine. His wife? Either way, she'll know those she loves will have it all because this father of fathers was rearranging and adapting with his children as his number-one concern. Headaches. They go away when a person figures out what's causing them. This man figured that he was doing a very good job at home and felt so rich because of his newly minted relationships with his children—stock options be damned. This man's about to have a balance in his life that he knows is necessary, and I felt him relax as he accepted this obvious necessity. Did he know it before he sat on my chair? Probably. Yet having a sounding board, even with hundreds of stranded people all around, generates an intimacy that allows for self-reflection like no other. Very cool.

LIVER CANCER

I will forever love this man. I will forever think of him.
Washington to Boston, deep winter 2009

DURING DELAYS, I set up a massage chair and invite the customers to partake of this, another of my professions. I've been a licensed massage therapist since 1983, and I run the MYO Clinic in East Berkshire, Vermont. While I massage their cares away, people open up and tell me a great deal about themselves. Such a blessing for me!

What I saw first were his enormous brown eyes floating in a sea of yellow. "Can I be next in your massage chair? Can you guess what's wrong with me?" He was dark-haired, young, and jaundiced, so the evidence made it pretty clear that his liver was compromised.

"Is it your liver, sir?"

"Liver cancer."

Into my chair he came, leaving the little photo album and

a stack of loose pictures on the sterile-looking airport seat.

"How's it going, then?" I asked.

"Not so good."

"What should I work on, sir?"

"I have a major headache."

Working on cancer patients has always left me hurting, but with this man, I felt nothing bad at all. He wasn't strong enough to cast any of his pain upon me, even subconsciously.

I felt my hands going beneath his very skin and into his soul. It's magic when this happens to a massage therapist because it symbolizes the duality of intent without interference of predefined, tangible mortality. It's all good at that point, and it doesn't happen with every patient. His sense of humor was obvious, and like most that are in the position to laugh at the silliness and inanities of daily life, he did. We soon settled into an honest warmth.

I asked this handsome man, in his mid-forties, how his mom was handling his sickness.

"It's really terrible. I mean, she shows up at my house without calling first. I'm sick. I'm tired. I'm not dead! I can still do my own laundry, cooking, and cleaning and all that. Everyone just figures they're supposed to hang around and help me, but I just don't want that. Jesus. I'm tired!"

I wondered aloud if he'd ever been honest with the interloping do-gooders.

"I want to tell them to get the f—— out!"

We talked more about his time on earth and the friends in the snapshots he had with him. I looked at them; he was in many, his arm loosely slung over this one's shoulder or around another's waist. He wore a baseball cap and smiled broadly, and

I fell in love with that man's life. He had friends and family. He loved and was loved. He had laughter and good times. Maybe he'd had it all; if so, he definitely knew it as he shared these pictorial vignettes with me. We both understood the fleeting moments that might only happen again in the review of these captured images, but we were sharing them, and I felt blessed.

During the flight, he took a turn for the worse. His head went forward, and he seemed to disappear within himself.

"I'm cold. I'm so cold!" he told me weakly.

I wrapped him in a blanket and rubbed his arms to warm him. I turned the heat up to the maximum possible. Nobody in my section complained. Man's humanity to man was in play.

I made him mild tea, and he had a few sips, but mostly he just held the cup for additional warmth. I didn't want to be that mother who just showed up, but I am a mother and, by definition, sworn to that role.

He sat in the first aisle seat. I was facing him from my jump seat just before landing, so communication was easy. He seemed to rally just before we landed and said, "My neck always hurts."

I innocently asked, "What kind of mattress do you have?"

So everyone could hear, he pulled out a Groucho Marx attitude from somewhere within his cocoon of blankets and said, "I'd be happy to show it to ya' if ya' come ovah to my place." He'd not accepted my care as maternal but instead, very subtly, on his terms because he's "not dead," and he wanted to affirm that fact to me and the other passengers. Everyone knew I'd been giving him special care before and throughout the short flight. Perhaps some understood the inevitability of his situation. There was a warm and universal chuckle, and he knew he'd entertained us with his Groucho imitation. If anything were magically possible, most of those sitting around him would someday show up in his photo album as friends. He was just that sort of guy.

When he was getting off the plane and being tucked into the awaiting wheelchair, we hugged and looked each other straight in the eyes. "I'll be thinking of you," was my parting comment.

"I'll be thinking of you, too. I love you, you know."

"I love you, too, sir."

And I do think of him. Of his honesty, humor, frustration, smile, and pain. I think of his mother, no different than myself in that role. And I think of him doing his own laundry, cleaning, and living.

I'm thinking of him now, with love.

FROM A CULT TORN

From a southern to a northern airport

SOME DAYS ARE rife with drama: medical emergencies, hysterical customers, passive mothers.

Before boarding I like to meet everyone waiting to get on my flights, so I mosey through the gate area just saying, "Hi! Are you coming with me on the next flight to Boston?" For some reason, getting to know the folks at this point makes for a lovely time in the air, no matter what transpires between departure and arrival. The interchange is usually light and fun, but there are multiple occasions in my memory bank that hold fast to a place in my heart. When the expression on a person's face is dour, they've probably had a bad day, or maybe they're expecting one upon arrival at their final destination. If one has a sad face, there are other things going on in that life. The worried look is common and can be caused by anything from a son's motorcycle accident in the arrival city, or because the person is giving a speech and doesn't feel great about their delivery capabilities. The average customer has a normal life with enough emotional baggage to fit into an overhead bin coupled with all the space under the seat in front of them. In some cases I can get them to gate-check this burden just by holding a hand or listening as they purge their personal angst. This is the best part of my job as a SkyNation flight attendant. The listening. And when my mind's working, I hear words left unspoken, but not always.

Yesterday, a normal Saturday in Orlando, began this way. I schmoozed; held a crying baby; examined a fabulous hairdo created at the Bippity Bobbity Boo salon that transformed little Sarah to the rank of royalty; then met an older woman and younger man, also at the gate. The black-haired woman was portly, with eyeliner applied a bit too heavily to upper and lower lids that framed dull eyes. Not stupid eyes, but numb. I thought, "There's one tired woman!" I sat beside the man because, when I reached to take his hand in introduction, he held on to mine. He was trying so hard to speak that I thought he might be suffering from some sort of laryngeal impairment. When words were finally expelled they were clear but strange. He was communicating through a third party.

"The spirit within says that you are at peace."

True. I thanked him and looked at the woman, whose expression was totally unreadable. Blank. I assumed she was totally accustomed to this pattern of speech, and I felt it a harmless interaction. Even nice.

At the next gate a woman was prostrate on the floor because of some sort of allergic or emotional reaction. She wasn't on my flight, but because I was there, I held her hand until paramedics arrived. While awaiting the medics, the man I'd met during my sweep through the gate area came over and knelt close to her head.

"The Presence within says that a wall will come down and the pain will be released."

Hmm, thanks but no thanks, sir.

The man was slight in build, very clean shaven, and wore black pants, a nylon jacket, and running shoes. His female traveling companion was standing just behind him, so I signaled her to take him away from the downed woman. She just said, "Come over here," and the young man rose and returned to his waiting area. He was very compliant.

"I'm not in pain," stated the woman on the carpet. She didn't seem upset by the sudden appearance of one who spoke in third person at all. You see, his presence was just that, an ethereal nonentity that couldn't make waves in the world if he tried. Just a slip of a man who's spirit was a bit closer to the surface than most. A gentle breeze rather than a cutting wind.

Our flight boarded without incident. Folks leaving Orlando are usually tired, satisfied, and happy because they're coming from a place that evokes childhood memories or makes new ones for their own offspring. There's absolutely nothing wrong with living in a fantasy world for a while, but when one inhabits such a place permanently, there's a social stigma attached. Isn't that a totally obvious double standard? One is deemed a healthy escape. One is christened aberrant behavior. And let's not forget the entire gray area between both poles. This is a vast chasm inhabited by most of us. Those who fall between here and there, imagination and realism, the gaseous or concrete stages of physical and chemical reactions make up the majority. And those so placed in the middle and without overt behavior patterns that elicit extra attention are the ones who judge all. This isn't fair, it's just the norm.

I told my crew, just before closing the doors, that a man in the back, named George, spoke in third person but seemed more spiritual than antisocial. However, I told them to be aware and not surprised if he ordered chips for his "Presence" within. I wasn't making light of his condition, just sharing something, in a positive way, with two of the best flight attendants in this company: Sam and Jenn. Both make me so very proud to be in this uniform.

Before takeoff Jenn suggested I ask the mother if she was certain her ward was good to go. Jenn was working in close proximity to the lad, and her eyes are as sharp as her mind. I'd venture that her intuitive senses are also highly evolved.

"Ma'am, is everything fine with you?" I quietly asked. She nodded. No smile. The young man's eyes were closed so I leaned over and whispered in her ear, "I know you're traveling together, is there anything I should know before takeoff? Is there any medication involved? Will everything be okay here?"

Her response was to level her eyes at mine, and without a facial muscle flexing, she said, "It's fine. He's fine. He traveled a couple of weeks ago. He's fine. He doesn't need any medication."

Right after takeoff, my number two, Sam, saw George kneeling on his seat. 22F. The woman was in 22E. A young man, as stylish as any walking the streets of Paris, sat in 22D. I watched but remained in the forward galley before calling Jenn to the front so I could go back.

A Boston-based flight attendant named Bob sat in one of

the rows close to the one inhabited by the disruptive force, his mother, and the Presence within. Before joining this trio, I leaned in and asked Bob, "If, by chance, I need to sit with the young man, would you be willing to do my service?" This man was totally into the entire situation and nodded vigorously. Great, I thought, we'll get to Boston as a team.

It was obvious at this juncture that the man was having some sort of emotional episode, so I moved in, sat on his guardian's lap and took his hand, looked him in the eye, and we connected. He sat right down and held firmly to my hand.

"The Presence within believes we should land this plane now. The Presence within is aware of the need for landing this plane *now*." This warning, given in a firm, very slow, clearly enunciated manner was said very quietly.

"What makes you think this is necessary, George?"

"The Presence within says that we must overcome fear."

I asked the woman. "Are you the mother? Fill me in, please."

"I don't understand. He was fine at the airport, but we waited too long. We were there for four hours before the flight. It was too long."

"Is he on medication?" I asked again.

"No. He's fine. He's fine. I don't know what to do. I don't know."

Sam and Bob moved the dapper man from 22D to the back galley, the mother took his place and I sat in the middle seat. George and I held hands and locked eyes. He was trying to communicate that we must return to Orlando because he needed to be there. Every syllable came out like some large object being forced through a tiny hole. Still attached to my disturbed row mate, I turned slightly to the mother to ask what caused this outburst. In answer to my string of questions, the following facts emerged.

"He's a member of a cult. He took a vow of silence. He hasn't spoken until today. I'm taking him home for reprogramming. He joined a year ago and was home at Christmas. We had a reprogrammer set up at Christmas, but he had a fight with one of my other sons and went back to Orlando. His girlfriend is pregnant—and she's breaking away from the cult. She called a couple of days ago because she thinks he's getting worse and should be taken back to Boston. He was living with his girlfriend's family, not actually within this cult. He's taken a vow of silence. He's a professional man. He finished tenth in his graduating class at college. He was a very hyper child but never a problem. There was never a problem with him. And now this. I don't know what to do. His girlfriend met him through this chanting cult, and now she's trying to break away. She's only got a high school education. I've never met her family. I went to meet him yesterday, but he'd disappeared from their home. I tried to get him on my cell and found out he was at the Ivanhoe Hotel. It was a miracle I found him in the lobby there. Just a miracle. And now this! He was fine this morning and all day. He ate a good meal, and I don't know what's going on now. When it started he just took off for three months and traveled around. He gave up his business and just did his thing."

What makes an educated man join a cult? What could have been missing from his life to make a high achiever succumb to the teachings of an organization that steals identity and individualism? What would make hundreds of people in a

South American jungle drink poisoned Kool-Aid? It happens. It happens.

From the mother I gleaned more information during the out-of-the-corner-of-my-mouth interview.

The mother has a boyfriend of ten years who believes all George's issues will clear up if he only gets a job. This lack of sophistication and insensitivity seems to have erased any deep initiative on the mother's part. She's stuck in the middle of intervention and ignorance. One younger brother has a problem with drinking. Another is married. The three sons are thirty-one (George), twenty-seven (the drinker), and twenty-four (the husband). They're not close. ("We all do our own thing, you know?" she offered.) She went on to tell me that George's father and she had divorced while he was in college.

It was my impression that the mother is a passive person and not one who stands up and believes in herself. ("I had to leave work the other day for this. I don't want to involve his father too much. He doesn't understand what's going on.") What work would need her more than a troubled son? And what father needs understanding alone? Might a father not offer love and support at a time like this? I don't know anything more than what my imagination holds up for immediate speculation, and that's certainly not enough to build a reality around this disconnected family unit. Assumption lead me to believe there existed a family composed of individuals who didn't thrive in a collective society—and apparently didn't evolve as happy sorts in their autonomous states, either.

All information volunteered by the mother was given without any inflection; her affect was flat. She was shell-shocked. Stunned. Totally without any control, and she knew it. Perhaps this was her entire way of life? Maybe her existence is one of passivity and acquiescence? Her brilliant, beautiful son had been replaced by a brainwashed nonperson. One of the people of I AM. The cult of I AM had permeated every cell of George's body. He rose and took his knapsack from the overhead. He needed his CDs to reaffirm his connection to the I AM, and I thought this was a good thing and might serve to assuage his separation anxiety. He let me listen to the music of one song. The only word I remember from the acoustic sound was *revolution*. And the tune was innocuous and rather grating to my ear. Boring stuff. Little rhythm and adolescent in its musical style.

For an hour and twenty minutes all was well. We communicated, held hands throughout. Then George's eyes closed, and he gave a loud "aaaaahhhhh." I responded by taking his cheek in my hand and whispering in his ear, "George. A quiet *om* with me, now, please. Just a quiet *om*." I crooned that universal mantra into his ear, and his hand tightened around mine. I thought all was well, but his "aaaaahhhhh" came out again. Then again. And again. I'd lost him, I thought. How to bring him back to me? I held him in my arms. A passive body leaned against me. Spent? Not even.

"The Presence within me says that you must admit your fear."

"I'm not afraid, George."

"The Presence within me says that you're afraid of my screams."

"Those weren't screams. They were just loud aaaaahhhhhs. I'm not afraid, but please, George, think of the others on board because they might not know that you speak from a Presence within. They might be scared when they hear you. That's all."

There were no more outbursts. Only an hour left before landing. It was now 18:48 by my watch. I felt that the flight would continue without incident, because the man was going deeper into his meditative state. His hand released mine and paralleled the other with index finger to thumb, palms up, resting upon his thighs. Legs akimbo. Complete relaxation of body and mind. Good, I thought. Very nice. I affixed his once-shared earphone properly to his ear and his eyes flew open.

"The Presence within says that you are not to touch the headphones."

I felt he was pulling away, and this wasn't good. Not good at all. Somehow I felt he was revving up internally to cut me off even further. Somehow he was alienating me, and that didn't feel good at all.

A classic anxiety attack?

Then George's body went rigid. He became an automaton and stood. I held his narrow hips tightly and asked him to sit, please. He was catatonic. His body, robotic, rigid. He stood above my seat, my eyes level with his waist. Sam placed his hand on George's chest and asked him to sit. There was a continued forward motion as George forced himself past me and into Sergio's outstretched arm. Suddenly, I was looking at a belt buckle, and I was being pulled backward and dragged in one quick, steady, irreversible motion toward the aisle by some great physical ability or cohesive force. I remember two things: the armrest blocking my progress and my feet suddenly straight up over my head. I flipped fast and took a seat on the downed man's thighs as he was already face down, arms behind his back. I swear, in this nanosecond that marked his entire time afoot, Sam had the cult member completely subdued, two seatbelt extensions already around George's wrists, and a rather large customer had George's ankles pinned to the floor.. All was well. Sam's unbelievable ability to size up a potentially threatening situation wasn't lost on me. But even then, I hadn't seen that the cockpit crew was using the facilities and the barriers were up, so I didn't realize that Sam acted so quickly because of the potential breaching of the flight deck by our unstable customer. Sitting in the back, in a middle seat, with all my attention being consumed by my charge, hadn't allowed me position or opportunity for such an observation.

After the cockpit was secured, Bob and Sam carried the restrained customer to seats 25DEF, while the customers from these seats were reseated.

Bob kept the captain informed of all events. Sam guarded George, who was face down and acquiescent in his restrained condition. Bob had taken a belt and affixed George's feet to the armrest with it. Sam had fastened seatbelts around the customer's midsection. Because he was face down, George's breathing was monitored throughout the flight from this point forward.

I divorced myself from this suffering young man and visited every person from row twenty-five to the front of our aircraft to inform them of the situation and inquire about their comfort. With only two exceptions, the feedback was positive on the crew's behalf. One customer was "pissed" that someone would act this way on the plane and thereby disrupt the status quo. This gentleman was in 21D, and I'd asked him, before seating myself beside George and after

I'd asked Bob to take my service, not to react to anything George might say to him. You see, upon takeoff, when the cult member got up for a second, the man in 21D had turned and started telling him what he thought of his behavior. I arrived at the scene and whispered to the man that we'd be okay and "thanks." I didn't know he'd get upset by my intervention. I was polite but this one man was very angry with George. One shouldn't react in an abusive manner to one who's having an emotional/psychological episode. One woman, traveling with two children, told me she was afraid of flying at the best of times and would never fly again. I knelt and told her that I was totally afraid of snakes, and no manner of consolation would alleviate my phobia, "however, please, ma'am, know that the young man is under control and poses no threat to you, your children, or this plane." I asked if she needed anything to make the last forty-five minutes better and she just said, "No."

Jenn told me that throughout the dramatic takedown and afterward, the customers were universally willing to help, and they were offering their services for a multitude of imagined or real scenarios. Policemen on board. Firemen on board. Two women who weren't nurses but "understood problems" asked to be pressed into service if need be. Jenn, an absolutely amazing and forthright woman, with common sense, grace, and charm equally distributed in her every cell, handled all customers with élan. God, I love her!

With his quick thinking, immediate physical response, and tremendous bravery and leadership talents, deserves a commendation from SkyNation. Bob, who did nothing less than prevent a diversion by eliminating the need for my presence in the aisle, must be recognized for his initiative, leadership, strength of will, and dynamism during a time of duress.

You all know the rest of the story. The passengers were asked to remain seated while the Massachusetts Port Authority personnel boarded the plane as the doors opened and moved hastily to the rear galley. The customers filed off and, without exception, were thankful and openly full of admiration for the teamwork and professionalism of my crew. The angry man took my hand and gave a half smile as he deplaned. The frightened woman smiled then hugged and kissed me.

Hindsight is twenty-twenty. Had the mother not completely assured me of George's ability to travel well, I'd have had him removed from the aircraft before departure. Yet, as religious zealots go, he had offered healing, a wish that a downed woman's fear be released, and he'd held my hand as he wished me peace. Never was I afraid of the man. And that "Presence within"—although holding this man's heart in a fist and his soul in an enclosure bound by musical propaganda, a loud mantra, and silence—hadn't completely killed that young man who'd finished tenth in his chiropractic graduating class.

Not a happy ending, to be sure. Yet, as way leads onto way, we can only hope that George finds peace and the Presence within releases his grasp on this young man's soul. Blessed be.

Injuries to the crew: Sam had an enormous bruise on his upper left arm. The bruise extended lengthwise across the middle of his biceps (approximately four-and-a-half inches in length and one-and-a-half inches in width). It was a deep and painful injury.

Me? My right shoulder was untouchable. The right side of my neck, likewise. My right rib cage was sore to the touch. I couldn't raise my arm without extreme pain. I was nauseated all day and slept only three hours that night. Emotionally? I can't second guess anything done on board; we all did our very best and used the best judgment possible given the information provided by the mother and the initial behavior of George, the peaceful warrior, the soul in transition, and, according to his mother, the man who'd spoken not a word to anyone in a year until he spoke to me.

SHANE

JFK to New Orleans, December 2009

"AS A REMINDER, all SkyNation flights are nonsmoking. Tampering with smoke detectors or smoking in the lavatory may result in a fine."

So sayeth the flight attendant.

Until recently, I thought that the word *will* should be substituted for the word *may* in this fine warning to our guests. In recurrent training—the annual reintroduction to things we know but need to review—we're told of the "Invited Not to Fly" list and hear stories of customer foibles. Our security department sends those who hear it all, after flight attendants see it all, to entertain us with accumulated tales of the flying public's daring deeds. I love this portion of training because it never ceases to amaze me how far people confined to a tube flying five miles high will go to bend, fold, reinvent, or break the rules of the airborne road.

We hear of folks who throw fits, baggage, drinks, cuss words, or worse in the general direction of our crew members. There are others who swear that their carburetors fit in the overhead bins and that tiny dogs are supposed to be draped around their necks as accessories to outlandish outfits. There are some who think that to pop a few Valium and wash 'em down with a few shots of vodka is the only way to fly. Some insist that carry-on baggage, even if it's the same size as the average coffin, not only deserves to be in the cabin, but only partially under the seat in front of them; the rest should stick out in the aisle because, "Dagnabit, I paid forty-nine dollars for this ticket, so the space around my seat is mine!" Others can't resist the romantic urges that they've been denied while spending two weeks at the home of strict in-laws.

Some smoke in lavatories.

I love the individuals who march onto my planes. Everyone has their own internal ethics, logic, and moral barometer, right? Rather than judge the myriad personality types and their accrued social behaviors, I choose to enjoy most of them for who they are and whatever habits, eccentricities, or behavior patterns they bring onboard with the rest of their carry-on baggage. If they know I not only respect them but genuinely find something to like about each, getting them to cooperate can be fun for both sides. As the song goes, "Ya' got to give a little, take a little, and let your poor heart break a little."

When it comes to safety, we not only need charm but the Federal Aviation Regulations to hold up as the gospel according to the Federal Aviation Administration. There might be a softening of consequences for any number of customer infractions, but one I've never thought would cause me to bend was the breaking of that smoking in the lavatory rule. As far as I was concerned, life doing hard time was the sentence I'd have imposed. It took a nonbureaucratic, think-out-of-the-box pilot to soften me up a bit.

On the way to New Orleans, I learned that there are different levels of retribution for the smoking in the lav offender. We were on the plane, and my number two was none other than Ben, one of the best there is at SkyNation. He's a giant of a man with a gentle spirit and beautiful heart. To top it off, he admits to being nonconfrontational.

The plane, holding a hundred customers when full, is super easy for service, and the configuration is such that the flying public is close, but there's room to breathe. The lavs are not made for giants, but they'll do. Just last week, I bent the wrong way and my cell phone plunged into the abyss of a commode. Oh well, worse things can happen in an aircraft lavatory than the loss of one's cell phone. Fire, for instance! The fact that we have sensitive smoke detectors and ashtrays doesn't eliminate the possibility that a contraband cigarette might be surreptitiously placed into a trash can. Of course, that might lead to a fire alarm sounding, but who wants anything to go that far? Certainly not me!

As gentle as I am with the usual wayward customer, I always thought that my wrath would be without sympathy for anyone I'd ever catch smoking on board. The very idea that someone might put the entire population of one plane in jeopardy just angers me. I do not like narcissists.

I used to teach in a prison. For years, I've had a television talk show in Vermont. There was about a year when the camera crew and I would go into a correctional facility to tape shows. From murderers and pedophiles to arsonists and thieves, the full spectrum of evils was right there in front of me. Of all the people I've interviewed in prison on my television show, the criminals who are the most willing to talk about their innocence are born of narcissistic personality disorder. Remorse is nonexistent unless it gets them "good time" or removes the powers that be from their weak, incarcerated backs. Narcissists don't care about anyone but themselves. Not all self-serving, self-involved, self-promoting people end up in prisons. And some really good but terribly unlucky men and women do crowd such institutions. How can we, as servants of the people, judge? Intentional insults to society delivered by a sociopath or the momentary weakness of one who's been stressed beyond his ability to cope leaves a lot of gray area. The poles on the breaking-of-laws spectrum, and every graduated sin between the two, present themselves to crew members. I think the time I've spent behind bars in my roles as teacher or interviewer has left me wondering if my unconditional love of most folks is justified. Yet, at what point should we draw the line and become judge and jury of our fellow man based on first impressions? What do we really know of the culture of an individual's mind, after all?

When Ben called and told me about the suspected smoker in the rear lav, I drew a hard line. I marched to the back of the plane and was told that a man had definitely smoked, and there were two witnesses. Calling the captain was our next move. I figured our felon would be instantly vilified and arrested upon landing. Why? Because I didn't understand the powers of a captain at this point, nor did I feel any sympathy for the perpetrator's cause.

Ben hadn't seen that fellow in 15C smoke. The folks in another row had entered the lav immediately after our suspect had vacated it, and they'd seen and smelled cigarette smoke. They were incensed (pun intended) when reporting their findings to Ben.

The captain asked the smoker's age. This I thought totally irrelevant because a crime's a crime, right? Would he be prosecuted as a minor if he was under eighteen or something? Then the captain said, "If he refuses to admit that he was smoking, we'll have him picked up in New Orleans. Tell him if he admits it, things will go easier on him. That is, if he's very, very sorry."

After these comments, I was mixed up. Does that mean if I get a confession, he doesn't get arrested at all or simply that he doesn't get the death penalty? And I was truly miffed about the age question. Before ringing off, the captain said, "Let me know what happens."

I approached the seat of the wrongdoer. Looking down I saw a guy closer to boyhood than manhood. His hair, parted on the side, was a grand example of what good genes can do for the crowning glory of a man, and he had a face that should be in front of a portrait artist: Thin and chiseled, it was a tad feminine in its beauty. The skin, that of one who might never need to shave because it was like a baby's. The eyes, dark and in a permanent squint, suited the face. Suited the man.

"Sir, it's been reported that you may have been smoking in the bathroom. Were you?"

That face became even more angelic. "No." And I thought he'd either been drinking or perhaps taking some sort of barbiturate—just the slowness of his speech and his inability to focus on my face, I guess.

"Sir, it would do your cause more good if you came out with another answer if it applies."

"I wasn't smoking."

I knelt down beside him and told him about the rules, and he looked at me like I was a long-lost mother. Oh, he wanted to tell me the truth. He was bursting with it, but the fear of something inevitable held him back. Like anyone, he thought he could bluff his way out of trouble and was giving it the old college try.

"How old are you?" I asked, with my hand on his arm.

"Twenty-four."

With that, I stood up and impulsively pushed his beautiful hair off his face, like any mother would when a stalemate is reached with a favorite child.

I went back to share this denial with Benito and asked him to relay this to the captain. Ben said, "Tell him we have two witnesses, and it'll go better for him if he tells the truth and even better if he gives up his cigarettes!"

Back I went. This time I knelt down and told him the truth, "I don't know what 'going easier' on you really means. But if it gets you less of a fine or anything, wouldn't it be worth it? We have two witnesses. You know, you remind me of my own son. Dave's twenty-six, and I miss him right now very, very much. We live close to each other, but he's busy. You know how that is. I'm actually worried about him, and—well, why are you going to New Orleans?"

"Just to go, you know?"

"Do you have family there?"

"No."

"Friends?"

"No."

"What's your name?"

"Shane."

I reached out and took his hand, "I'm Heather. It's very nice to meet you, even though I'm a major thorn in your side right now, Shane."

Oh, I thought. It's the day after Christmas, and this boy's so terribly alone.

"I'm hoping you can tell me something. Our captain says that things will go better for you if you admit that you smoked, if you did. There are two witnesses. Were you smoking, Shane?"

"You've got to understand. I've been at sea for two months!"

"My, that couldn't have been easy! I guess a smoke felt necessary, eh?"

"I smoked."

I patted his arm and said, "I know. Do you think you can go without doing that again until we land?"

In a rather relieved, relaxed and nice way, he nodded.

"May I have your cigarettes, please?"

He reached into his jacket and pulled out a half-smoked pack of Kools. "Thank you," and I took them, got up, patted his shoulder, and returned to Ben, who called the captain and told him of the confession and confiscation. It became obvious at that juncture that the question of age did weigh in the handling of the situation. A young offender isn't always to be grouped with the hardened criminal. A slightly impaired young one might be better served with a warning and a scare than a stiff fine or sentence.

As everyone got off the plane, I saw him coming up the aisle. He was nearly the last one off. You see, this young, vulnerable sailor-of-sorts had no idea if he was to be slapped on the wrist, taken off in a paddy wagon, caned, or ignored while getting off the plane. He stopped in front of me, and I pulled him down to whisper in his ear, "Promise me you'll never smoke on an airplane again, Shane."

"I promise." And I believed him.

The pilots watched this little interaction and, as Shane deplaned, I said, "That's our little smoker."

You know, I do believe that confession is good for the soul. Moreover, I believe that a loving warning and a compassionate way of handling things, as our captain did, is good for the world. Not only at Christmas should authority be meted out sparingly, but all through the year. I really learned something that night. And from a pilot, no less. That's a Christmas miracle right there!

To finish that old song I started earlier in the story: "That's the story of, that's the glory of love."

But remember, smoking on a plane is not allowed *ever*. If a fire starts, it takes only ninety seconds for the entire aircraft to be engulfed. Do not try this because it *will* result in a fine!

SMART IN OUR OWN WAYS

West Palm Beach to White Plains, December 2010

HE WAS PRETTY, and she was absolutely model perfect as they sat side-by-side, awaiting takeoff from West Palm Beach to our destination, Westchester Airport. I was talking to everyone in their vicinity as I stood in the aisle, when the gorgeous, young twenty-something lady asked, "How long will it take to get there?"

"Two hours and forty-three minutes."

The response to this answer was one of sneering disgust. The throwing back of the head and openly disgruntled facial expression was surprising. I didn't know that such a vision of loveliness could transform so quickly from cover girl to backstreet girl personality. This Jekyll and Hyde switch took less than a nanosecond.

"Okay, you don't like my answer so let me rationalize for you. If you were to get onto a stagecoach now, you'd arrive in White Plains sometime after Christmas. That's if the snow didn't stop you in your tracks. You'd probably be snakebit before you left Florida. The cook would have died or deserted before South Carolina, and you'd be served very bad coffee every day."

"What's a stagecoach?" asked the pretty young man.

Everyone in the vicinity was smiling by this time because they understood that I was just trying to be funny. My facial expression must have looked like a cross between total incredulity and bliss because now, besides rationalizing, I could be a teacher.

"Well, a stagecoach was pulled with four horses, usually. It was an enclosed wagon and it helped open up this country because it was a pretty good mode of transportation in those days."

"You did that?" he asked.

"That must have been so cool," the girl added.

I look my age. Really. I have wrinkles and knobby arthritic knuckles. My vanity button is nonexistent. However, the young man's question really threw me. More teaching on my part was necessary, for sure! The crowd was now totally enthralled by our interaction. They couldn't wait to hear where this verbal volley would go next.

"Yes. It was tough, but it made me the man I am today. I actually discovered America."

I don't usually like anyone who patronizes innocents, and I guess I was kind of mean. You know, playing to the audience rather than softheartedly letting ignorance pass as their problem. Yet we were taking these young ones to their folks for Christmas, and I'm sure the parents would have encouraged me to enlighten or introduce their offspring to our past.

"What do you do? Are you a historian, by chance?" I asked the fellow.

"No. I'm a hairdresser. I go right for the roots!"

"Have you read Alex Hailey, then?"

"Who?"

"Never mind." I felt pretty badly by this time. The sarcasm was lost on the boy. The girl didn't respond either. All those sitting in the seats around them were chuckling. By now, I was actually feeling terrible for my own part in this interchange. No child left behind, indeed. These young people really don't know very much at all. But is what I know more important? Does my knowledge of history, so filled with propaganda and revisionist redirection, give me the right to consider myself smarter, more informed, more aware than these two beautiful people? It shouldn't. It doesn't. Maybe they have a brighter future because they aren't anchored to the past and the stories told in books about the people, principles, and ethics that built our country. Maybe they're not hooked into the dogma and rhetoric of corporate America media now. Good for them.

"I love my hairdresser! She totally fixes my mess and listens to everything that's going on in my life. She's a great woman!"

He nodded. "We do that!"

So who cares if he thinks I discovered America in a stage coach; he knows how women feel today, and his sister made our plane that much lighter and sweeter even she presented the apogee of physical beauty crowned with her smile.

Before takeoff, I hugged that young man and told him

that he'd made my day. Sweet innocence. Where has it gone? Gone to history books every one. When will we ever learn? When will we ever learn that to know facts doesn't always allow us to get to the root of a problem and come out with a beautiful ending. Blessed be.

HIT BY LIGHTNING

Washington to Boston, deep winter 2006

ANOTHER WEATHER DELAY. A ground stop in Boston halted departures out of Washington Dulles, again.

It's now pretty well-known that, when I'm working a delay, I'll pull a wheelchair up to the gate of my nondeparture and make an announcement.

"It's really, *really* tough to live through a delay, and we know that your shoulders, arms, necks, and backs are carrying more stress than usual! So, there's a licensed massage therapist who runs a clinic in Vermont right here to offer free muscular therapy to anyone on this flight. Just line up or sign up here at this wheelchair!"

Of course, it's usually the extroverts who will be first to volunteer, and the camaraderie around the gate area is usually beginning to gel before the first massage is halfway finished. It's my side show; the players are those who sit in my chair and share themselves with me as I massage away.

First up on this night was a man who asked, "Have you ever been hit by lightning?" I had no time to respond before he told me, "I have! I was in a coma thirty-eight days, and now I work with NOAA [National Oceanic and Atmospheric Administration] and travel all over the country talking about the dangers of lightning strikes. You know where most strikes occur? Within fifteen miles of Crawford, Texas! You know when most are hit by lightning? Walking to school! I work with NOAA and travel all over to talk at schools and teach about lightning!"

He was a very handsome man who appeared, as his oral biography continued, the ski instructor, hiker, and hearty, life-loving, zesty man he'd always been and would be. There was a devilish twinkle in his eyes. There was also warmth and wisdom therein. He'd been to hell and back again, and something told me he'd enjoyed every bit of the trip!

His life had changed dramatically when that high amperage hit. "My daughter was just two, so she didn't really know me before I changed. No short-term memory. She never knew me before, so I'm it. I'm what she knows now." It was the way he told me about his daughter that was the catch. The hook had been set, for I was working on the shoulders of a man not removed from his own truth. All the couldas and wouldas might have taken a lesser man to the dark side of life instead of inspiring him to become the evangelical educator on ionization who energetically and positively related his experiences and blessings to me.

He'd been laid low and damaged in a flash, but his own personal energy was electrifying me. He had turned this wrong-place-at-the-wrong-time accident into a life's work with his family intact, and he knows he can still love and be cherished. He is a force of nature stronger than that which shot through his body and exploded out of his heel so many years ago. And I got to hear his story and work on his sore shoulders and neck, and have my faith in miracles renewed. Sometimes bad things happen to good people because they've been chosen to take their experience to the world as "learn from my mistakes" educators. How many lives has this man saved already? Log onto www.struckbylightning.org to learn more about this incredible man. Is the perennial light in his eyes residual electricity? Yes. I felt it!

SYNCHRONICITY

Burbank to JFK, October 2007

ON WESTBOUND FLIGHTS there's plenty of time to meet people and find out all about them. I always hope for multiple verbal exchanges to keep the time flying by and to deepen my understanding of the human condition. Miracles happen. I've seen strangers bond, anger assuaged, sadness diluted, anxiety peaked or evaporated. Anything can happen between New York and California; that's one thing that's a constant, and one of my great expectations every single time I board a cross-country flight.

She was a beautiful woman. She carried her thirty extra pounds so well that I couldn't imagine her any other way. Hair, although coifed professionally, didn't look unnatural or hard but like a gentle crowning glory. It was soft and flowing to her shoulders even as it looked fresh out of rollers on top. The glasses were suited to her face in such a way as to be a part of it. How many times do we see people whose glasses are the focal point of their entire bodies? The Elton John look that screams, "Don't look at the rest of me; aren't my glasses to die for?" Well, this statuesque woman of class didn't need overstatement. Her clothes were unrevealing, but their lines were soft enough to invite guessing. Now that's style.

Although reared in Montreal, a fashion mecca, I now live in Vermont, where checkered flannel reigns supreme. If we had a heat wave in the Green Mountain State, there'd be a meltdown worse than Three Mile Island once the polyester around home hit the right temperature. That's why the gorgeous wardrobes on my planes tweak my store of Quebec memories but allow for gladness in my new role as the clotheshorse understatement I've become. I digress.

The woman. When she spoke with me up in the forward galley, her poise was tangible, but there was a tremor of something just beneath the surface. She was returning from an informal reunion. The solidifying of her new self in the face of preconceived expectations of peers was winning out. Little did I know how this woman would symbolically bid adieu to her former shy self within a few hours of our meeting.

The man. The gentleman and I first engaged in conversation in the back galley. He was a man chock-full of twinkling energy. It surfaced like the tides, beating its way out of every pore in a wavelike cadence. A natural rhythm. If that wasn't a dead giveaway as to his profession, his long scarf certainly was. It was all of six feet long and sported multiple muted-black musical notes on an off-white background.

"Ah, let me guess. You're a musician?" was my opening line.

He was just exploding with positivity and was instantly easy to like. There was no egocentric ownership of his obvious interests. None of the usual, "Why don't you just know who I am, what I do, and everything about me because, geez, I'm on a flight to Burbank so you should intuit my life history." No, there was only a joy skipping out of his eyes and filling up all the air between us. I loved his energy, and if I had had a butterfly net, I'd have captured as much of it as possible, to hold in reserve for a day I might need to mainline it into my own soul.

"Do you know the 'WIM O WEH' song by the Tokens?"

"Well, of course, I do. 'The Lion Sleeps Tonight.' I love it."

"Well, that's my song. That's me. My name's Jay Leslie."

Well, rarely have I ever met a performer so full of easy glee and willingness to just be among people he didn't think of as fans, but as spiritual peers in happiness.

The flight was a good one, just long enough to make contact on every possible level with a lot of the travelers. I'm so lucky.

Up in the forward galley, again, the woman came up to visit. She'd experienced some sort of catharsis recently and wanted to share but needed a little scraping of her surface before the entire story was exposed.

"I was with a lot of old friends this past week. In high school I was known as a lion sleeping; you know that old song?"

I was shocked by the unfolding coincidence. "God, are you talking about that 'WIM O WEH' song by the Tokens? You're kidding me, right?" I said, my eyes popping out of my head.

"Yeah, you know, 'The Lion Sleeps Tonight'? Well, I was that lion sleeping in the jungle in high school, and everyone would sing it to me all the time. Well, I'm not sleeping anymore, and now all my old friends know it."

My heart was racing, and I grabbed her hand saying, "My God, meeting you tonight is like a period at the end of a long sentence. You'll never guess who's on this plane in a million years. I can hardly believe it myself. I love my life. Oh—it's him, Jay Leslie, the actual singer of that song. Do you want to meet him? Come with me."

"Oh no . . . you're not serious. No, I'm fine, I'm fine. I can't believe it. Really? It's my song. It's my life. How my life was, you know?"

She returned to her aisle seat in row three. I respected her resistance to a meeting with the singer because, like me, she was in shock with all the synchronicity in play. She'd recently shed her sleeping-lion persona and evolved into the confident queen of her chosen jungle. Had she announced to her old school chums her new self-definition? Had they, perhaps, redefined her themselves after picking up on her new, assertive life force? Whatever. The coincidence of being on the same aircraft, going in the same direction, as the very person who had sung her old identity into concretion was the ultimate coincidence. To meet the man who'd put a caption to her former life, at that very moment, would be too amazing to feel real. That door to her past, still open a tiny crack, would be forever slammed shut and never again could she access the hiding places of her past if Jay Leslie touched her at that very moment. That mighty jungle where she once slept must have held a tiny comfort zone she still needed.

Before landing, she would change her mind.

Now to tell the musician of my find. I did, and the gracious fellow said he'd sing a duet with me to the lady in 3C. As his "agent on board," I proposed this to his fan. "Oh, maybe later. . . . Would he really? You're kidding me, right?" Hah. Never kid a kidder.

Before the end of the flight I brought the two together. Mr. Leslie was buoyant. I was informed later of his recent hectic travel and performance schedules. "Rock 'n' roll does take a lot out of you," he admitted. After a couple of notes, he zipped back to his seat. That little bit of up-close-and-personal singing left that woman in 3C glowing. What a gift she'd been given by this down-to-earth singer/songwriter.

What's it like to find yourself on a new and improved plateau of self-acceptance and personal best? Wonderful, I'd imagine. And how perfect would it be if, just when you think you have it all together, a sign was given. A sign that says, "You're right. You've made it. You've evolved. You're okay. You've overcome your demons. You're on the correct path."

Wouldn't it be wonderful to get that sign, the one that gives permission to wake up and keep moving forward out of the jungle?

As a postscript, Jay Leslie and I have become friends, and he graciously and generously came up to headline the 2009 Highbrow to Hoedown concert at the Enosburg Opera House in Vermont, which you'll read about on page 315. If you get a chance, please find out where the Tokens or 'Jumpin' Jay Leslie are playing. They put on a most amazing show! You'll laugh, dance, tear up, and wish the concert wouldn't end. Thanks for everything, Jay. Love you!

AUTHOR'S NOTE: Jay Leslie (Jumpin' Jay) has come to Vermont to headline one of my Highbrow to Hoedown shows at the Enosburg Opera House. He brought down the house! Jay's one of the most talented, most genuine, most amazing of men. Meeting him, seeing his kindness aboard this flight and writing the story, laid the groundwork for our enduring friendship. I have the best job in the world! HM

SOMETIMES THERE'S NOT ENOUGH TIME

JFK to Burbank, November 2007

TAKING OFF FROM JFK at the international push time has been considered either one of our worst national disasters or the eighth wonder of the world, depending how you look at it. *International push time* is the term given to the hours when the volume of scheduled flights supersedes the time and runways available. In short, it's a complete cluster. Time in line on a taxiway gives crew members more time to get to know their customers. It gives the customers an equal amount of time to write their congressmen about this ongoing air-traffic and flight-scheduling issue. We boarded the 128 customers and pushed back early that evening, another unanticipated blessing given that it was Black Friday, and we expected the shoppers would have multiple bags, all filled to overflowing with things "too delicate" to be rammed into the overhead bins. (A capitalist's dream, Black Friday is the day after Thanksgiving, when stores open before dawn to start the holiday shopping season and give consumers their money's worth.)

The flight to Burbank is always rife with characters. Open and effusive is the personality norm. There's usually no need to intuit a person's station in life because most introduce themselves by their main interests. Actors, producers, directors, writers, film makers, singers, and several other titles with extroversion as the major prerequisite.

While meeting and greeting during boarding, I usually pass out smiley-face stickers to willing passersby. This serves a number of purposes: eye-contact, an attitude adjuster, a surprise, and something 99 percent of this California town's flyers accept gleefully. God, I love my Burbank people!

Before any flight, if there's time, I meet the customers at the boarding gate. In my youth, I was a commercial-fishing lady out of Newburyport, Massachusetts, working from four in the morning until four every afternoon, without even a snack break on good days. I learned the vocabulary of the old salts. One set of words I use, whether I'm flirting with potential advertisers for my newspaper, building a new patient base in my clinic, or preparing to board a flight from anywhere to anywhere, is *chumming the water*. The customers, be they fish or fowl, sponsors, patients, or our traveling public, respond to free anything. The travelers need only bit of handshaking, humor, information, and introduction before they get on a plane to become positive people once on board. (This might also be referred to as "tenderizing the meat," but that's another chapter.)

However, on the day after Thanksgiving '07, by coincidence or divine intervention, I missed someone both at the gate and as she boarded.

"Hey! I want a smiley face!" were the first words I heard from the comfortably reclined young lady in seat 1F. I whipped my head around, and there sat a pair of twinkling eyes surrounded by long, two-toned waves. One of those soft scarves was draped loosely around her neck and covered most of her arms and torso. The long legs, held prisoner by tight denim, went all the way down to fabulous, pointy-toed boots. I sure wish I didn't have bunions, Achilles tendinitis, and heel spurs, then I'd wear boots like the ones this fun lover sported! She was a really well-assembled Manhattan/Los Angeles combo, I thought. Sharp looking and sharp tongued? I obliged, and she just beamed when I presented the sticky expression for her lapel. Her reaction reminded me of any child on Christmas morning in receipt of the best gift in the world right from Santa! She was like a female Peter Pan, and that sort of spirited attitude demands reciprocity. I was thrilled that she was sitting in my section!

First impressions on the way to Burbank aren't usually way off their marks, as I said. So far, I'd missed her at the departure gate, and she'd slipped past me during boarding. My net was coming up empty, and I didn't have the wit to realize it!

Just before we closed the doors, a gentleman moved to the first row. This left my happy woman at the window, the handsome thirtyish gentleman on the aisle, and the blessing of an empty middle seat. For the lively sprite at the window, the open space between the two was being defined as an invitation to respect an age-old truth: nature abhors a vacuum. For the newer occupant of row one, it was a coveted and not-to-be-violated airspace that, in his mind, guaranteed him a few hours of peaceful solitude.

We pushed back a few minutes early.

We taxied straight to the runway and took off.

We'd arrive in Burbank ahead of schedule for sure! I was happy about that initially.

I overheard the woman begin to carry a conversation. The fellow, now strapped in and required to remain thus until after takeoff and beyond, was listening intently. A tropism of the two was at play, their heads and shoulders leaning toward each other during taxiing, and it made their mutual interest in each other obvious. With hands gesticulating and her volume set on high, the monologue was easily heard from where I sat. Burbank people, so jubilant and extroverted! The catch of the day was going to entertain from New York to California, and I felt lucky to be in close proximity to this happy party. Ah, first impressions, so rarely are they as misleading as they were that night. In the air, her voice still conquered the noise of the engines, and their shoulders now bridged over the middle seat. "How nice," I thought. "Maybe it's a match!" Neither one wore a wedding ring.

As we leveled off and I was preparing for drink and snack service, this energetic extrovert was suddenly beside me. Like a specter in the night, she was suddenly almost skin-to-skin with me. When I turned my face to hers, I detected a slight smell of spirits. She seemed alright, but her first question was, "When can I order a drink?" This was after gushing about how funny I was, how incredible the safety demo was, how the uniform was just perfect for me, and on and on. As prepared as I was to enjoy her company for the remaining five and a half hours, I was a bit surprised by her overwhelming persona. Thanking her, I asked what she'd like to quench her thirst.

"A vodka with just a smidgen of orange juice, Heather. Just a splash of juice because it'll be stronger that way."

"As soon as I finish setting up, I'll get that for you."

Red flags were still at half mast, but they were creeping higher up the flagpole of warnings.

"Heather! I'm buying a drink for Hal, too!" she called from her seat as she pointed to the man. He looked me straight in the eye and firmly said, "I'll have a Sprite."

As I delivered both drinks, I overheard her confession to Hal, "I'm a lush. It's the Irish in me. You know how we are, don't you?"

The self-described lush was overtaking all air space above the empty seat and some of his. The man's body was now listing to port in an attempt to evade the intrusive girl. I mouthed, "Would you like to change seats, sir?" just out of the exultant woman's range of vision. He bravely shook his head.

I advised my fellow crew members that our little lady in row one was officially being cut off. No more alcohol would pass her lips. That one vodka had already been the crystallization point for anything taken on before we set sail. Was it a shot with her favorite uncle? A cocktail with a friend? A toddy or two all by herself? I judged it to be the last.

She made the inevitable request for another vodka as I was running her credit card, and instead of refusing, I asked her name and what she did for a living.

"Bridget," and with a cutesy, apologetic can-you-believe-it expression, she added, "I'm a lawyer." Without skipping a beat she asked if I was cashing out everyone on the plane or just her. I sidestepped and stalled for a minute. This was a common thing in her life, and she knew that she was about to be cut off. Still smiling and fairly jumping in her seat, her hand firmly on the thigh of her new best friend, she laughingly tossed her head and said, "Are you not serving me because I'm inebriated? I'm quitting. I'm joining AA when we land."

"Well, my goodness, are you really?" I asked.

"No!" she beamed. "Will you bring me one more vodka?"

"I'm pacing the flight, ma'am. What's your name?" My face felt like it was giving a nonjudgmental but maternal smile at this human conundrum.

"Bridget." We shook hands and smiled at one another over Hal's shrinking form.

"It's absolutely great to meet you formally, Bridget! You're a very interesting young lady, and it's no surprise that you're an attorney. What kind of law do you practice?"

"Civil," she said in a very self-deprecating way. Then she jutted out her lower lip in a faux pout as if this minimized any personal pride or indicated that she was less than satisfied with this professional choice.

I was dutifully impressed but my mind raced. Why would this pretty, educated woman be a loud, forward drinker? Why would she behave in this way? What could be missing from her life now or during her formative years to make her want to imbibe to excess and pretend to be embarrassed about her excellent career? And why had she referred to herself in such self-deprecating terms—lush, alcoholic, the stereotypical Irishman?

One reason became obvious just over halfway to Burbank

when I found myself skin-to-skin and face to face with the tipsy litigator in the forward galley. "How old do you think I am?"

I guessed, "Midtwenties?"

"Hah! No, I'm thirty-seven, and I'm not married. My mother wants grandchildren, and I'm thirty-seven, and there's no hope in sight!" She was allowing a bit of her real self to bleed into the galley and into my heart.

"Your mom will get a grandchild when that grandchild's ready to be born. Do you want children? Do you want to get married? If you had a magic wand, what would you wish?"

"I don't know. My sister's twenty-seven. She lives in England with her *boyfriend*." The last word was said with disbelief; a roll of her eyes was the punctuation point. She raced on with all sorts of disjointed comments, but there was a sense that these bright eyes, now glazed then blazing fire, had not seen many positive things in decades. The feeling I got was that her accomplishments, which would make most proud, were constantly devalued by the domestic expectations of her family, like a little girl who completes her first somersault only to be told that she'd dirtied her hair in the sand. There was a quitter's acceptance to her station in life. An attorney. A beauty. A drunk. A complete disappointment to her mother. So every new candidate for matrimony or sperm donation is engulfed by the vacuum in which she dwells. That vacuum is the panic she harbors behind all her other gold medals in life.

As close as Bridget was to me, having no concept of anyone's need to breathe, I didn't mind anymore. I was staring deep into her eyes and seeing a storm. It all made sense, how this child-woman was. The duality of goals, hers and her mother's, were chasing each other around in her body and creating a vortex that was failing to pull anything up from Mother Earth intact. Like any tornado, that spinning, directionless mass just sucks up perfectly made structures from the ground, rips them apart, and spews them out as wreckage and waste. There aren't enough good parts left over to build anything worthwhile, but that destructive top just keeps gaining speed. What's a tornado hoping for, anyway? What are its goals? Why does a storm like this keep going?

The pilots informed us that we'd be landing half an hour earlier than scheduled. Unbelievable. Three breaks on one flight!

I'd denied further vodka treats, but Bridget came to the back galley to find me. Her eyes fell hungrily to the bottle of wine in my hand. "We're not getting there for another hour or so, are we? Can't I have another drink?"

My crew knew I'd had the cut-off conversation with her, so we stood our ground. "As soon as you told Hal that you were inebriated, I had to resist the temptation to serve you, Bridget. It was really your call, and I have no choice after an admission like that."

"My sister gets totally blasted on all her flights, and it's okay."

Another refusal by all of us. A united front, but a kind, friendly one.

Initial descent.

Then Bridget was in my face and space again. "Hal's just sort of acting weird, like he doesn't want to talk with me anymore. Do you think I should just go to sleep or should I go back and ask him if there's something wrong?"

"Bridget, you've answered your own question. You're not

socially illiterate, and you can certainly read a room," I said.

"I did, didn't I?" she said disbelievingly. Then the star-crossed teenager she seemed to be at that moment emerged. "But why did he pull away? We were having such a great time!! I just can't get a guy. My sister's twenty-seven and has a boyfriend! What do you think of my mother calling me the only old-maid or spinster in the family? There just aren't any good men out there at my age." That tornado had done it again, destroyed a good thing by grabbing it up in a frenzied yank instead of slowing the winds down to a gentle breeze. Probably an established pattern in her life.

I gently put my hands on her arms. She was deflated and looked so fragile. Those Irish eyes weren't smiling. "Bridget, you're an accomplished woman, but you've been drinking and admitted to being a lush, inebriated, and a candidate for AA. When my better half took me on our first date, a forty-five minute walk, he asked me if I drank. I told him I didn't. It was one of his major qualifiers, you see. He didn't want a minimized relationship or to share me with another lover—alcohol. You might not want or need the life your mother prescribes, but you won't be able to get a decent man if you're never really clear. Many good men don't want a perpetual party girl. They don't want a drinker to be the mother of their children. Quality men aren't that few and far between, you're just not using the right bait to hook one." Then I added, very seriously, something I've said often, "Oh, by the way, the terms *old maid* and *spinster* were coined by jealous women who secretly crave missed freedom, autonomy, and/or independence!"

"I should quit drinking, but life's so mundane without alcohol! It's all just a big facade!"

"Bridget, life's not mundane. It's exciting and scary and fun and full if you experience it with clarity. It's quite a blast, and the sky's the limit! I think generalizing life as mundane is a copout." Now I was gushing.

"Yeah. I should quit drinking."

"You might do that. You might not. It's 100 percent up to you, Bridget."

Final descent.

And then the flight was over. If I'd had a magic wand, I'd have given it to Bridget, or I'd have waved it myself and asked for just another five hours with this rosebud yet to bloom. Sometimes there just isn't enough time.

THE VICTIM

Richmond to JFK to Boston, February 2009

AS SOON AS she stepped aboard my plane, I knew she'd suffered a loss. I took her forearm and looked into her veiled eyes only to see the emptiness of a wounded bird about to breathe its last. The large eyes must once have been bright, because even when clouded with some drug, a huge sadness, or both, they had a depth of their own. Her youth was in place on her skin. Light, freckled, and taut, a face of someone more comfortable watching life than jumping into the pulsing throngs of teenage extroversion. Yet this appearance of delicacy might have been one recently adopted after an enormous shock. A refugee of a war-torn universe had just let me hold her arm. There wasn't the pulse of vibrancy within her atmosphere. I could have passed my hand clean through her body and there would have been nothing of substance to stop the infringement. She was dead on her feet.

I pulled her closer to me and whispered, "You've been hurt, my love."

A resolute nod.

"Where are you sitting?" After checking her boarding pass for the information, I told her that I'd be over to see her as soon as possible.

A passive agreement. Did she know I could feel her incredible pain somewhere to the left of my heart? Even I wondered if my bronchitis or a heart attack was responsible for the absolute sharpness of my reactive empathy.

Alone by a window, she was an inert nonentity, not trying to attain invisibility but having accepted this as her new accessory, a statement to her destroyed self. Sitting down beside her, the tailored crone I am and the vulnerable beauty she is must have made for a contrast of before-and-after possibilities.

"What would you like to tell me?" I asked.

"I was a victim of an assault," she quietly told me.

"Ahhh. It shows. There aren't many of us who escape life without such things happening to us. How can I help you?"

"Were you ever assaulted?"

"I was."

"Was it a sexual assault?"

"It was."

"Did they catch him?"

"No. In those days the victim was treated as the instigator, my love. Women were always blamed for the attacks and were interrogated without mercy. My brother took me to the emergency room and told me to tell the doctor that it was a one-night stand because this would be more believable than the truth itself."

"I have a hearing on March 8."

Her eyes held the storm clouds seen in saturated skies over Tulsa just before tornado warnings sound. Yet the precipitation wouldn't release, just that steady state of near release brimmed just behind the dams. I wished she could just break down and cry in my arms like any daughter should with a granny who'd been there. The corners of her mouth were scab crusted where they'd been torn either by the exertion of screaming or a physical insult. Poor baby. Seemingly alone in her new world of reality.

The serendipitous path of life is fraught by misfortune and blessed by chance meetings. That's life. I told her that I'd never spoken of my brush with violence until my own daughter reached an age when hearing the story could be a great part of her education. To live in a state of blind naiveté is bad, but to know that horrible things can be followed by normal, even exceptionally wonderful experiences is marvelous. To be thankful for a rape would be an overstatement of optimism, but to be enormously grateful for the education gleaned therefrom is a saving grace.

Turning points in life. This youngster, sitting in a seat on a jet to Boston, breathing the rarified air shared by everyone else on that flight, was on the cusp of falling to one side or the other of life. Telling her that, in my experience, life just got better from the worst night of my life until present day wasn't the pep talk of a Pollyanna but words from one who's accepted what was and invited survival skills from somewhere in the human genetic memory to help. A good, even exceptional, life is possible after a personal violation. Trust can be rebuilt. Love can bloom. Healing and strength can combine to form a new alloy of a tempered steel will. Resolve and contentment can be allies in a newly matured mind and stronger body.

Chance meetings. Perhaps that moment in time some thirty years ago happened just so I could relate to the little girl I flew to Boston yesterday. If this is so, then I must allow myself to thank the universal energy that binds us all for the favor granted.

Her bright yellow T-shirt sported the old slogan "Virginia is for Lovers." Ironic. That a nearly broken entity can wear the happiest color and words that combine the location of her attack and the word 'lovers' was a vivid contradiction in terms. Who could have given her this apparel? A sick mind or a cockeyed optimist, surely nothing in between. Yet think of it; what a prediction this shirt gave—enlightenment and a crash course in situational adaptation to survival! She'll return to Virginia for the hearing. She'll survive. She'll love again. She'll rise to the expectations of an accidental T-shirt. Please let it be so!

Deplaning, carrying three plastic hospital bags with a room number scrawled on each one with garish felt marker slashes, she allowed me to hug her, and little arms encircled me in response. It was a weak hug, but there was life in it. She'll live to hug many times, and with each one, may there be more strength. More love to give. More trust to share.

PART THREE

CRUISING ALTITUDE

TWO SOLITUDES, GIVERS OR TAKERS

Florida to JFK to Rochester, November 2006

THERE'S A BALANCE in our human population, and it's obvious, in microcosm, on flights.

One flight was delayed out of Florida because of weather (naturally). I filled my apron with animal crackers and began my ground-delay routine at the front of the plane. "Would you care for some delightful animal crackers? They come in this lovely green tinged bag! No animals were injured during the making of these cookies!" It begins quietly, and by the time I'm at the fourth row, folks are usually participating in this little sideshow with good humor, even glee! However, when I arrived at the fourth row, I was met with a stony glare from an ultrathin woman on one side of the aisle. Her two teenagers were in the center and window seats, and her handsome husband was across the aisle oblivious to all things because half of his head was ensconced in ultracool headphones. My snack offering was dismissed by the alpha female with a frigid facial sneer. Okay, I thought, it'll be tough to bring her around, I'll just betcha'. Down the aisle I continued, enjoying everyone along the way.

Delays offer their own special opportunities to make the best of the situation. I personally fell in love with all things airport-related when my dad and I were snowbound in the Montreal International for three full days in March 1971. The Canadian Alpine Ski Team taught me songs my mother wouldn't understand, an opera singer performed the music that would become my lifelong pastime, a flight attendant encouraged me to become one, and a great time was had by all! That delay set my life into an avionic love affair, so I try to re-create that absolute fun when I'm lucky enough to be in an airport with marooned customers. Sometimes it works. Sometimes it doesn't. That microcosmic balance strikes again.

This was a flight that was stopping at JFK, dropping off some, and picking up new customers. Some who began this trip at its point of origin were scheduled to continue all the way to Rochester on this same plane.

Once up in the air, as I was taking drink orders, the mother asked bluntly, "Will you be serving anything to eat on this flight?" I told her about the snacks that would follow the drink deliveries. She didn't even acknowledge my response. The service was completed with many an extra snack bestowed upon the wife and children in 4A, B, and C. Nothing for the dad.

Not a thank you emanated from any member of that family.

There wasn't even any noticeable communication among its members. The father never looked at his offspring or wife but stayed in the protective embrace of his headphones.

Upon landing at JFK, already an hour late for the Rochester departure, we deplaned everyone but those who were continuing on the same plane and began our furious cleaning process. Flight attendants, pilots, the cleaning people, and any SkyNation employees who'd come in from Florida on that flight were whipping around that plane for a quick turnaround.

The woman grabbed my arm and said, "We'd like to get off this plane, because *you're* late, and we haven't had anything to eat!"

I told her that our turnaround time would be quick, and I couldn't recommend her leaving the aircraft. I also stated that the flight to Rochester was going to be only forty-one minutes. She had let go of my arm, but her nail imprints remained. Whew! The gate crew member got on and asked if she could begin boarding the awaiting Rochester customers, and I was about to answer in the affirmative when this woman, who didn't look like she'd eaten in years, let alone hours, stood up between us and, pointing at me, screeched, "She said we can't get off the plane, and my kids haven't had anything to eat! Can we get off?"

Bless that gate agent! Her response was ultimately patient and professional, "You're welcome to get off the plane, but the computer has counted your family as 'checked in' in West Palm Beach, so the flight might leave without you."

The mother continued her loud argument until the daughter said, "I'm okay! I don't even want to get off the plane!" End of discussion because the fulcrum of her argument had been the hunger of her children. That husband-father didn't once involve himself in this discussion; he never even noticed, or pretended not to anyway.

As customers began to board, I noticed a woman laughingly coming on with her teenage daughter and guess what she was carrying—a medium-size pizza.

"Ma'am, may I ask a huge favor of you, and please feel no obligation to comply!"

"Fire away!" was the happy response.

"Ma'am, it's a forty-one minute flight to Rochester. Do you live near the airport?"

"A few minutes' drive—"

"Well, ma'am, is there a bunch of good food in your fridge awaiting your return?"

"Fer shure!"

"There's a very hungry family on board tonight, and if I could buy your pizza, they might get home a bit happier than they've been since leaving Florida late!"

The mother and daughter looked at each other and without exchanging a word said, "We'll just go back and cut out a piece to share and you just tell that family it's on us, okay?"

After takeoff I went down to get the pizza and give all my cash (six dollars) to the willing pair. "No, no, bad karma, please just take the pizza to that family!" I did. With the delivery I knelt down and said to the family, "Aren't people wonderful? Pay it forward."

As I was collecting trash, I took the empty pizza box from the mother, who didn't look at me when she passed it to me. I asked the teens if they were feeling better now that they'd eaten the pizza. The girl, about fifteen, said yes. I then looked at her brother, about fourteen, and he said, "My sister ate it all and didn't even give me one bite."

If my face registered shock it was only to mask my disappointment. Isn't it funny that strangers can be so willing to share all, but some families won't even share among themselves? Both kinds were on one plane, going to the same destination. So different, eh?

HUGS AND HOMELAND SECURITY

West Palm Beach to JFK, June 2006

Hi everybody, The FBI removed a young man from my plane the other night. A big to-do. Just as the boy was about to be taken, I gave him a big hug. The FBI came back later to question my motives. Here's a story about why we should continue to give unconditional love, in any way we're able, to our fellow man before it's deemed illegal. I totally accept that we must be vigilant, but a mother's love is infinite and irrepressible. Love to all of you, Heather

Maternal nature. I needn't say more by way of explanation to most Americans, but some dismiss the need or reality of this driving force.

I have a son. Twenty-five years of age and still my sweet baby whose voice I miss when several days go by without an exchange of words, no matter how innocuous. Our reunions are usually initiated with the same conditioned response; I fling my arms around him and pull him close with pure joy and kiss his neck three times.

I have a daughter. Twenty-seven and a mother with the same obvious affliction as her mom's—that irrepressible urge to grab her son and cleave him to her bosom. With obvious physical energy, she closes her eyes and transmits every positive emotion from her being into her sturdy child. The absolute transference of adoration, unconditional acceptance, and love is an osmotic process made possible when one sweeps another into one's arms. The spontaneous encircling of a being in a tight embrace must be a necessity surfacing from ancient genetic memory.

NECESSITY

There grows an overwhelming need within my being to give people something from a deep cellular level of my soul—love. Simply put, easily offered, usually accepted. When I can't give my own loved ones a hug, there builds a steam within. Compression. Suppression. Implosion. Explosion. Something's got to give as this pressure cooker heats up. The friction of every passing stranger causes static electricity, and the shock runs to ground when two hold each other.

My mother died thirty-seven years ago. What if nobody had taken it upon themselves to give me the motherly love needed? So, so many people have thrown an arm around my shoulders over the years, and perhaps this has saved my life. Without self-consciousness, those who've dragged me to their breast have proven time and again that everything's okay. All's right with the world in that nanosecond where two become knotted under the umbrella of succor.

KARMA

I must give back what's been given me. So many mothers in the world and so many orphans. If I'm a thousand miles from my offspring, I want another mother to give them a hug! The universality of caring is compulsory in our transient, global society. It would be so selfish to say "Only I, the birth mother, will hug this child!" I mean, what if every mother forbade another the opportunity to give love to those not born to herself? Possessiveness would really hurt the world, wouldn't it? And what if shyness prevented women from giving of themselves to those who seem to be adrift on a sea of anonymous, impersonal humanity? What a lonely world it would be.

And the biggest "what ifs?" are:

What if Homeland Security put every mother on notice, and touching became suspect?

What if some suspicious, paranoid, machine of a human being dictated that "to offer consolation to strangers" means instant indictment and a one-way ticket to Guantanamo Bay?

What if I died and no other mom was allowed to hug my son in my stead? My God. My God.

What if that boy-man taken off my plane is incarcerated from here to eternity? Will not that last embrace, so full of unconditional love from an aged mother, be something he might remember in his darkest hour? Every man, be he the salt of the earth or the definition of evil, is some mother's son. Maybe yours.

SELFISH

Washington to JFK, July 2009

AS HE BOARDED, the proper, preppy, popular type of young man passed without acknowledging my "Welcome aboard" greeting or accepting one of my proffered smiley-face stickers. I said, "Sir, did you lose a case in court today?"

"Yeah." He responded more with his eyes than anything else. They were glassy with something. Was it disbelief? Anger? Disappointment? Sadness? Whatever was causing the outward appearance of dejection was something rooted deep.

During the flight, I found him sitting in an aisle seat near the back of the plane. I stopped and said, "Well, there'll be other cases you know."

"You knew I was kidding about that, right?"

"No. I thought you really had lost a big case because you looked so upset when you boarded. What do you really do?"

"I'm in finance."

"I live in Vermont. We don't have finance there. Well, not in East Berkshire anyway."

"You live in Vermont?" he asked, and this was the first time he smiled. Even those cowled eyes opened with a bit of light shining out. Only a flicker, but enough to meet my eyes halfway and give me a bit of an opening into his unlived part of life.

"Oh, it's my dream come true. I love my little village."

"I'd love to live there," he said, but in such a wistful way that I knew he'd never believed that this pipe dream would materialize into reality.

"What's stopping you from moving to Vermont? In fact, you don't seem too enthusiastic about your present job either. If you had a magic wand, what would you be doing right now?"

"Well, my wife and I used to travel a lot. Now we have a kid. We used to travel two and a half weeks a year, but with a kid, we can't do that anymore. He was born a year ago, and we just don't have a life anymore, so I can't just go and do whatever I want. He's got some problems, you know? He's always having ear infections and stuff. We don't get cut a break with this kid."

At this point, I kneeled down in the aisle beside this young man. I was hurting for his one-year-old as I looked at this beautifully dressed and perfectly groomed professional. So handsome. So beautiful. On the outside. Inside—what I couldn't see, but what was oozing out of every pore, was something I've only seen in a few people in my life. It was selfishness. Narcissistic personality disorder, perhaps. At least the symptoms of this sort of disorder. Is it created genetically or by the materialistic world of the Me Generation?

"Do you love your baby?"

His eyes closed and he said, "Oh, I love that little guy so much."

"Does your wife work, too?"

"Yes. She puts in about fifty hours a week and makes ridiculous amounts of money. I work long hours, too, and make a ridiculous amount of money. It's sick how much money we make. The kid has nannies and babysitters. You know how it is."

Well, I've seen how it is up close and personal, to be sure, but as long as people think that business is more important than time with a child, such conundrums will occur. Sacrifice isn't the same as investment. The man thought that to give up the money and prestige he presently has, he'd be somehow self-castrating. He also admitted that he lives in the best neighborhood and has targeted another level of success on his five-year plan. But, now, with a "kid," he feels guilty for working so hard for those goals.

"My wife loves her job, and she won't ever leave it. She's knows the kid ruins our chance for traveling, but she's not about to let him take her career, too."

As he was getting off the plane, I took his arm and pulled him to me. "Oh, you have a magic wand. We all do. Just wave it and make your world into what you want it to be. Vermont will always be there for you, but that child, that beautiful son whom you love so much, won't be. Freedom can't be bought. Wealth in Vermont is measured in buckets of contentment in my village. We don't have much but we have enough. We don't have two and a half weeks off a year. We take what time we need to do what we have to do. It usually works out for us. I was far from being a perfect mother but I was there. My children wore secondhand clothing, and I could only afford to heat one room of the house in winter, and for that I bartered massage therapy for firewood. I didn't have everything then, but I felt like I did! I didn't go around the world when they were in school. Yet I didn't feel like I was missing anything, although by your way of thinking, I didn't have a life. They didn't have nannies or sitters very often, and I never resented my position as a parent. Remember Annette Funicello from the Mickey Mouse Club? She now has multiple sclerosis and stated; 'Life doesn't have to be perfect to be wonderful.' I say, use your magic wand and get happy!"

The man's face contorted into what I thought would end up as a full-blown crying jag. Then he just looked defeated and slowly shook his head before saying, "I can't."

TABLE OF ELEMENTS IN CHILD DEVELOPMENT

The "weight of touch" on planes: some parents cuddle and read, others put on headphones and ignore

---

MADAME CURIE KNEW that there existed an unidentified element within coal. When distilled, the raw product's known properties didn't add up to 100 percent. What was missing? Radium of course.

Now the weight of babies, infants, and toddlers has known and identified elements. Yet there must be in existence a particle of tangible input that hasn't been included in the sum of parts.

Observing year-old children with their caregivers, there are several notable differences in the physical and intellectual properties between those who have tactile relationships with their young and those who withhold the universally accepted touches—hugging, kissing, holding, and other indications that the child is cherished. The offspring of those who don't interact on an emotional level often have a vacancy. This isn't to say that these unfortunates aren't full of potential in the intellect department, only that heretofore, with the example of dour, undemonstrative role models, these children just haven't been handed the tools for self-expression. Nor have they been given even tacit encouragement to emote.

Now back to the weight issue. The child of a roughhousing, dancing, laughing, crying, and expressive parent has the will to thrive because he's been exposed to a variety of realities in the house. Action and reaction. Like exercising a muscle group, these young ones bounce from one set of emotional and physical stimuli to the next and realize, perhaps subconsciously, that there are patterns in human behavior. This fact is added to his gray matter and stored for cognitive reference throughout life.

The physical moves and touches of the people in his life awaken his body to everything from coordinated movement to the confidence in his own body's actual presence in the world. He becomes, unto himself, a tangible entity aware of his own impact on his world. In short, he grows from an observer of what's real to being one more reality within his environment. This is added weight.

Life for the child who has physical and emotional input from his immediate family is full. His cup runneth over with the elements required to move forward in his natural developmental process. The other positive attribute generated for this lucky child is the *retention of energy*. He is not required to rev his own engines and waste valuable vigor reaching for some unattainable star he can't really see or understand. He can use this stored energy for answering a multitude of questions bombarding his psyche through his senses of taste, touch, sight, hearing, and smell. In short, he becomes an efficient package of positive and natural progression. The stored energy has weight.

When a child is denied either intellectual or physical stimulation there is a minus on the scales of child development. If he intuits that he's an invisible, intangible being without actual acknowledgment other than the minimum daily requirement of care for his survival, there is a void that has no weight. This hole in his being might well become a sucking vacuum with the vague sense that something's missing. That something is necessary for survival in all individuals. As the maturation process progresses, these lightweights will, in order to fill that empty space, use their "will to thrive" to seek out and ingest the stimuli from others not in their immediate family. The danger in this hunt is that often these individuating youngsters do not possess a vocabulary that will efficiently ask for what's needed. These empty vessels, unless in the presence of altruistic, loving people, may well fall prey to predators. The lucky ones enjoy the fruits of the old African saying, "It takes a village to raise a child."

The weighted matter or *missing element* has been defined by words for decades. Yet, as Curie discovered by pursuing her resolute faith in the definite existence of radium, we must endeavor to accept that external stimulation, that invisible energy that passes between parent and child, is transformed from weightless, ethereal nonmatter to a definite element during the transfer process. (Matter is defined as that which has weight and takes up space.) By definition, the end product of physical and emotional input must be added physical weight to a child.

THE BLESSINGS OF A BLIZZARD

West Palm Beach to Washington to West Palm Beach to JFK, January 2005

I'D JUST WATCHED the inauguration, many Januaries ago, when I was blessed with a three-day trip. I was thrilled. Being new to an airline job has many blessings, and multiday trips to new destinations, Sky Cities, worked for me. The news of the day carried more than what was happening in our nation's capitol. There were also ominous predictions of a huge Alberta clipper coming down the pike to slam into many a SkyNation destination. The frigid air in New York was already causing discomfort to most. So where was I to fly that day? All over heck's half acre with a twenty-hour layover in West Palm Beach. Yet another Trump wedding was happening in that town, and the place was hopping with anticipation.

Waking in a hot and sunny Florida location is far from what this Vermonter is accustomed to during winter months! I headed out for a run and planned to meet the rest of my crew by the pool eventually. Our outbound flight to JFK was scheduled for late in the afternoon, so pleasure and recreation were to reign until departure.

The best laid plans of mice and men don't last in the airline business. We were ordered to the airport by noon. A preemptive attempt to bring the chickens home to roost before the predicted storm would force a flying freeze. We mustered and caught the airport shuttle. No poolside was to be ours that day because that blizzard was closing fast. We boarded and aimed for JFK but knew that a diversion to Burlington, Vermont, might ensue if conditions at Kennedy worsened. Wow! All this schedule changing and I might end up in my state of residence? I was ready for that. Diversion or scheduled landing would work for me. There's no place like home!

My crew wasn't working the flight. The word *deadheading* means the company puts uniformed crew members on a flight just to get them from one place to another. Being in uniform on any flight, deadheading or working, we are expected by customers to be "on." The questions started immediately as I moseyed down the aisle just to stretch my legs.

"Are we going to be able to land?"

"Are we going to divert?"

"Is JFK going to close?"

"Will I make my connection?"

"What are the snacks?"

Staying optimistic and reassuring while being completely

honest in the face of incoming weather reports is like walking a diplomatic tightrope. I was sure only of the snack list and admitted this.

On the last bit of the flight we learned that a Polar Air 747 cargo plane (there's irony in this mishap given the weather conditions and the name of this airline!) had gone off the only available runway, given the quarter mile of visibility at JFK. We'd now land at Dulles. Gosh, I'd missed the Trump wedding in West Palm Beach and the inaugural events in Washington, D.C., by only a day or two. It wasn't my week to schmooze, that's for sure.

The passengers were, understandably, miffed. Some reacted philosophically, others with disgust, and still others with curiosity. Before landing, I'd decided to interview customers. During social sweeps up and down the aisle, I'd chanced upon interesting individuals.

One, a friend of Donald Trump's father, another, a seventy-two-year-old artist, and there was also a singer from Haiti. It was my lucky day! People are what this job's all about, and I was being indulged. They had stories to tell, and I was all ears. Learning history, art appreciation, and feeling the musical energy of a middle-aged Haitian gave me such a feeling of joy. Yes, we were not where we wanted to be, but it did feel to me that we were exactly where we should be at that time.

There was a couple who were trying desperately to get to New York for cancer treatment.

A small, tired family had no remaining energy after visiting family for, what may have been, just a few days too long.

The young rapper who just had to have a cigarette or he'd die came to me. Well, he didn't die, I pressed the craving pressure points on his arms and gave him a Coke. He decided he didn't really want a smoke, after all, nor did he wish to expire. How cool was that?

Some folks just got off the plane to drive home to wherever that might have been.

When the news came that the remaining travelers were to be moved to another plane and flown back to West Palm Beach, it could have spelled bad feelings to the uniformed among us. Yet it was, overall, such a mature return trip. It was great to have been assigned this flight to actually work when the original crew timed out with too many hours of flying on that day.

To end this story on an even happier note, the northern airports reopened the next day. As luck would have it, the same folks who had traveled up and down the East Coast and shared their goals, interests, and worries with me the day before boarded my flight to JFK. Familiar faces! Smiles, hugs, and a genuine appreciation for each other and the shared experience of flying to nowhere for a day were in evidence during the entire flight back to JFK.

So, I missed the big wedding and the inauguration fun, but the trade-off was worth it. Sometimes it just takes a darn good snowstorm to give us time to really get to know and appreciate the wonderful men, women, and children we call customers; I call them "my people."

THE EYE OF THE BEHOLDER

Long Beach to Las Vegas, May 2010

MEETING AND GREETING before boarding is a favorite pastime of mine. It sets a tone of familiarity and entertains the onlookers, but more importantly, it serves as a warm-up to the individuals I'm lucky enough to interview as I vet out the interesting from the inconspicuous, the needy from the overconfident, the happy from the morose. Every single sort of person is an inspiration, and it's such a lucky thing to be able to embrace the masses one by one by one.

It was Long Beach, and I'd already interacted with the wheelchair bound, the dog owner, the young, the elderly, and everyone bracketed by these extremes. I'd played a game of gin and won it with a young lady as her husband talked on his cell. Everyone was coming to Vegas on my flight, so even the mild-mannered first cousin of rummy wasn't out of place at the gate.

A twentysomething girl on crutches approached the gate agent's station. The agent wasn't there, so I sallied forth to see if she had a question.

"Are we boarding, yet?"

"Not yet, but you can preboard when the flight's announced, if you'd like. Would you like ice on that braced knee when you get on?"

"Yes, that would be great. I was hit by a car."

She was traveling with her handsome boyfriend, and this was good because she looked so tiny and frail. Vegas? That's a rough destination for the injured or weary, in my opinion, but what do I know of the tenacity and inner strengths of the young? Or the older for that matter.

The last to arrive at the boarding area was a couple. He was round to the point of confusion over his gender. Without a tooth in his head and in such attire as to shout, "This is my best so deal with it. I'm comfortable." I totally appreciate such a way of life; the lack of vanity and self-acceptance is paramount where I live, too. I respect and even admire those who just beam the truth about themselves without any need to adapt to the general demands of fashion. Comfort over vanity because of financial constraints, practicality, and general comfort rule in Vermont, and in the lucky parts of the United States where to hold one's head too high or to cover one's socioeconomic reality with designer duds would be considered suspect. I consider the uniform of the poor to be a noble one.

I saw the woman from behind at first. She was very tall and, from behind, gave the impression of African royalty. The majestic skeletal system covered by the strong, beautiful, and stately musculature of a reigning queen. I wanted to meet them and did so. As the man fell into a chair with a loud expulsion of breath, the mere descent having taken every ounce of his energy, I asked if he'd be on my flight.

"We're going to Las Vegas."

These were the last words he had time to utter. The woman turned to me with a huge smile and enormously twinkling eyes and said, "We've got one of those systemwide passes. We've been visitin' family, friends, places, and just havin' the best time. Now we're going to Vegas. This is my brotha' and we've just been havin' the *best* of times."

Her infectious good humor and enthusiasm were contagious, and we just gave each other the biggest hug for the joy of being on this adventure at the same time in the same place.

The woman had no face, really. She appeared to have suffered the torture of fire or acid; I really couldn't describe it then or now. And the skin on her neck, such as it was, could be any other material, really: mottled silk, tie-dyed cotton, or the screen mesh from a cottage door. But even without the normalcy of bone structure or enough skin to allow for a real smile or eyelids, this woman was radiantly beautiful.

The brother and sister preboarded and sat in the first row in seats A and C. It was a joyous flight and one of shared excitement. Being alive, being on a plane, being able to feel with a heart and soul instead of nerve endings and conditioned reflexes is perhaps the best way to truly receive the messages from our Universe. Or to send needed communiqués to the vapid masses who don't appreciate the inner being.

We had time to chat about life and love during the flight. I somehow knew that they were from South Chicago and was correct in this assumption. I knew that they'd seen the hard side of life and survived. Having lost my own brother twenty-four years before, I knew that, had he lived, my sibling and I would have traveled well together, too. I guess I vicariously watched brother and sister sit and share silence or inside jokes with one another. Ah, everyone has something that others don't, eh? I have skin, but the queen had a brother. Yet we both have joy, so we're sisters after all.

"I have five children. One biological, four adopted," she offered without prompting. Her inner strength poured out with her words from the deformity that could once have bordered the lips of the lover she might have been. Pride in her accomplishments as a sister, mother, and friend were evident, and that royal bearing was very pronounced with each shared bit of information. Would that every American woman realizes that external, status quo appearance is fleeting, but the beating heart of a mother and sister is where the beauty really lies.

That day was her birthday. "I'm sixteen today," she laughingly told me. Her brother joined in the joke. "Yeah, she be sixteen a'right. Yeah."

Facing them as we were landing, the woman and I locked eyes. Our link felt physical. Oh, the gorgeous soul I felt jumping into me was tangible. There, there before me, was a goddess. I'll always think of her as one of the most beautiful women I've ever met. Or will ever meet. Blessed be.

THREE-YEAR-OLDS

West Palm Beach to Newark, March 2008

AS I WRITE this, my grandson Shea is three. If you ask him, though, he'll tell you all about what's being planned for his fourth birthday. I remember being three, actually. The little soft-pink smocked dress was my favorite. The red crinkle material with little white hearts was my second choice. I always felt so squeaky clean—that's another memory. When we'd get a very rare treat, like a stick of black licorice or a tiny one-cent bag of potato chips, we'd always save a bite of the candy or a handful of unbroken chips for my dad upon his arrival home from work. We lived on Empire Avenue above the Fishlocks, across from the Anglican church's manse and next door to the Wrights on one side and the Blynns on the other. I first saw my mother faint when I was three. I saw my dad cry when he lost his business. My cousin Judy taught me how to tie my shoelaces before we all went to Montreal's Santa Claus Parade, which I stopped by walking out to the center of the road to pet the Royal Canadian Mounted Police horses before they passed me. I received a big doll in a baby carriage that Christmas and christened her Joni. Joni wore those little dresses of mine for years after I'd outgrown them. I think I really liked being three.

We were delayed in West Palm Beach, so I set up a massage chair and started working on the customers awaiting an eventual boarding on our Newark-bound flight. Everyone was in a decent mood, and as usual, I heard life stories as well as golf handicaps and health concerns as I massaged necks, arms, and hands. Two mothers told me their reasons for leaving their temperate winter residences for the chill of New Jersey.

"Moy son's just had a haht attack. He's fawty-two. Whataya' gonna' do?" I told this woman, who looked about fifty herself, that I'd be thinking of her and hoping her son's life got healthier. "He was such a good little boy . . . and now, he's not married, and he just works all the time. Whataya' gonna' do?"

"My daughter, thirty-seven, just diagnosed with blood clots in hah leg. If hah sister hadn't noticed that hah leg was twice its nawmal size, she'd probably be dead. I mean, thirty-seven! My daughters, the most wonderful children they were! Why one's got this thing at thirty-seven, I'll never understand." I told this mother that I'd be thinking of her daughter, too, and hoped that all would be well.

"She only works! I remember when she was a girl. . . . "

The eyes focused inward at this point, and that elderly mother was seeing a child. Perhaps a three-year-old at play? A bouncy, bright, healthy child with twinkling eyes and maternal love all around her? Both mothers were worried sick and couldn't wait to get back to New Jersey to hold the hands, kiss the cheeks, and be in the presence of their afflicted babies. Yes, to most mothers, a forty-two- or thirty-seven-year-old is still three. Just because mothers will always be mothers. Most. Not all.

Just before we were to begin boarding, a latecomer barreled up to the podium with her small child. The mother was berating the child for some transgression in a husky, unrefined voice. I was three feet away and noticed the interaction, making mental note of the mother's striking appearance and the daughter's acquiescent little face. This little one's been told off this way many times, I thought to myself.

The mother was very tall with longish, bleached-blonde hair. Her figure was one of those long-legged, flat-stomached, and buxom sorts. She would be the perfect woman to saunter down a long, sandy beach, sandals casually dangling from the fingers of one hand; oversize sunglasses and a vainly and perfectly placed straw hat would be the only attire besides a string bikini. Her tan was dark, but the sort one receives from year-round tanning under UV lights. Had she not been so harsh and rough-edged, she could have been somebody.

During boarding, I was working the cabin. The woman came on board giving the appearance of one harried, stressed-out, overwrought babe. I took one of her wheeled suitcases and escorted her to her seat. Up went the first bag, and then, behind this woman, some distance away, toddled her child who also pulled a suitcase on wheels.

"Hurry up, wouldja'! Yah impossible. Yah so slow! Hurry up!" The child complied as fast as her tiny legs would carry her. The mother was in the aisle, and I couldn't get her to step aside so I could help the little one.

"She's *always* like this. Just impossible!"

I finally got the suitcase from the girl and put it up. There were about a hundred more folks to help so the idea of intervening on the child's behalf was only fleeting. I was shocked by the way this woman treated the child, however.

The flight was going well. Service was fun and my number one and three were amazingly helpful; I'm quite a slowpoke in this department. Everyone gets their drink and snack, but I usually converse with the folks during distribution. The youngster in question separated her mother from another woman but every time I passed, that mother was leaning over her daughter and talking in the face of her row mate. Under the human umbrella of her mom, the daughter scrunched down to make it easier for that embodiment of maternal neglect to converse with a stranger. That one-way conversation was loud, too. The look on the face of person in the window seat was one of appalled fascination. Every time I passed this row, the person in the window seat, being subjected to the verbal onslaught was nodding, but I had the distinct impression that she had no choice at all in this matter. The child was there, too. Right in the middle and looking at her shoes. An invisible nonentity between her outrageously overstated mother and an imprisoned audience of one.

Every once in a while, I'd hear the mother telling the child, "You just stop that right now! Do you hear me? You just be good! Can you do that? Do you think you can be good? You're being terrible!" I truly hadn't seen or heard that little girl so much as move or make a peep since first laying eyes on her at the gate! Was I missing abhorrent, delinquent behavior, or was that mother simply creating excuses to minimize her daughter?

"God," I thought, "that poor little girl!"

At one point the mother brought the child to a rear lav, opened the door, roughly yanked down the child's knickers, and plunked that tiny thing onto the commode like she was just a horrible thing for having to urinate. I closed the door on that scene because, not only did the woman treat the child roughly, but she didn't register that there were people standing right there in the galley, totally able to see it all, whether we wanted to or not. Poor little thing!

I waited until the duo had returned to their seats and stepped in to ask, "Ma'am, how are you doing? Is everything alright?"

"Yeah."

"And, what do you do when you're not flying around the country?"

"I build houses."

"Great! You actually design and build them yourself?"

"Yeah."

"In Florida and New Jersey?"

"Actually, I went to Florida to buy a house! I'm coming back next week to close. You'll see me next week!"

"Congratulations on the purchase. I'll bet it was pretty stressful to go to Florida house shopping with a youngster, eh?"

"I've been down for three weeks. I haven't told my husband a thing. He doesn't even know where we wah. The son of a bitch won't know anything about this house!"

"Oh! You just up and left and he didn't know anything? That took some strength on your part, I'll bet. I hope it gets better for you."

"It's the in-laws. Theyah crazy."

There's always a reason to hurt a child. Was it because this woman was afraid of the reception she'd receive upon her return to the daddy? The in-laws? Her life in New Jersey in general? Or was she just a rotten person and horrible mother?

I was hoping it was just temporary jitters and poor maternal skills while under duress that made this woman overtly insensitive to her child.

Another pass down the aisle, and the child had been placed in the aisle seat. The mother and her new best listening post were now totally engrossed in a continuation of the original one-sided, loud chat. The little girl stared at her shoes.

I knelt down and looked at this pixie in her eyes.

"Hi. I'm Heather, what's your name?"

"Sage. *S-A-G-E.*" She spelled her name!

"How old are you?"

"Three."

"I'm fifty-five."

I reached over and took her little hand, and we started a little conversation of our own about flying and other things important to a little girl. Her eyes were alight, and she was almost smiling at me when her mother leaned over, shook her, and asked, "Did you tell the lady about this?" At this time her mom whipped out some glossy photos of a zoo and flipped through them, all the while asking, "Did you tell her about the elephants? The lions? The tigers?"

In a tiny voice with eyes downcast, the girl said, "They made me afraid." This admission was lost on the mother as she continued her verbal inquisition;

"Did you tell her about the beach? Did you?"

Obviously, the narcissistic mother couldn't bear to have the spotlight directed, even for a nanosecond, at her daughter. I should have known this by the fashionably chic clothing that couldn't shroud that woman's crassness or complete lack of good breeding. Class was not something she'd ever be able to buy no matter how many houses she built, purchased, or used as ammunition against her husband.

I'm sure if that woman had been capable of reading a room, she'd have been able to translate my well-aimed glare and would have stopped her verbal onslaught. Not a chance. The fact that her daughter was having a one-on-one with me was lost on her. "I was speaking with your daughter, ma'am."

I gave the child's hand a little squeeze and managed to get her to look me in the eye, and then I told her, "Thank you for talking to me, Sage. It was very interesting talking with you."

The flight ended and everyone was getting off en masse. Like that little red-coated girl in *Schindler's List*, who wandered innocently through the streets of the Warsaw ghetto, a tiny figure came up the aisle with the throng. She was alone. She was completely alone. I picked her up and held her tiny self in the crook of my arm. So light. "How are you, sweet pumpkin?"

"My daddy's lives here. He's going to give me a piggyback," she said solidly.

I made eye contact with another crewmember and we were both hurting for that little girl. The mother, way at the back in the aft part of the plane, hadn't even noticed the absence of her baby. No, she was still immersed in conversation. We waited for her to notice. She finally did. But was it with an air of panic or fear of loss? No, it was with rage. I called back to her, "Don't worry, we have her up here with us." The mother made her way to the front and hissed, "You're nevah wheah ya' supposed to be. You nevah help. Look! Ya' didn't carry your bag to the front!" Well, neither had the mother, actually. That woman in the window seat who'd spent the entire flight listening to abrasive chatter had wheeled the child's little pink bag up the aisle. As I reluctantly put the little girl down, I whispered in her ear, "You're a wonderful, smart, beautiful little lady. Never forget that!"

To the mother I said, "Go easy on her."

"She's just impossible. She nevah helps!" And they were gone.

Will Sage remember being three? If she remembers one thing, I hope it's the ten words she heard that night;

"You're a wonderful, smart, beautiful little lady. Never forget that!"

All little ones are so good, eh?

ZERO EYES

Boston to JFK, April 2007

FIRST IMPRESSIONS, NO matter how bleak, should include a modicum of optimism. The rude might become polite. The mean have the potential for kindness. The imperfect possibly harbor greatness at a closer second look.

Today I met four children and their mother. They were in a departure area at Boston's Logan when first I saw them. What struck me most as I spoke to them was their inability to respond. From the youngest, a two-year-old girl, to her three stairstep older brothers, there was what my better half refers to as "zero eyes." Were these children traumatized? Was this a temporary condition? I hoped it was a uniform condition caused by separation anxiety, but on some level, I knew that these four youngsters might never volunteer a smile, laugh out loud, or have an opinion of their own. They just seemed to be missing a chunk of something they needed to thrive intellectually. Physically, these children could have been beautiful, but their lethargy didn't allow for an appearance of strength. There was no display of outward energy, let alone interest in their surroundings. None at all.

There was a mother. She was a complete blank. Her children seemed invisible to her, but by some cohesive force or basic instinct, all hung within close range of her. Did she even know they were around her? It didn't look like it. No verbal or physical contact—not even a quick look—did she impart to them. I approached and told her that she could get on the plane first, and she just looked at me and said in a monotone voice, "Nobody's getting on now."

"Oh, I mean when the boarding starts, please bring your children on before everyone else if you want to."

She just looked at my face but I could tell she wasn't really focusing on me, or on anything at all.

During boarding, there was a herding of this group to their seats. The mother couldn't make out what the numbers on the boarding passes meant, so I just took them one by one and placed them into their designated seats.

As the flight progressed, I tried to engage the eldest boy, who was sitting on an aisle across from his family, in chatter. He couldn't answer me and just kept staring at his television. The mother held the little girl on her lap and never interjected any comments as I mined the child for any sign of brain activity.

The children became sick. One of them, very sick. At no point during these episodes did the mother offer comfort to her children or help in their cleanup process. She just kept watching television and was inert.

At one point during the flight I noticed the mother had a

cell phone and it was on. "Ma'am, do you mind switching that off, please. Just until we land."

"I'm trying to make it go dark."

I asked for a peek and pressed the End button.

"How will I get it to go on again?" she mumbled.

I turned it back on, then off, then on, then off. "It's not easy until you know how." I told her. Then I knelt down and asked what they'd done in Boston. "We stayed there."

"Were you visiting friends or family?"

"Family. Maybe my kids got sick because they caught what my sister's baby had." This seemed to prove that although there had been no maternal involvement in the multiple bouts of sickness among the four children, the mother really did understand what illness was. Yet none of these disconnected souls ever acknowledged one another or spoke to each other during that flight. There were no sparkles in any of their eyes, no wisdom, humor, or discernable spark of anything that could be considered alive. Enthusiasm would have been the least available commodity if I could pick one trait missing more than any other.

To quote a famous line from the movie *Cool Hand Luke*: "What we have here is a failure to communicate." Or did we?

As they were leaving the plane, I heard, "My boy got sick again. In a bag. Could I get another bag in case he throws up in his daddy's car on the way home?" We gave her some bags, and they were gone.

The children, although they appeared numb, knew who their mother was. The mother, flat affect intact, knew who her children were. They were together. They knew who was going to pick them up. And they were going home. Blessed be.

FAILURE TO IMPRESS

Fort Lauderdale to JFK, October 2010

HE'D BEEN ON a flight of mine before and was easy to remember because he was one of the least approachable individuals I'd ever served. Jockey-like in size but with an attitude that thrust the unspoken as an almost tangible wedge between us. I just knew he detested flight attendants in general. Being a student of "the Four Agreements" by Don Miguel Ruiz, taking things personally isn't my problem. I have other problems, but most of the time, I breeze through my days feeling pretty unencumbered by guilt. If you're having a bad day, 'tis not of my creation. It's your karma or maybe just the weather, but it's not my fault. If you don't like me, it could be because you've missed your connecting flight or dislike those in the service industry as a group. Again, that's your problem. Not my fault. I love this agreement the most and use it all the time to prevent a plummet into the groundswell of the average man's unhappiness.

Anyway, the man sat in an aisle seat, and lucky for him, nobody took the window. As I took orders, it was obvious that the gentleman in front of the acerbic one was from France. Being a Montrealer by birth, I struck up a conversation in full Francophone bliss. It was obvious from the Parisian that he believed Quebecois French to be about as low on the linguistic ladder as you'd find. Yet I defended my favorite language and place with a bit of tongue-in-cheek acquiescence mixed with facial expressions that only a real Quebecois girl could offer. It's always a debate between the continental and the provincial when it comes to proper pronunciation and dramatic gesturing. What the former wins with perfect enunciation, the latter wins, hands down, with hand, arm, shoulder, neck, and face movements! We were enjoying this dual, that long-haired, casually clad but classy European and I. This slowed down my order taking a tad, so that hater of all flight attendants interrupted us by looking at me for the first time. His look and body language communicated his absolute disgust that I hadn't taken his order. I put my hand on the Frenchman's shoulder and said, "*A bientôt, monsieur*." (This is a friendly way of saying "Our conversation is over . . . until later.")

Taking his order, I swore to myself that I'd earn this man's respect. "Would you care for something to drink, sir?"

"Coffee. A bit of milk," came the demand without any eye contact whatsoever.

"Yes, sir. I have a full pot, so please ask for another at any time during this flight."

No response.

I served the drinks and was just returning from a trip to the rear of the plane when the man who hated me and my kind said, without looking up, "Give me another coffee."

"Yes, sir. A bit of milk, right?"

He gave me a look that said it all: "You stupid woman! Of course, with a bit of milk."

If I'd asked him, "What's the magic word?" I'll bet he'd have said, "Now!"

I returned with the fresh coffee right away and made a huge mistake. I reached for what I thought was his empty first cup. As I took it I heard, "No!" and was so surprised that I looked at him, but my hand kept that cup in motion until it hit the back of the Frenchman's seat. You can guess the rest—that half-full cup of lukewarm java did a flip, and the contents poured in their entirety on the beautiful hair of the innocent Frenchman.

After getting a gross of paper towels, I raced back to my poor drowning victim. His wife was speechless, and the fellow was expressionless as the lukewarm liquid continued to drip out of that long hair and onto his T-shirt. Only Europeans can carry off the carefree casualness that his mop of long ringlets and well-worn top evoked. Even covered in the milky liquid, the fellow looked nothing short of dapper.

I started squeezing excess coffee out of his locks. (What am I saying? The only kind of java anyone has in their hair is *extra*. Doesn't that go without saying?) Then I mopped and wrung out that poor man's shirt. Yes, he was still wearing it, but I'm an old granny, so it must have seemed to all like an elder cleaning off a little boy. That's what it felt like to me, and the way he availed himself to my ministrations, I'm sure he was remembering a time when his own mommy fixed him up. Little boys, so helpless. So sweet. So lovable. I so loved that time of my life when my own son needed me after falling into a swamp or some other unclean place on the dairy farm. I miss those days very much. This incident, I believe, returned the customer to a carefree time when his mom could solve all his problems. We were both lucky for just a few seconds to have memories of unconditional love when the biggest worries revolved around a dirty shirt. I saw this in his eyes. He felt this in my care. We locked eyes and all was well, but I wrote him a personal check for ten dollars and listed "cleaning expenses" on it. It was slipped onto his tray table as I passed by later in the flight. Later, he passed it back saying, "Zee gesture was enough. I cannot accept deese. *Merci, mais non.*"

I had been trying so very hard to impress that fellow who obviously could not be won over and failed miserably. The dismissive man behind my French customer remained disgusted from beginning to end of the flight. I don't take it personally when someone's miserable, but maybe trying too hard was counterproductive in this scenario. I had also been trying to win the always-waged war of words and movement that my kind has with those from the land of wine, cheese, and the Eiffel Tower, yet it wasn't wordplay that won him over. It was becoming his mama.

You win some, you lose some in the flight attendant business. Sometimes you lose 'em all. Never quit trying, though. Never, ever quit trying.

NEGLECT, COMPASSION, STRESS, SHORT FUSE, NO LOVE?

Point A to Point B one wintery night

SOME PEOPLE SHOULDN'T breed.

The sweet under-two child was one I immediately loved. Her eyes, enormous when compared to any others I'd ever seen, were full of the dickens. Her little body didn't walk but bounced and spun, propelled by the enthusiasm of what? Of her excitement in a flight with her mommy? I didn't know what the motivating factors were behind the complete joyous abandon she displayed on the jet bridge. The woman with her, I mistakenly assumed to be her grandmother as she closed up the stroller. She was probably in her mid- to late forties, but who knows these days?

"Where do I put this?" she barked.

"Right there by the door, ma'am."

The people boarding planes are vetted for sobriety, excess or too-large baggage, fear, and a long list of other notable characteristics that mark them as rejected, helped, encouraged, or calmed customers. All in-flight crew members are adept at generalization when it comes to the boarding population. Yet exceptions to the rule exist, and this is a story about one. First impressions don't always yield all the information needed to analyze everyone at the forward entry door!

The woman wrestling with the stroller finally came forward and physically closer to her child than she'd been since they'd come into my view. Until her attention was given to the little girl, I'd kept up a monologue with that precious babe who responded with arms waving and those magnificent orbs shouting how great life can be for a twenty-month-old.

The mother, with short brown curly hair and dressed in nondescript browns, was short and built like someone who was rippling negativity and stress. She schlepped a heavy red bag aboard and listened to my opinion of her daughter without a change of expression. I thought, "Wow, not a happy woman. Not a woman who knows *how* to be happy." Sometimes you can just tell when the skin is composed of the bitter veneer of resentments and self-pity. The child didn't know she was supposed to head down the aisle of the plane to seat-number something! That woman said, "Go down to our seat. Go, go, go now." Unbelievably, that mother didn't guide her child in any way but gave her a push with her right leg. "That way. That way." The rest of the customers who were lined up behind may or may not have noticed this, but I felt a pain shoot through me as I realized that this woman didn't want that child—not on the plane . . . not in her life. I felt it, and it hurt my heart.

Before taxiing, I noticed the child in the aisle and went back to ask the mother to hold her. I received an exasperated look, and the child was hauled back and into her seat. Seatbelt on or on the mother's lap were acceptable options to my request. The child wiggled in her seat, and I was told, "She doesn't like seatbelts!" I nodded but thought the mother would make things better. Taxi.

Takeoff. Still climbing. The passenger call button went off, and I went to it. "She doesn't have a headset." The mother said pointing to but not looking at her child. The mother was wearing a headset but I guess the thought of giving it to her child never crossed her mind. Selfish, I thought. Really selfish. I don't usually judge travelers, but when it comes to loving mothers, this one sure didn't qualify. We delivered a headset.

Just after ten thousand feet, another ding. Back I went. "Get her a juice or something!" No eye contact with me, just a demand. I was married to a man with autism once; I know the symptoms of this condition. She did not have a neurological disorder; she was just a mean, put-upon, spoiled, insensitive, and very defensive individual. Not a happy camper! I told her we would take orders very soon.

Seatbelt sign still on. Child bouncing around the aisle. Back I went to ask the mother to secure the baby. There was moderate turbulence in play, and I was holding on to seat backs!

With a hate-filled, disgusted look, the woman said, "Well, what do you want me to do?"

I swear, I've never been less charming on the job, but I was shocked by her irresponsible response, so I countered, "This is your child. It's for *her safety*." The mother's hand was holding onto her daughter's collar and pulling her by it. Then, when the child was within grabbing proximity, a little arm was caught, and the child pulled to the seat. I felt so awful for that child.

Nicki was my lovely partner on this flight. Tall, elegant and gracious, she is capable of handling all situations with élan. I just love flying with her! Nicki called and told me that the woman wanted to speak to me. Okay, and back I went.

"You spoke to me aggressively, and that set the people around me off, and they've told me that I should control my child better. They're all very aggressive, too. What do you want from me? She won't sit down. I have a son and he's not at all like this. He's exactly the opposite." I sensed she was defending her ability to raise at least one good child, and it hurt me because I'll bet that child gets applause, but no warm loving from her at all.

At this point, I knelt down and put my hand on her arm. Suddenly I felt like a child again myself. I, too, had a perfect brother. There were favorites, and I wasn't one of them in certain family circles. At large family parties, from the age of three on, my paternal grandmother would have me recite this poem:

There was a little girl
who had a little curl
right in the middle of her forehead.
When she was good
she was very, very good,
but when she was bad,
she was horrid!

Everyone would laugh, including me. Then I'd hear, 'She *is* horrid!" As an adult, I continued to encourage this pattern and even married a man who used me as a punch line to every joke. Not a healthy way to self-evaluate, I can assure you. Will this little child grow to feel that she must be the naughty, useless, unwanted child? That mother's setting her up to feel just this way.

Many's the time my paternal grandmother would tell me how horrid I was. "You're just like the little girl who had a little curl, Heather!" How wonderful my brother was. How destructive I was. How cheeky I was. Maybe she was correct . . . probably she was correct. But I remember being tiny and very alive and happy. The drip, drip, drip of insults didn't add up until temporary insecurities caused me to believe that, indeed, I was horrid. Certainly not as good, wonderful, bright, or fabulous as my brother (who, indeed, *was* all of these things). I'm different; I've been criticized and ridiculed for excess energy. Learning how to run a wire to ground the lightning-strikes of self-annihilation took me decades. I still run the risk of shorting myself out, but the sight of this little girl, so completely happy in spite of her mother's lack of understanding, empathy, and warmth just hurt me so very much. I remember, you see.

"Ma'am. I didn't mean to be aggressive, but your daughter could have been hurt during that bumpy time. Really! "

"Oh. She's just awful. That woman sitting across the aisle said she'd raised six children, and none of them behaved like my daughter. Well, they don't know me. They're just aggressive. My son's nothing like this one!"

I said, "I have two children, and their as different as night and day. My son's kind and loving; my daughter has other great qualities. They're so different, and I really think a mom needs two children, if only to appreciate the differences in each one. I know it's tough to have two but I also know the joys! There's a preschool teacher and one of her friends in the front of the plane, and we all love little ones. Won't you move up to my section?"

I moved her up. Put her heavy red suitcase up and introduced her to the young ladies across the aisle. They had noticed the child and the disconnected behavior of the mother. "She's not warm or loving to that child at all," said the teacher after watching the two go up and down the aisle pell-mell without communication or contact.

Once seated, the mother hooked up her headsets, and the preschool teacher gave a ballpoint pen and a big yellow legal pad to the child. That little girl drew and scribbled and talked to herself and was loved up by the women across the aisle for the duration of the flight. Nobody was thanked. The efforts of strangers were ignored, as was the child.

On final descent, I saw the wee one unattended, standing at the bulkhead. "Please, ma'am, we're landing, and you should hold her or strap her in, please."

Again with a disgusted look the tiny thing was pulled onto the mother's lap. The crying became a wail, the wailing escalated to a yell, the yell exploded into a crying jag that lasted for a full five minutes. Making eye contact with others around the first row was startling. We all had pity on our faces. We all hurt for that child. The mother wrestled her into a nearly suffocating arm lock, and there was nothing any of us could do. That poor little girl. I don't think she'd ever sat on her mommy's lap, you see. The closeness was imprisonment, nothing like the nurturing embrace that most of us give our children.

We all heard, "*They* want you to sit in my lap. They're the ones making you do this. I'm sorry but they say you have to stay on my lap." The martyr. The obedient passive-aggressive. The mother who didn't mother.

When the door was opened and I turned to invite people to leave the aircraft, I heard, "Take my bag down."

To this I answered, "I hurt my shoulder putting it up, ma'am. I'll ask a pilot to help you with it when everyone's off." No more favors, lady. No more favors.

The captain did get the heavy bag for her. The stroller was retrieved. I saw the woman assembling the vehicle as her daughter walked around without any sort of connection to the mom. The woman was grunting her dissatisfaction with the stroller, baggage, and other miscellaneous items, but she wasn't watching her baby.

"Let me help you with that," I said as I took her suitcase "You just get your little girl situated. We're going your way." She passed me her bag and tried to talk her child into the stroller. Not a gentle process at all.

One more favor, I guess. But who'll do the favors for the little girl for the next few decades of her life? Who will love her up? Who will accept her for what she is at heart? A little girl with a mother who doesn't love or want her. Well, at least not to the naked eye.

Like me, she'll probably have a fabulous life because of

the kindness of strangers and a great brother who sees what's happening up close and personal. I also hope she has at least one side of the family that loves her unconditionally. I did. I survived. I'm thriving.

It's funny how we can relive our past and, for better or for worse, be so very grateful for every facet of our upbringing. Like having two different children, we all have different sides of our families. God bless the child that has it all. God bless the child that has enough. I did. Will that little girl? Her eyes say she has everything she needs right now. Blessed be.

GO TOWARD THE LOVE

Fort Lauderdale to White Plains, August 2009

PEOPLE GET OLD at different ages. There came aboard a regal black woman in her very late sixties. She'd earned a PhD some decades back when women were kept in their place and black women were kept below all others. What was great about this woman? What made her ultimately impressive to me, besides her obvious self-confidence and erudite sophistication, was the fact that she was in the presence of her mother. Now I wondered, what gave this woman of color—from her era—the strength to overcome all odds and earn a doctorate? I was about to find out. It was, of course, the influence of her unstoppable mom.

The mother, tiny and almost-but-not-quite frail, boarded just behind her daughter. The wheelchair pusher was thanked and apparently quite touched by his little passenger. She didn't quite have a spry step, but she had a sure footing with every graceful forward thrust. It was that: *thrust*. A force field of good energy preceded her belted cotton dress, fetching little hat, and dainty shoes usually reserved for the under-forty set.

I extended both of my hands and took this little woman's hands in mine. This wasn't done to steady or lead her. No, it was an automatic and necessary (for me) move to catch some of her essence. She beamed at me.

I asked, "Do you sing?"

"Well, course I do, chile. Course I do."

"Good! We'll sing a duet when we get up in the air, okay?"

"We'll do that!"

The duo was in the first row, but the eldest was at a window, youngest in the middle, so I didn't have easy access during the flight. There was a sleeping man on the aisle. Sometimes, three seats abreast are too many!

We parked at a gate at some airport, and all the announcements were made. The mother and daughter decided to deplane last so I had time, between fond adieus to the other 148 folks, to chat with the older woman. I lamented, "I'm so sorry we didn't have a chance to belt out a few hymns!"

"Well, next time, then. There'll be many a time. I go to visit my otha' chillen. My husband, he passed three years ago, and now I just fly from chile to chile. They jes cain't git enough of me. It's tirin' though. I'll be ninety-one next birthday. I cain't do much when I git to they places, but I kin sho love them all, and that's enough. That's surely enough." She twinkled. She gave me that sly little look that only the ancients can deliver with impunity. Conspiratorially, she was planning the next twenty years of her life. "I'm lettin' everyone else git off foist because, well, I don't want to be bowling them ovah in my rush to see my son. You know I could, girl. You know I could!"

Another day, another flight. He approached the entryway in a wheelchair, but two canes in strangleholds made it possible for this very big man to make it to his front row aisle seat. 1C. He was jolly enough as I took his carry-on, canes, and other needed belongings and popped them into the overhead bin.

"Do you need anything before the rest of the people start boarding, sir?"

"No, thank you. I'm just fine. Oh, on second thought, how about a new back?" He laughed at his impossible request but I countered, "Hey, nothing ventured, nothing gained, right? It never hurts to ask."

"It hurts all the time, actually."

With this comment, his jocularity ceased, and I saw him shut down, go deep within his own self, where his humor, masculinity, virility, and perfectly functioning body were stored in a vault only he could access. And it hurt him to look there at what was. I could tell.

The flight was long but smooth, and my 1C man snoozed or gazed at his TV screen without expression. I gave him whatever he asked for, but he only let a bit of himself out with each of my little forays into his space.

Then we were on final approach. That flight seemed so quick! A young man who'd displayed faux gangsta' behavior, and had ignored his woman and baby with malevolent attitude and cruel intent, decided to storm up the aisle. I got on the PA right away and said, "We are landing, please, we ask everyone to insure that they are in their seats with seatbelts secured." Still the young hood just kept barreling up the aisle with a hateful look on his face. I thought, "Geez, is he storming the cockpit or coming to get me?"

I exchanged a quick look with my man in 1C, and he got what was happening. Then I saw it. Whatever past this man had lived, he was in his macho knight-in-shining-armor mode again. In reality, it would have taken a Herculean effort to come to my aid, but he was ready to try. We both knew it, and I felt grateful. This was all taking place at Mach 1 velocity, so this wordless exchange was a catalyst for my confidence.

My next announcement was without the benefit of the mike, as I fiercely signaled this upstart to take 1B. "We're landing—sit down there! Sit down immediately!" I didn't have time to do anything else, really. It was a last-ditch gambit before a full-body tackle. When seated, the young fellow with such a bitter attitude said, "I want to go to the bathroom." I was terribly relieved and immediately conciliatory.

"I'm sorry, do you think you can hold on until we land and are parked at the gate? It'll only be a few minutes, and you'd be safer strapped up."

"Yeah."

"Good. Stay where you are until we're parked and then you can scoot right up here, okay?"

No response, but he did give a wan smile, fastened the seatbelt of the aisle seat he'd occupied, and set his body in an accusatory "I'm so relaxed and you're so uptight" sprawled position. I called the flight attendant in the back to inform her of the incident then assumed the posture—hands under my thighs, feet flat on the floor, back and head pressed against the jump-seat—in anticipation of imminent landing. With speed and coordination that surprised me, the young man whipped open his seatbelt and jumped up and into the window seat. The customer in 1C and I locked eyes and just shook our heads as we shared one thought: “This guy’s got no respect or smarts. Just a disrespectful punk.”

In one more quick motion, the youth was up and stomping quickly down the aisle to his seat in the back. Was he nuts? Just someone the world owes a living, I thought.

By now, my kindred spirit in 1C and I had bonded enough to get lots of conversation in before touchdown. He so wanted to be my hero but must have been relieved when that fellow moved back to his place far away from the flight deck and me.

“Thanks so much for being aware of the potential danger in that fellow, sir.”

“I had your back.”

“I know that. It felt super to know you were there to help me. When will you be flying again?”

“You know, I don’t really know. Maybe never. I just visited my daughter and her new baby. My wife stays home. Because of my back, I can’t work anymore, so my girl says, ‘Dad, come and stay here, you can help with the baby.’ I can’t even lift up that child, so I’d be no good to anyone there. My wife, she stays home and thinks I’m in the way. I’m not much good to anyone anymore. I’m not old enough to be so useless! I guess I was a pretty good dad though, because both my daughters have graduate degrees from prestigious institutions of higher learning. They both married well, too. They’re both doing well. They both miss me, but I can’t just go to see them anytime because, look at me, I’m barely able to get around, and I’d be such a burden. Such a pain in the ass. I sure love their babies, though. I sure do.”

Now, I thought this man was seventy, and I said, "I'm pushing fifty-eight, and I hurt when I get up in the morning. When did all this start for you?"

"I'm fifty-six."

This revelation shocked me. I remembered the ninety-year-old woman who, although stiff and sore, kept moving toward the love of her children. She was as smart as this younger grandparent but wasn't burdened with the male ego whereby, to be useful, one must earn his keep, contribute to the common purse, or any other such fictions.

"Sir, please, know this: if you're a presence in their lives, that's enough. Your love is enough to justify any space you think you're just taking up. Just go and be there and know that you're giving your smarts and persona to the little families of your busy daughters. When that guy was a possible threat to me, just knowing you were right there in your seat and totally aware of every single move that guy made, gave me such a great feeling that I was not alone. In that nanosecond when I wasn't sure exactly what was going to happen, your strength of mind came right out and stood between me and any danger. I felt it. Your daughters and grandchildren will, too. It comes from your brain, heart, and smarts. You may have a bad back, but the rest of you is worth more than mobility because you can project it all. You just did!"

"No. I think it's all over for me."

"Well, in the darkness of night, think on what I've just said. It's a seed that'll need some of your energy to germinate and grow into a reality for you and your family."

He gave me a smile and said, "Okay. I'll just think about it."

The captain waited for the punk and gave him a talking-to

on the jet bridge. The man in 1C employed the two canes as his legs slowly carried him to a waiting wheelchair. He'd be met by his unsympathetic wife and returned to a home where he was not accepted in his physically imperfect body. He must first accept himself, I believe.

I still think this man could live to be ninety-one if he just realized a couple of things. He's loved, and his daughters desire his company; his wife might accept him on nicer, more loving terms if he accepted and loved himself as he is.

When working isn't possible or when our bodies are stubbornly resisting direction from our minds, we should go to places we're invited, where there's unconditional love. No man is useless if he can give and receive love. No woman either. I hope I have the love of my children in my old age and that I'm not too proud or lack the self-esteem it takes to have them take me in just because they feel my love.

WE'RE ALL JUST REFLECTED LIGHT

Boston to West Palm Beach, December 2010

EXAMPLES OF SILVER linings abound in this industry. Yet who among us has the energy or presence of mind to look for them when fatigue hits? It's tough, but the effort of digging deep and extracting those subatomic particles of ourselves known as our humanity and our joy is worth the effort.

On the night of the winter solstice in December 2010, my crew had to reach into our collective gut and pull out the "fake it till you make it" smile. Conditions? Boston's Logan closed because the snow was piling up faster than the plows could remove it on the only runway with a chance of opening up. It was the week of Christmas. Folks are stressed on perfect days, so a night of "maybes" and "we'll sees" added to their woes.

We'd already had a long day trying to get into Boston so,

by the time we arrived to take the next payload to their Palm Beach destination, we were nearly comatose. Before any of you think I'm tooting my own horn, let me clue you in to a secret that I employ to replenish my supply of positive life force. The whole crew did this on the stormy night in question.

I steal the energy of our customers. I do! If a person offers a tiny bit of positivity to a few people, then the energy returned is greater than that expended. (Positive energy to the power of one when returned by one hundred people equals a return of positive energy to the power of one hundred. I know this equation is in an earlier chapter, but it bears repeating.)

The earlier story about how I learned to effect change in a group when I was stuck in the Montreal International Airport for three days and two nights is important, too. The snow had hit hard. The mood for all stranded individuals turned from anger and frustration to laughter and music because some airline agent set the tone. By the end of the first day, disparate individuals had bonded with others to make the party of the century come to pass. The Canadian ski team, an opera singer, storytellers, and the less extroverted among us found places within that group to enjoy and pass the time. I had a blast, and that one airline employee made it happen for hundreds of us. She must have been exploding with returned positive charges by the end of her shift. Copying her has turned my airline experience into one of joy and satisfaction. I've always believed that everything happens for a reason and that three-day delay in 1971 was a springboard into a really positive life. Boy, am I ever thankful for that experience!

So in the aforementioned delay, we mingled with the disenfranchised customers. Believe me, they all watched as conversations were begun, a laugh here and there was shared, and the uniformed crew members wove their personalities through the group. Until this personal touch was introduced, this crowd was ready to lynch us all. I did my thing, by setting up a massage chair and working on the folks who were in no mood to be nice—at first.

By the time everyone was boarded and we finally pushed back, we were four hours late and hadn't even de-iced! Between takeoff and landing, so many of the folks asked about our welfare! "Are you tired?" "When will you get to rest?" "Is this what you do every day?" "God, how do you keep smiles on your faces?"

Well, we kept smiles on our faces because, as the crew moved among the people at the departure gate, we were all touched by their humanity. They were transformed from the angry mob to a crowd being entertained, encouraged, listened to, and massaged by flight attendants who were about to work their flight—if it ever got off the ground! We stole their energy. We siphoned off their vibrations, adapted to each of their frequencies and became energized. Personal histories were exchanged, reasons for their trips shared, anxieties were assuaged, and the crew, with our empathy, transmuted the negative vibes into a supercharged alternating current within our own bodies.

Most of the travelers slept throughout the trip. Too bad. They missed the lunar eclipse on the winter solstice. The crew saw this once-in-a-lifetime occurrence, and this was partial payment for the hours of sleeplessness we were experiencing. Isn't it funny how the Universe gives us perks to remind us how lucky we are to have this great profession? A full lunar eclipse on the stormy night of our winter solstice, viewed from our office at thirty-seven thousand feet. We'd have missed it had we left Boston on time. We counted our blessings as we watched the shadow darken the moon for a time before the brightness of its reflected light peeked out again.

If you think about it, our job's like an eclipse. The bright side is sometimes hidden, but if you look for it, it's there; it's just lurking behind a temporary shadow.

"I HAVE EVERYTHING"

Long Beach to JFK, July 2007

HE WAS BOARDED as a special needs customer because of profound deafness. A slight man of indeterminate age; pencil-thin mustache; thick, slicked-back black hair ending in a short ponytail. Olive skin over Cherokee bone structure (I thought). Nails, not too long but evident, at the end of long fingers on the veined hands of an artist. Black, shiny eyes that were a mixture of hunger and innocence. Searching eyes that didn't twinkle like those of an excited explorer, but they did present the incredible incandescence of someone on the brink of something.

That something was the fish recently hooked after a long time jigging with a souring bait. And that mighty adversarial catch is still being reeled in. Sobriety. Being clean. That illusive but not impossible catch of the day is being brought to shore one hard crank of the reel at a time. One day at a time.

He spoke to me with large swoops of his arms, each poking out of his short-sleeved cotton shirt but screaming with actions louder than words: "I shot up. I shot up for twenty years! I'm thirty years old now. I don't do it anymore! I'm smiling!" He gave the sign for "thank you" and pointed upward, then formed the praying hands. He was thanking God. His higher power of choice. I mouthed questions and moved my arms and hands in grand gesture, and we reached a point where emotions and passions for life, success, and freedom overcame us both; he signed for a pen and paper.

Down came the drink order pad and out came a pencil. Neither of us completed fully spelled or punctuated sentences during the "dialogue." We were too excited. One as a neophyte drug-free addict, the other a mother wanting to hear all about the success of a long-gone son. The lead in the pencil broke after the first couple of questions and answers. We were not looking at each other but instead at whichever word was put down next. A new hunger? The impatience with which he wrote and the intensity of my need to know made for a perfect marriage of input and output. No word processor or abbreviated text messaging could have made the exchange faster.

"I am visit my sister and brother house for 1 week. I am first to visit my family to [say] sorry. Steps 6, 7, 8, 9. My sister's son, 8 year old. He love me. My grandma, 8 years ago. I all time [took] care of my own baby—drugs. Now I stop. Feel so great. Drug controlled my life." He'd believed his nephew to be his own son during the earlier years of drugging. I could envision him holding and gazing at the child with those shining orbs. There was enough love in his eyes to merit ownership on some ethereal plane.

I scribbled, "That's okay. You're who you are *now* because of what you've done! What are you learning?"

Between every frenzied note he'd do the sign for gratitude, spread his arms as if for Crucifixion, and send a smile from the forward galley to the aft lavs. He was casting his joy toward every sleeping customer and then looking up to take one more deep breath of energy from his Lord and Savior. I was exploding with each infusion of blissful energy he gave to me! He'd been saving his gifts for twenty years, and now, after walking his own painful "green mile" for two decades, this deaf man was being heard and felt by a granny and anyone open to his glee. Can a speechless man yell? Until last night, I wouldn't have believed that the quiet, rarified air required by the hearing world could be so loud and filled so fully with tangible life force and wordless speech.

"Are you Cherokee, Osage, Pawnee, Crow, or Blackfoot?" His hands and face, black eyes, and noble profile had rekindled the memory of my friend Tom, the Cherokee-Creek medicine man with whom I'd apprenticed for years in Tulsa, Oklahoma. Tim descended into the quagmire of chemical abuse and is lost to us presently. But no, my wordless fellow is descended from the Russian and Spanish ex-patriots of the other oppressed natives; his ancestors are the Jews, the gypsies, the expelled.

"Ah! You have genetic memory of great injustice! Stay clean!" I said, wishing I could reach into my old friend Tom and bring him back into the world of the coherent.

"Will you become ordained? Have you felt the call of your God?"

"Yeah. I called."

As serendipity's presence is a constant, another traveler

joined our powwow and, with permission granted, I shared the reasons for the conversation he was witnessing. He asked the recovering addict, "Are you a friend of Bill?" Instant understanding between both parties. "I've been his friend for seventeen and a half years. I'm sixty now."

"Me, eleven months!" countered my penman.

They sat down together and the pen and paper was passed. I left them and was never missed, of that I'm positive.

Later, I asked the older man, "What were you writing?"

"I told him that this year would be the toughest of his life. Every day's a struggle and the longest of his life, but, in a few years, he'll look back at the gained years of sobriety, and they'll seem like they've raced by in a flash!"

Life races by no matter what. We've got to grab and experience what every second offers. Sharing ourselves and appreciating each other is why we're in this mortal coil.

In August 2007, the deaf-but-great communicator will hit his one-year mark. One day at a time. One year at a time. There's hope for Tom then, isn't there? I needed to know that and feel the potential, and I did as, by some rich osmotic process, hope came to me from one who could neither hear nor speak in the common manner. Yet he'd heard his God and he'd told his story. Maybe we're all deaf at times in our lives, eh? One written sentence contained the words, "I have it all!" Yes, he does. He knows it. We all do, but how many of us know it?

SHE WHO HESITATES IS LOST

San Juan Airport, midnight on a winter's night 2008

IT HAD BEEN a magnificent flight from New York to San Juan. The warmth, mutual respect, energy, and innate joy the Puerto Ricans bring onto each plane always fills me with the gladness only gospel music, a hug from my grandson, or the handhold of my lover usually awakens. As midnight struck, three of us stood at the arrival gate waiting for the pilots and the last in-flight crew member to deplane. We were a contented trio.

A few straggling travelers passed down the corridor toward some other gate or exit. One tiny two-year-old seemed to be wandering all alone. He was crying. I wondered aloud if he was alone, and we all looked for some missing mom or dad. Walking about fifteen feet in front of the toddler was a tall, well-dressed tourist. The man occasionally looked back but never offered a word or signal of encouragement to the sad little boy. The obvious was painful. This father was not in any way, shape, or form consoling his son. The boy lurched forward at a constant, if slow, pace occasionally raising both arms toward the distant parent. The spectacle tore me up, and I preached my disdain for the coldness of this father to my coworkers.

My mind and heart were not one. I wanted to rush up, embrace the boy, and never give him back to the man who so cruelly ignored the pathetic sobs of his son. I wanted to race after the father and ask him to put himself in his son's shoes.

Some men think they will make men of their sons by ignoring their emotional needs. Some think that any form of movement that tires a child will invite sleep better than lullabies or bedtime stories, rocking or rubbing a tiny back.

I'll never know what sparked this horrible action and reaction for this pitiful twosome, because I did not intervene by sweeping the child into my arms and kissing his tears away. I'll never know the motivation of this father because I didn't ask. I didn't involve myself.

Yet I'll always be involved at a cellular level with both parties because there I was, full of joy and love, energy for support, and the training to understand family dynamics and respect the culture of each individual's mind, yet I did nothing. I'll be crying inside forever now. Was it because it was after midnight? Was it because I thought the father must have reasons for his lack of nurturing at that time? Was I being too politically correct to step up to the plate and grab that youngster so the tears would fall on my shoulder and the baby could feel love? Was I a coward or lazy or just feeling holier than thou?

Maybe I need to be inside a plane to be empowered to intervene. Maybe I'm only true to myself at high altitudes. There will always be a huge hole in my heart because the second chance to do the right thing won't present itself. Not with that tiny human, anyway.

TO CALL OUT OR NOT TO CALL OUT; THAT IS THE QUESTION

Las Vegas to JFK, August 2008

AT 2:15 A.M. IN the crew hotel, I knew. Food poisoning again! It's the third bout of this affliction in four years, so the symptoms were totally patterned. The wish either to become unconscious or just die is the most common sensation. I resigned myself to become one with the cool bathroom floor and did just that until some invisible hand helped me back onto the bed.

By my van time, I was sure I was on the mend. Oh, what power the mind has to fool the optimist within. In actuality, I was on the precipice and about to fall into that pit of "I don't care, just let me die," but I was in denial. Pride goeth before that imminent fall.

By the end of boarding, I was feeling squirrelly but still thought the day would improve with time and distraction. During take off the walls began to close in on me. Before ten thousand feet, I removed myself to the confines of the forward lavatory. Before service, I'd ended up on an aft jump seat hoping that I'd be able to do my job. The question was immediately answered by Jamie and Corinne, as my fellow crew members, who took over and told me they'd do my section. I was determined to get better by the end of the flight, because this was a three-day trip that had been fraught with delays, and we were a team.

I went into an aft lav, and the urge to lay down was overwhelming. In fact, I couldn't have remained upright if I tried. Laying down my head on the commode wasn't enough. The mind is so playful when the body isn't functioning. There's really little or no common sense involved, so everything seems possible. Like laying down in the lav. I knew I could. Here's how you can make it happen, too.

HOW TO GET STUCK IN A LAV: PART I

1. Sit facing the commode.
2. Let yourself slide down with your back to the door, legs up over the commode while aiming your feet at the back wall over the sink's counter. Got that?
3. Let your head come to a stop as close to the floor as possible in the corner between the lav door and the rear wall. This hurts, but it's as close to being prone as you'll ever get in such close quarters.

4. With your right hand the only appendage able to move at all, you can consider yourself safe when the realization that you're unable to move anything else becomes obvious, because you can knock on the door until a crew member unlocks it and helps you up!

Corinne heard my soft knocking, and, because she's fabulous in the cabin-awareness department, opened the door to hear, "I'm stuck!" I knew it must have been a very funny sight, what with my legs over the facilities and my head scrunched into a corner—not what you'd see every day on an A-320! But, seriously, I was too weak to extricate myself. Corinne hooked her arms around me and flipped me up. She was amazingly strong and so terrific about it all. She made me laugh, and that took a lot of talent, that's for sure! I asked to be left in the lav after being righted. Sweet Corinne closed the door and locked it for me. The floor beckoned yet again. This time I'd be smarter, or so I thought.

HOW TO GET STUCK IN A LAV: PART II

1. Sit facing the commode.
2. Rest on your left hip.
3. Put your head between the commode and the back wall.
4. Let your entire body collapse into a fetal position while resting on your left side.
5. Fall asleep.
6. Wake up and realize your hip is in terrible pain, your face is cold, and your feet are completely wedged and imprisoned between the base of the door and the floor! You cannot move!

7. You pray that your brother or sister in Sky will think of checking on you before you become permanently disabled.

Once again Corinne did three things: she checked on me, rescued me, and made me laugh.

There's a lot that can be said for being sick on an airplane. It's tough. It's limiting. It's scary. But at least we're closer to Heaven than we'd be in our own homes, I guess. What a way to go! Anyway, note to self: call out sick before you find yourself ill at ten thousand feet. My poor crew. They did my section, rescued me from compromising positions, and made me laugh. Even though there's a funny story to tell, everyone would have been better off if I'd just admitted at the get-go that I wasn't airworthy.

PART FOUR

A BIT OF TURBULENCE

DRUG-SEEKING BEHAVIOR

JFK to Rochester, July 2006

AFTER PUSHING BACK from the gate and becoming entrenched in a long line—wait estimated at a minimum of an hour and a quarter (seventy-five minutes on the taxiway) after an already multiple-hour delay in the terminal—my crew member, Holly, came up to the forward galley and told me I'd better get back to the aft galley because a woman was having some sort of tough time.

Back I went. The customer appeared to be a well-groomed, in-shape, contemporary woman approximately forty years of age. I asked her what was wrong, and she told me she didn't really know but described to me the symptoms of an anxiety attack (shallow breathing, rapid heart rate, shaking, and all-around nervousness). I stroked her forehead and hair and asked if she'd ever had this before, was there a usual fear of flying, or if some stress in her personal life might be causing this reaction. She consistently answered "No." to every question. I smelled alcohol on her breath, but she assured me she'd only had two glasses of wine that day (fib number one). There were no symptoms of intoxication, but it didn't smell like a wine aroma.

I asked if she had taken any medication that day.

"No."

I asked if there was ever a time when she employed a medication to counter these symptoms. "This has never happened to me before." (Fib number two.)

I asked if she'd like to go back to the gate and get off the plane, assuring her it would be alright and maybe a good thing given her condition. "No! I'll be fine. I'll be fine in a minute."

While I was calling the captain, she laid down in the back galley. We had an hour to wait in line, so the captain suggested we give her a chance to relax before pulling out of line and attempting to get another gate (not a likely possibility given the massive delays in play that night).

Holly paged for medical assistance and a registered nurse responded. After examination and mini-interview, the RN determined it was a mild anxiety attack, which appeared to be abating.

Her pulse was taken; it measured at ninety-five beats per minute. We administered oxygen, and she relaxed. "Do you have any sedatives you could give me?"

I said no, and I became suspicious. "Has this ever happened to you before?" I asked again.

"A few times." Fib, fib, fib.

Holly went for her stowed carry-on baggage because suddenly the patient "had medication in her bag." I took out the pill container, and the RN administered the pill chosen by the patient. Xanax. When asked what the other pills in the container were we were told, "multivitamins." (Fib number—ah, who's counting?)

I had been told that she was traveling with her daughter. However, when we went up to her seat, it was her next-door neighbor who was retrieved and brought into the galley to help. Immediately, the neighbor sat in front of the patient, pulled her into a sitting position and started breathing exercises that I liken to Lamaze techniques. It looked like these two had been the panic attack victim and the calm down coach team of the century. Hand in glove they were.

The neighbor asked, "Is there any way you could give her a shot of something?"

I said, "Absolutely not." I was becoming more suspicious.

The nurse and I spoke and thought it to be hysterical drug-seeking behavior in play. It was now twenty-five minutes before estimated takeoff, so I called the captain, and said, in a voice audible to the patient, "If we go back to the gate now, this customer will be deplaned. I'll give her ten minutes to pull herself together before making a decision."

He said, "The flight will probably be canceled because we'll be toast before we're able to get out of here." I said, again so she could hear me, "So if we go back to remove this customer, 149 others wouldn't be able to get to Buffalo tonight?"

The ploy worked. The customer immediately stood up and said, "I'll be okay. I'll be okay." She zoomed back to 13A and her neighbor took 13B. Just like that. All seemed great with the world.

We gave our volunteer nurse two Dewar's Scotches and had a lovely, incident-free flight. The neighbor talked to me privately saying she'd never, ever witnessed this behavior in the mother of her daughter's best friend and was shocked. When I asked about her instant response and co-breathing therapy, I was told, "That was Lamaze. I didn't know what else to do." I believed the neighbor, who has decided to reevaluate her friendship and trust level for our anxiety-ridden woman who listened to the worst-case scenario and miraculously returned to her seat symptom-free.

I'm not unsympathetic to those among us who are drug users. Yet an upper-middle-class woman who tries to hide her addiction by creating dramatic scenarios to play on society's desire to help is a sad commentary. Her poor family. Her disillusioned friends. Her uncertain future. It gives one pause to either count one's blessings or just know that, "There but for the grace of God, go I."

SECOND CHANCES

Orlando to JFK, May 2009

GIVEN TIME AND some profound listening application, most difficult people become compliant. If not putty in our hands, at least responsive to the subtle touch of compassion. If not understanding, at least accepting of our ways. At the end of the day, mustn't we all close our eyes, thereby bringing an end to the pains inflicted by those who've hurt us? Spontaneous healing isn't always acknowledged by our society, but ya' nevah know!

When I arrived at the departure gate I was informed of an explosive individual: "Don't look now, but that woman over there with the red suitcase is crazy! She came up to the podium when told of our half-hour delay, swearing her head off, saying how much she hated our company. I think she's been drinking."

She was a woman whose face was a roadmap of self-imposed aging. The skin, tanned to a crisp brown, eyes made up with black eyeliner and yesterday's smudges of mascara. No lipstick. No softening pastels to make the dark circles or fine lines less evident. Her hair was chemically ruined and would have benefited from a savage clipping with a hedge trimmer. Yet with all the harshness imposed by hard living and misunderstanding, lack of mind-broadening education or environmental stimulation, I thought her sparkle was still twinkling deep inside that armored exterior.

She first marched by me as I stood by the agents and our eyes met. She drew her eyelids to better aim her penetrating, contemptuous gaze at me. I just nodded and hoped I presented an "I hear ya" attitude. She threw her handful of trash into the can, and I cocked my head and gave another expression that I hoped would let her know that I wasn't the enemy but maybe a possible ally. It worked. She came to me and gave her uncomplimentary opinion of our airline. "I hate you guys!"

"Why are you in such a rush to get to LaGuardia?" I asked.

"LaGuardia? *LaGuardia*? I was supposed to fly into Westchestah. I live in Scawsdaelle. I don't even want to go to [big bad expletive] LaGuardia! You made me miss my flight and then charged me $220 moah fah this [nasty, nasty expletive] flight."

"God, I hate it when that happens, ma'am. Why were you in Orlando? Vacation?"

"My brothah and I had a huge fight. He tried to choke me. He tried to kill me! And now I'm out $220. Why do you guys kick us when we're down?"

"Ma'am, when the flights fill up, the prices go up too. I used to commute to my job in Manhattan before working for SkyNation. I used to buy my tickets months in advance and saved a bundle! It's a shame about your brother. Will you ever be able to patch up the relationship?"

"No. I hate the son-of-a-——. I'll nevah talk to that f'er again. So you used to work in the city, and the tickets were cheaper if you bought 'em ahead of time? I want to come back to Orlando in November, should I buy my tickets now?"

It was obvious the woman was scattered. I smelled no alcohol on her breath but didn't discount the possibility that there was some pathological condition at play. She was all over the emotional map. Not a bad person, just disturbed and volatile. Bringing up her brother caused instant flare-up. Money, instant resentment. Saving money, a cunning businesswoman. Typical American, eh?

We introduced ourselves, and I told her that I was about to set up a massage chair for the folks delayed and sitting around the gate. "Oh—I'll be first!" she screamed. Excellent, I thought, because I'd be able to assess her behavior and determine whether or not to let her board my flight , or just get to know about her life and outburst triggers.

"I was in a car accident a few years ago, and it messed me up. Surgery on my elbow, hurt my back, and I was in a coma for forty-five minutes!"

I asked if she was still on any medication for those physical insults.

"Not any more. None. My lawsuit's being settled next week, and I'm gonna get a lot of money."

I asked if that's what caused the fight between her and her brother.

"You got that right. He wanted half of it, the ——! Can you believe that?"

Of course I could. It saddens me to hear of family breakups because of money. What's really important in the final analysis? Material or blood? Some unlucky folks lose everything in the pursuit of the former. My own brother died over two decades ago, and I'd give anything to have him back. This woman's lost her sibling while he's still alive. Tragedy of tragedies.

Suddenly this manic person had a trusted ally. Would she behave properly on the flight northward? I was willing to bet she would, and I was right. She fell in love with the copilot on sight—but no future there. (She's married to a "businessman" in Scarsdale, and the pilot is young, gorgeous, and probably doesn't want a hit man to end his life really soon.) She developed a clinging chumminess with me. This was a small price to pay for seeing a woman who hurts on many levels come to the realization that delays can bring out our worst and still have a positive result.

Her final question of many? "How do I get to be a flight attendant? I could do this job. I love people! You can see I love people, can't you? You really do see that I love people. Tell me you do. You see, I don't work. My husband's in his own business. Do you think I'm too old? I know I could do this job!" Her tone was so desperate, like we might be the last lifeline she could grasp before falling forever into the empty-nest abyss in a possibly Gotti-style existence, and oh how she was reaching. Reaching to have some sort of uniform that would mark her as someone who's allowed to be good. Allowed to give. Given permission to be a part of something greater than oneself. SkyNation. My second family. Perhaps it would be her first. I hope she knows it's never too late. At forty-nine, with two sons already out of the house and a spouse who pays her little attention, she hasn't much—if anything—to rush home to see.

She'd hated us. She'd fallen for our copilot. She'd adopted me as a long lost sister. She'd developed a healthy admiration for the rest of the crew. She now wanted to join our family. Well, she's lost most of hers, hasn't she?

UNWELCOME ADVANCES

Fort Lauderdale to White Plains

AS THESE MEN boarded, I hailed them because they came in as one. A huge threesome of large, loud men that begged attention. "Oh, you'll be my trouble row, I can tell," I laughingly said. The response was more laughter, and I felt enveloped in whatever they may have been celebrating.

"What do you do that makes you so happy?" I asked them.

"He's a fighter!" one said, pointing at the last of these behemoths to board.

"Oh! We'll have to talk about that!" I promised as they disappeared down the aisle. . . Little did I know that two of these men could cause the atmosphere of jubilation to descend to belligerence and filth when a young woman was at their mercy.

Before takeoff, my number two, Ned, told me, "Those three guys in the back were on my flight recently. During final, I noticed that the seat back was down so I had to wake one of them up and ask him to put it up for landing. The guy told me, 'Your disturbing my f——g sleep!' I couldn't believe the attitude!" I made a mental note of this story, but didn't think it would be a factor on this particular flight. Oh, how naive am I?

Three-quarters of the way through the flight, Ned (in the number two position), Diane (our number three), and I were in the aft galley. A young lady, perfectly groomed and dressed in a tweed skirt and matching blazer with a modestly buttoned blouse, stood among us. "You look so professional, young lady!" I told her. She looked at me, eyes behind conservative glasses suddenly showing white fear.

"What's wrong?" I asked.

"Oh, I can't tell you. It's nothing." Yet she looked imploringly at Diane, a young lady of her own ilk and age. Ned, too, moved forward in an attempt to support the woman.

"Really, if there's anything we can do, please let us know." I think we all said this together with variations on the theme.

"I don't know what to say. I don't know what to tell you. I just can't go back there. Those men beside me started in at the beginning of the flight. I'm on the aisle and they said, 'Why don't you jes' sit between us. We like a little cream between us.' They're asleep now, so I came back."

Ned asked, "Did this happen after we closed the doors?"

"Yes." At this point, the tears began their downward tumble. She'd said it. She'd allied herself to us. "I don't want any trouble."

"No trouble! We'll fix it, don't you worry."

At this juncture, I knelt down beside the gentleman in 25D. "Sir, are you traveling alone?"

"Yes."

"Sir, we have a bit of an issue concerning a young lady. There have been rude overtures made, and we would very much appreciate a man sitting beside her tormentors so we could place her close to us and further from them. The flight's completely full, so there aren't any empty seats to offer her."

In a heartbeat, the man in 25D proved that, although there are scumbags in the world, there are also perfect gentlemen, because his seatbelt was unbuckled and he was halfway out of his comfy leather chair before he'd finished saying, "No problem!"

Ned wasn't surprised. "I knew those guys were scum by their animal behavior and lack of manners last week."

The young woman thought they were drunk from the onset of her SkyNation experience. I didn't have that impression as they boarded; I had smelled nothing, nor did they act out of order. I love boisterous friends who seem proud to be together and happy to be going somewhere, even if it is to LaGuardia! Being up close and personal, our little lady was insulted, harassed, embarrassed, humiliated, frightened, and totally hurt by two of the three men.

I told her, "Never *ever* believe that you deserve or must tolerate such disrespect for even one second. We wish you'd come to us right away with this. It's not for you to be embarrassed by this!"

Poor girl. Made to cry as she admitted what had been going on during the flight because of her naive belief that flight attendants weren't allies. Oh, we are. We're also advocates for women's rights, civil rights, human rights—the right of all people to be shown respect on our flights and beyond.

A report was filed and the rude men now have a permanent record of their behavior attached to their stored names in our system. They will be educated and warned before ever boarding another one of our flights.

"APPEARING INTOXICATED": CONUNDRUMS AND CONSEQUENCES

JFK, February 2010

IT'S ALWAYS RATHER tragic when a customer appears to be intoxicated, because, thanks to the Federal Aviation Administration (FAA), we are obligated to remove such malcontents before leaving the gate, that is, if these individuals have passed inspection from the ticket counter to security to gate agent. These bastions of protection can be fooled, bamboozled, or misled, resulting in the easy passage of an inebriated customer from point to point without apprehension. In fact, I'd wager that some under the influence are more wily than the sober among us! Either by design or guile, these folks often slide unnoticed with the chameleon ease of Darwin's nominated genetic wonders. So slipping through our firewalls could actually be attributed to survival of the fittest, adaptation expertise, and conscious or unconscious camouflaging techniques. Brilliant.

The fellow on Flight 112 passed me without exposing symptoms for several reasons. My olfactory system was inop, and my entire respiratory system was operating in name only. You guessed it—I had a cold that manifested itself nasally. Not at all attractive, I might add. So, when said individual was greeted at the door, I did not notice his presenting symptom—an extremely strong smell of alcohol. Now I don't just stand there in the front galley nodding to folks as they file onboard. I touch, hug, ask questions, and get to know each of them. On this flight, I was putting smiley faces on a high percentage of those who marched blindly into my web. A girl's got to make her own fun, right?

When everyone was seated, my wonderful number two, Fred, took over the forward galley so I could walk the aisle and ensure all were comfy. As I reached the center of the cabin, a man stood up and said, "I won't sit by this guy. He's so drunk! Can you move him away from us?"

I leaned over to the accused and he admitted, "I'm drunk."

I asked if he had any baggage in the overhead bin or below decks and was told only carry-on existed. I retrieved same and asked him to come with me to the front of the plane. I took his hand and led him forward without any problem at all. Once in front, I whispered that altitude has a strange reaction with those who appear to be intoxicated. I broke the news that he couldn't fly on this flight and apologized sincerely.

"You mean I'm being kicked off this flight, right?"

"Yes, sir. I'm so sorry, but thank you so much for being so gentlemanly about all this. Will you be okay here at JFK?"

"You mean I'm being kicked off this flight?"

Point made. He was removed by the gate agent and was quite nice throughout this interaction.

The Corporate Security fellow arrived, and, owing to his line of questioning, I felt as though he thought I was removing a customer for my own satisfaction. He was forceful and accusatory in his questioning of my observations and said it was up to him to evaluate the condition of the removed customer; that's doo-doo, my friends. It was topped off with the comment that our visionary founder says too many customers are being removed from flights!"

Well, maybe too many customers drink!

If our founder did indeed utter these words before leaving, I'd wager it wasn't to plant the seed of mistrust in the judgment of flight attendants.

The FAA has laws: and one of them is those appearing to be intoxicated can't board a flight!

Once removed from a SkyNation flight, no customer is to be allowed to board for the second time on that particular flight.

I have no ego-attachment to my own authority, nor do I need to take on any sort of altercation for the sake of self-aggrandizement. Corporate Security and other crew members are supposed to be on the same team and display mutual respect for each other. I understand the bottom line, but here's the kicker that, perhaps, isn't understood by both sides: the

SkyNation experience is for the well-behaved majority and not for those who are breaking the law.

The customers who remained on the flight—no fewer than ten within the original seating area of the rejected man—thanked me for removing him in such a professional manner. I was thanked by his traveling buddy, who said, "Yes, he really drank a lot," for my consideration and concern for his friend.

The customer who appears to be intoxicated doesn't have rights that override those of other paying customers, who are in the majority, on any flight. And, there's not a flight attendant who passes through training who doesn't understand this rule. The cross-examination imposed by Corporate Security left me feeling undermined.

Just before closing the door, the Corporate Security representative smiled at me and said, "He's going on another flight!"

"When?"

"Tomorrow!" he beamed. That's when I felt like we were of like mind. I extended my hand, we shook, and a mutual respect was there in spades, finally. You see, he was doing his job, to be sure, but there must be another way to communicate that from square one. We're on the same team after all.

In the Buffalo arrival area, I stopped to speak with the travel companion of the man who was removed at JFK. "We were scammed. Eight hundred people bought tickets and transport to the Pro Bowl, and when we were in Vegas we realized that there was nobody to get us to the game! We were all scammed, lost our money. We left yesterday and came back today—no game, no money. Yeah, he was drinking alright. I could have sat beside him on the plane and taken care of him though."

I responded that it wasn't possible to take off with such individuals on board, and he said, "Yeah. I know. Thanks for your consideration though."

It was so sad that these fellows lost their money and the Pro Bowl fun. It's always too bad when someone misses a flight home because of poor behavior or chemical impairment.

Please let your airport personnel know that we're all in the same game when it comes to customer care and respectful interactions, and that we all understand business and bottom lines, litigation potential, and FAA law. Most of all, we are all crew members and shouldn't appear to be at cross-purposes ever.

HOODWINKING US

San Juan to Orlando, December 2010

UPON BOARDING, THE gate agent at San Juan presented me with three youngsters; I asked for the paperwork, whereupon I was told that none was needed. The eldest child was thirteen, and the dismissing San Juan adults had insisted that the trio would be met by an employee upon arrival at Orlando.

As the children passed me, I noticed that the young boy was being led by the forearm by his older sibling and was unresponsive to my attentions. I sent for the agent and said that I wasn't sure these customers were capable of flying without the supervision of an adult, so she went back to them and chatted. The agent ascertained that this was a common practice and that the eldest would be able to relate well to the socially challenged child in all circumstances. Once again, I was told that thirteen was a respected age of majority in such circumstances and that the adults who'd passed the three children into our care at the departure gate were totally comfortable with this arrangement. It was arranged that the children would be met and assisted upon arrival at our destination. I was led to believe, or assumed, that the MCO adult was a SkyNation crew member, but I admit that this might never have been said to me literally.

I watched the children before closing the doors and during the flight, and all was well. I did note that the boy who had been unresponsive upon boarding was fed the store-bought chips throughout the flight. He ate continuously. The group was quiet, and their affect was unemotional and flat no matter how I tried to initiate interaction.

The trouble began when we were at the MCO gate and had opened the main forward exit door.

The wailing and crying sounds generated from row six were loud, so I asked my brother-in-Sky, Alan, to take over the farewells and worked my way back to the noise. Taking the boy gently by the hand, I led him forward because he was kicking out into the aisle. I thought by getting him erect and moving he would feel less imprisoned.

Once in the galley, I asked the eldest where her relatives who worked for us were; Alan translated, but we received zero answers. I had expected the relatives to meet them at the door, so when there was nobody, I sent the MCO agent to look for anyone who might be meeting the children. The boy had quieted to normalcy at first introduction to the galley, but within moments of the agent's departure, he began yelling, wailing, and using physical force to push me as I tried to be the wall between him and the deplaning masses. Alan stepped in and became the protective shield between the child and me, but the boy collapsed in a heap and began kicking out with his feet! Alan raised him to the standing position and tried to assuage this sudden onset of hysterical behavior. The boy walked into the lav, and when he came out, he faced the departing customers, stuck his fingers down his throat, and induced vomiting. The pilots became involved at this time and were made aware that this unfortunate was socially challenged. My layman's diagnosis: direct appositional disorder combined with an explosive, combative reaction to stress or denial of will.

The MCO adults were found, and the children delivered thereafter.

Upon request, an MCO gate agent retrieved and printed the children's names and information from the manifest for me. I called reservations and spoke with the supervisor, and was given a bit of history on this family.

They traveled in 2005, and a note was placed on their file that stated "uncomfortable with allowing them to travel without adult." Somehow, the trio had slipped through the cracks. A different credit card had been used. When such circumstances present themselves, flight attendants make a report and submit it to Corporate Security.

Corporate Security did a great follow-up, and the children in this story will not be welcome on board without an accompanying adult again. As a team, we get it done.

PART FIVE

INITIAL DESCENT

CANAL STREET ENCOUNTER

My first post-Katrina run in New Orleans

THE NEW ORLEANS persona is transparent when it wants to be, veiled if need be. The facade of this steamy place has chameleon ability. With all the outrageous behaviors, high pulse rates, and slow speech, the range of permeability is controlled perfectly by any man on the streets of this Louisiana mecca for the socially inspired. What you see is just what you're meant to see. No more. No less.

And there's the person behind the behavior. The one who's been to hell and still lives there.

If the joyous feel like sharing, any passing stranger can catch the mood through some osmotic process. The humid air is the perfect medium for transfer of all energies. It's a dangerous place to be if you have an impure intent. If you think just because some person is gutter bound and decaying that he is therefore unworthy of your respect, think again. He can cast a spell with one sharp look. One that might turn your life from self-satisfied superiority to a moment of such darkness that you won't know what hit you. So you'd better not pass anybody on those cobblestone sidewalks with the false impression that you're the better person just because you have teeth or finery, obvious money or a job that gives you a certain status. You're a fool if you do.

Sitting in a bar entryway is the musician in a witch's hat who sent a lightning flash of humor my way as I jogged by on the other side of the road early that morning.

"Yaw runnin' away with mah haht!" he cackled.

"You've got mine, too!" I responded and we smiled across that little side street because we both knew that it was just in fun to do the counter-banter jig. The few passing on Bourbon Street were just as mellow as any who knew more, and let on that they knew naught. I said something to everyone who came down the streets toward me and was blessed with the normal responses.

"Mawnin', dahlin."

"Mawnin, now."

"Mawnin', girl."

Softness and warmness was in every elongated syllable, and these tones enfolded me like a grandmother's quilt but didn't really leave an opening for intimacy between the native and myself. Just niceties from genuine folk. The acknowledgments were necessary here because the early risers in this place slowly unfold as the day ages, and vocalizing is part of their blooming cycle: comfortable, natural with a bit of compulsion involved, a formidable genetic memory that makes token verbal greeting a core requirement from one race to another. There are innumerable secrets untold behind every offered *petit mot*. God knows, I don't deserve their respect or love. They have definitely earned mine, however.

It was my first time running in the French Quarter since Katrina's attack. I don't know what I expected, really. Boarded-up, tumbled-down buildings, malodorous air, unclaimed bodies of the long dead? Did I expect the ghosts or shadows of former inhabitants to be hovering in bewildered groups, or the disenfranchised survivors to be standing around with vacant eyes in postures of hopelessness? The descriptions from friends who've spent time in the Big Easy since the storm are rife with the negatives. Most of these stories have a similar climax that directs a pipeline of disgust at the fund-sucking politicians who, for some strange reason, won reelection despite track records of gross malfeasance.

I admit to few talents, but I do have one gift. If I want to, I can get answers to unspoken questions from just about anyone, anywhere. My desire was to glean some information on how the inhabitants of post-Katrina New Orleans really felt. When I stepped out of the hotel to run for an hour or so, I wanted an answer and knew, given the predefined time allotment and my chosen route, that there was a good chance I'd bump into someone who'd give me the truth. Verbally? In a song? In a look? In a touch? That's how it works for me. As a sensitive person, I have to protect myself from being overwhelmed by the tides of emotions, feelings, and physical pains from people. Putting on an armor that still allows for good reception but bars entrance of the negative is second nature for the intuitive. So after donning this invisible shield, I put forth my questions and started to run. The back streets, the river front, over to the bleak side of town on the far edges of any tourist's stomping grounds and then onto Canal. I like this street because, even so early on a rainy morning, the air-conditioning from the open store fronts cools me off as I pass.

I'd seen all manner of people already. A thin woman sitting by the river drinking something encased in a brown bag was having a really good conversation with a groundskeeper as he sat in his little maintenance vehicle. Men in small groups, just waiting to begin some street job, planned their day's strategy amid shoving and good humor. The people walking to their jobs had purpose in their step and universally responded kindly to my "Good mornings" and "How are you todays." I love these people. Besides me, the only non-African-American I encountered was a tourist from Asia taking pictures of those wonderful upper balconies on Bourbon Street. I passed him coming and going, and he never once acknowledged me or any other individual in his path. Architecture is nice, but it's not the meat and potatoes of a town like New Orleans. He missed that. He walked right by the people and just kept looking up and snapping this or that flower- and light-adorned edifice. I don't mean to judge, but he was passing flesh and blood and spirit and history with every step and never once looked one of those working people, down-and-out men, or working girls in the eye!

Mind you, for all those who made eye contact with me, I was still aware that they were not revealing their innermost feelings. I felt no malevolence, bitterness, anger, resentment, or curiosity about my presence in their midst. I did feel kindness and a kinship but no intimacy. The strength of a Louisiana soul is that it feels no need to turn itself inside out to satisfy anyone's desire to know what it's feeling. But they all knew what I wanted, although I'd never be gauche enough to ask out loud. They knew that, too. New Orleans is a spirit world full of omniscient ancients embodied in every size, shape, and demeanor.

As I said, I finally started running up Canal, a broad thoroughfare with cable cars following tracks and announcing their presence with the clanging of bells. Tourists know this street. The rich shop on it. The population I wanted to feel uses it, too, but I didn't expect to be noticed on this route.

Yet there they were. Two wiry black men. And when they came into view, standing on the edge of the sidewalk, every other person or thing within a city block ceased to exist for me. The wraithlike arm of one man extended to me, and I turned toward it. They were in faded everything. Shirts, jeans—even their skin was powdered and misty. All the surrounding cacophony ceased. I had no peripheral vision. There were only two lanky streetwise jesters. And as we all know, the truest words are said in jest. Sometimes no words are spoken for truth's revelation.

"You stop runnin'!" commanded the man whose arm ended in a very long index finger aiming at me. He had the posture of one who was joking, but his voice was from ages past, and although it was diluted by a good nature, it was an order nonetheless.

I smiled and jogged across the last fifteen feet. I couldn't have turned away even if I'd wanted to. And I didn't want to because I was running into his eyes. Those eyes contained an eternity of knowing, with folds of skin hanging over the top half of each orb. He was smiling a completely toothless smile, and as I closed the gap, my hand rose to take his. It was a ballroom dance as he swept the hand holding a cigarette behind me, our other hands, still entwined, fell to my right side. Our eyes didn't quite meet but there was a flash from his to mine in passing as he swept his face to my throat. Then, he kissed the lower left side of my neck, and I answered with a solid hug and hold. But it was so fast. Thank God for that, or his energy, the complete body-to-body embrace, which was meant for only one purpose, would have electrocuted me. The purpose of his overwhelming wraparound grasp was to answer my question.

His whiskers left a feeling on my neck that has remained since the kiss. Those bristles, sharp and coarse, have caused absolutely unrelenting discomfort on my skin. It's throbbing as I write this.

You see, I'd been watched as I paid the dues of running through the parts of town that only the real New Orleans black man inhabits in the early mornings as hot days come to life. I'd shared my trust, an immeasurable respect and humor that, although employed as yet another filter for a native's true thoughts in this city, is something I totally enjoy. For all the bawdiness within a proffered comment, I know it's meant to be a bridge to the common denominator that could save the world: a smile or a good chuckle. The ghosts I thought I'd see in this still-hurting city were there guiding me to the answer to one simple question.

"Are the people in pain, angry, unforgiving, irreparably damaged?"

The answer is the burning skin on my neck. The porcupine quills were embedded with that kiss. Each one is still plunged deeply in close proximity to a jugular vein. A humble writer's artery has been charged to bleed their meaning as words.

The kiss was one from a proud being to an inquisitive one. Somehow that man knew I'd be along one day and gave me the answer. No, not in words. In a pain that isn't dissipating with the passage of time, my friends. We might never truly be able to extricate in words the emotional, physical, and spiritual pain being felt by the disenfranchised of New Orleans. But who needs words?

The minuscule daggers in my neck were my answers. Too many to count and too quickly injected to resist the full force of what that man was sharing with me. I asked for it. That 100 percent unfolding of a complete truth. It's almost too much to live with, and I flew out of that town two hours after the embrace. He's still there, and most folks are still going to the French Quarter to take pictures of pretty verandas or to party hardy.

The pain. I was just given an abbreviated infusion of what is a massive hurt. A taste of what I asked to know. Had that old man given me the collective dose he could have, I'd probably have died in his arms. He knew that so he held back and let me feel only a tiny percentage of the total.

As I finish this story, I've had thirty-six hours away from he who was placed in my path to share something with me. I swear that the part of my neck he touched is still alive with intense discomfort. Will this tiny patch of pain stay with me until New Orleans is given its due? If it does, I deserve it. It will serve to remind me of my luck. It will serve to remind me that I'm not worthy to ask questions if I can't help when the answers are given.

THE ABSENCE OF COMPASSION

Troy, New York, on a visit to my son at Rensselaer Polytechnic Institute

---

AFTER CHECKING OUT of the Best Western hotel, I drove the couple of miles to my son's apartment. Troy, New York, offers very little in the way of scenic lookouts. One must be willing to notice the population if a cultural experience is to be had. Only one vignette caught my eye during that brief ride. My old Toyota was thinking about going into overdrive as it pressed up a steep hill. Coming toward me, a cluster of youngsters surrounded a motorized wheelchair on the descent. The entourage eschewed the sidewalk and whizzed past parked cars without apology. I remember thinking, "Wow! They're going to get hit! But look at all those little kids helping out." I didn't take a mental picture of the wheelchair's occupant;

rather I was left with an impression of an elderly woman and the multitude of young 'uns. Knowing I'd never again lay eyes on the group, I filed the snapshot away in the back of my mind under a "that was different" heading.

There was no answer to my knock, so I went around the house and climbed through the kitchen window. There was a toddler banging on a second-floor window across from my son's place. Curly blond hair, whiter-than-white skin, cute. Both little palms struck the pane with pretty good force; I immediately flashed on Eric Clapton's lost son. Remember? The one that fell out of an upper-level window to his death? I waved but the child only responded by continuing his attack on the glass. "Where's his mother?" I wondered.

The door hook was in its eye protecting the occupants of my son's room from intrusion. Well, he'd celebrated his twenty-first birthday the night before with his sister and frat brothers, so I thought it merciful to respect the need for sleeping past midmorning. Plus, the *New York Times* was sitting there ready to be read in the living room. The living room was almost inviting. Presents opened the night before, wrapping paper, a stray jelly bean, shoes, a knapsack, cast-off clothing, a terribly comfortable couch, and a fairly good breeze coming from one of the oversized open windows made for a good reading atmosphere.

The open window had no screen. None of the windows in that apartment did as far as I could tell. A ground-floor residence in Troy, New York, where crime and drug use are predominant realities, struck me as an incongruous combination. Oh well, fraternity brothers know best, and my son and his four roommates, students at Rensselaer Polytechnic Institute, are surrounded by an almost tangible invincibility (touch wood). I settled on the couch and read the *Times*.

Hearing conversation, I got up and looked toward the source. A woman, blue polyester from neck to slippers, was talking to a muscular black man in tightish charcoal sweatpants and a sleeveless gray singlet. The woman, legs akimbo, stringy hair uncombed, any exposed flesh pale and flaccid, occupied a kitchen chair on the sidewalk. The man, sitting in another chair, reacted to her every complaint physically. He leaned forward, shook his head, became incredulous. She just moved her mouth. She struck me as an Eeyore, a real "woe-is-me" character, replete with every excuse for not being able to go anywhere, get anything, feel any good, or have any fun. Her major worry was child support. I was rudely watching and listening. They weren't unaware of my presence, and I had the distinct impression that they wanted a captive audience. I think they were really getting off on performing for me. They live in a culture of inclusion, a dramatic netherworld of frustrated attempts to thrive.

Children began returning to the nest. Beautiful black children, sparkling clean in clothes that not only fit but were contemporary. It was obvious that they were excited and worried as they competed to get their apologies and explanations, excuses and cries of "it's not my fault" out the fastest. The black man yelled, "Where's Grandma? Where's she at? F—k!"

"We couldn't keep up to her!"

"She took off!"

"Her chair was movin' too quick!"

"We lost her!"

Panic. Frenzy. Swearing. Blaming.

The muscles in his arms showed their power as he swung them around. He spun and left at a fast pace down toward that hill that my car barely climbed without quitting. The children trailing behind all yelled that it "wasn't my fault! She just was going too fast!"

The polyester woman, her manner punctuated by pathos and lethargy, the excitement forgotten as soon as the horde of worried grandchildren disappeared with their father, uncle, or whatever relation they followed into the hunt, turned her attention now to an equally mundane woman who came out carrying that child I'd worried about as he pounded on the windowpane earlier. I returned to the couch and the paper.

A car pulled up directly in front of the living room. I returned to the window to see a late-model luxury vehicle deploy its front-seat passenger, a man who looked to be on his way to play nine holes at an exclusive golf club. Five grandchildren stood in the middle of the road speaking in unison to someone in the back seat. The preppy man went to the back of the car and started to wrestle with its contents to no avail. The polyester woman dragged herself over with her dim attitude and lack of spunk, offering a limp and useless hand in the struggle to extricate the wheelchair. At this point, I thought that everyone present was related, right? Well, think again.

It turned out that the folks who were returning Grandma did so because they'd recognized her dilemma; they were as foreign to this clan as I was. I hung out of the window, feeling as rude as can be but quite uninterested in being anything else in this place where no one knows me. The chair was on the pavement now, and the hunting party in full had returned from their foray. All of them were at the backseat of the car now, milling around, clucking, and pecking, but extending no helpful arms to the passenger. All words, accusations, and remorse. Escalating chaos it was. The preppy golfer stood at the passenger-side door not six feet from my window. I saw that no one was helping the elderly passenger out of her taxi in any way.

"May I help you move your Grandma?" I asked the preppy.

He just gave me a close-lipped smile, but I could tell he didn't want me or any other resident of the street to approach him physically. He had no intention of further imposing himself on the woman in his backseat or interfering with her removal. The wheelchair was being dragged across the street. It was an electric one with small wheels that didn't turn at all. It bounced as it was dragged to the opposite curb followed by everyone else. Grandma remained in that car. The large man who had returned and once again assumed the alpha male role yelled out, "Get ha walkah! Get ha walkah!" Five children at once tried to enter their front door. It was like a cartoon. Out they came with a walker. Over to Grandma with it they scrambled. Then something strange happened. Everyone just ran back into the house. The walker was left beside the car, traffic coming and going, and not one person stayed to help Grandma out of the car. The preppy golfer and driver didn't help either. Grandma just struggled by herself across the backseat to the walker at her door and somehow hefted her bulk to an erect posture on her own. There she stood, a death grip on the walker, catching her breath until she could shuffle across the street to the sidewalk.

Meanwhile, an extension cord had been thrown out of a window to recharge the dead wheelchair battery. Incredible. All attention was being focused on the wheelchair. All bustling activity was about fixing that damn chair! Grandma was completely on her own now. She stopped at the curb not able to get over it immediately. No one noticed. She stood there, thinking her next move out. I observed that her right arm was showing through a hole in her gray sweater. Not the normal heavy arm was exposed. No, it was a huge growth. Grotesque and round and bulging. Her dress was uneven and her stockings loose, her slippers floppy, her torso huge and pained. No one helped her, but she got onto that sidewalk anyway. I think this defined what her life must have been since day one. Impossible, but she could do the impossible. Slow, but she probably always got to her destination. Alone, but she was surrounded by a flock.

She plunked herself down on that old kitchen chair, and everyone gathered for a verbal flailing.

"Whatchoo leave me fo', boy? My chair stopped in tha middle of Congress Street! I screamed and screamed, ain't nobody stopped. Fifteen cars went by me! Then that car stopped. Ain't nobody was there to hep me. Why yo' run off and leave me? Where'd yo' go to, anaways? Ain't nobody. I screamed and screamed. Only but one anybody stopped to hep me! What yo' said? You ain't able to keep up witch me? What? Yo' sassin' me back? Yo' sassin' me?"

One of the flock stepped off the curb. "Getch off that road, child! You be careful now!"

Excuses from everybody. Excuses. Reasons. Why do those under twelve years of age leave a grandmother in a wheelchair?

They'll all regret this someday. Someday when she never comes back. She loves those children.

The man, his sweatpants rolled up to just below his knees as the day grew humid and the sun's rays intensified, stood in front of the matriarch and downed a soft drink. Everyone suddenly disappeared into the house leaving the Grandma alone with her shortness of breath and her thoughts.

"Would you like a glass of orange juice?" I asked.

"I would."

I found a clean glass and filled it from the gallon jug of juice I'd brought as a hospitality gift for my son and his roomies. They'd have preferred beer. I clambered out of the kitchen window, spilling juice on my arm. Crossing the street I had my first chance to see this woman's face. Ancient eyes. Not dull, but sharp and hardened by years of being at the helm of a sinking ship. Her face was unshaven. Perhaps for a week she'd not taken a razor to her mustache or beard. The hair on her head was thinning and spiked. Colorless really. Not gray, white, or black. Just a covering of ignored fuzz. I had stroked her arm as I passed it to her because she's someone's granny, and that counts big time for me. She took the glass and drank half right off.

"My chair died in the middle of Congress Street."

"I heard."

"I had to send a money order to my daughter. It cost me a lot. It was for $110."

Some kids emerged from the house and took up playing with each other. None of them gave me a second look, which I thought weird, seeing as I was a complete stranger giving their grandmother a drink of orange juice. I mean, that couldn't be a regular occurrence in their neighborhood. I asked her if she'd like a hat.

"Yes. One on the table inside."

I directed one of the children to get it.

Before she'd finished the juice, my daughter showed herself at the window that had been my vantage point all morning. Then my son joined her. I wished the woman would finish the juice so I could return the glass and get back to my offspring. You see, the night before, my son, Dave, had told me about the useless people who just sat all day in front of their house, drinking a forty-ouncer. I knew he detested these folk and all they represented. Welfare. Uneducated. Lazy. Pathetic. The basest of morals. Abusers of chemicals. Had he ever seen the youngest? Had he ever seen the eldest? The former with happy gurgling smiles and dirty diapers. The grandmother who'd sent all she could to a daughter but was deserted by her grandchildren in the middle of a busy downtown street to "scream and scream." Somewhere between the newborn and the tumor-ridden, nearly immobile elder there's a lost demographic of apathy and hopelessness. I agree.

But for a moment in time, I had a grandmother to love again. One who by her generosity enables generations to use. Use a system. She sent her Social Security money to her daughter somewhere. She got less attention than a wheelchair from those who live in her old house. She didn't get either libation or protection from an unrelenting sun upon her return. Raised in a time before integration, this woman has come as far as she was allowed during her prime. Now an octogenarian, with nothing but a parasitic, disorganized, dissatisfied population in her home, still she provides, enables, forgives, loves, and shouts out protective commands.

I retrieved the glass, wishing I could have just left it in her keeping, but it wasn't mine to give. Perhaps it might have been something to have as a reminder of a cool drink on a hot day? Of a kinder world? Of me? She said, "Thank you." I stepped onto the street and heard a strict, "Yo' be careful crossing now! Watch for cars!"

Through it all a grandmother shone forth. And tomorrow will be like today for her. The only one in that house who hadn't sunk to narcissism and the bitterness bred of an unfair society, genetic memory, or addiction. She's the glue at ground zero for bedlam.

To look out a window and witness the chaotic, disjointed trials of one's neighbors isn't polite. Even in a society with no expectations of etiquette there's a certain level of grace, if you're patient enough to watch for it. This grandmother. This woman who'd been to hell and back in one lifetime is capable of eliciting a group panic at her disappearance but remains unable to extrude compassion enough for a drink. Her only concern is to keep the kids from being hit on the road. Perhaps that's the only danger she can admit and keep her sanity.

When I drove off she was still sitting in a kitchen chair in the full sun. Without a hat.

WHAT HANDS ARE, WHAT LOVE IS

Newark to West Palm Beach, May 2010

THEY WERE BOARDED together but apart. He, delivered in a wheelchair pushed by a face I don't recall. She, behind him as a candle is, softly giving a bright but tiny flame hovering over a thick trunk of wax.

I reached out two hands and braced myself against the pull of his weight as he rocked himself out of the chair. He was laughing at himself, and she joined in.

"Oh, he can do it, just fine!" she chuckled.

"I think she's right. She always is, and she'd be the first one to tell you so!" He twinkled as he strained upward and steadied himself atop his slippers. His concentration, deep as it had to be as he tried to convince first his right and then his left foot into a shuffle, was broken by his constant banter to me. "She's a wonder. She's a wonder. She's my girl. Guess how long we've been together?"

"Oh sir, I'd say you were newlyweds."

"Ha, ha, ha. You hear that?" he said to her, never stopping that tiny foot movement or looking back at her. She laughed out loud, but not in an unladylike way. Hers was a genuine, guttural sound that was as rich as an AM radio morning man's after his first cup of tea. Rich and human and true, and it invited more bragging from her husband.

"We've been together sixty-three years." They both laughed.

Into the first aisle seat he sank with as little of a crash landing as I could make possible. "Okay, woman, come and sit beside your boyfriend."

"Anything you say," she said with a wink to me. "You have to make 'em believe they're in charge, you know."

I joined in the fun and loved their interplay. Before takeoff I'd hugged them both and told them how much it meant to me to see happy couples, in love and enjoying life together.

"Sixty-three years. Went by like that," he said, but he wasn't laughing when he said it. His clear eyes looked deeply into mine, and in that look I saw that he wouldn't know what to do without her. He was worried that something might happen to the love of his life, and he'd have to let her go.

Right after takeoff, I noticed they'd fallen asleep. Hand in hand, her head on his shoulder, his head resting on the top of hers. I wanted to take a picture but decided that I'd just never forget them. Ever. Holding hands tightly, they were.

Few mental photos are more vivid in my memory than those of the hands that I've seen. And held. As a child, the hands of my mother were as big a part of my nurturing as were her roast beef dinners or her gentle ways.

They were the delicate hands of an invalid, yet their strength was in their ability to create a beautiful knitted baby layette or any other knitted article. They were so very white. The skin was almost transparent, and all of the veins were visible, but not in an unattractive way; they were just part of the delicacy that was my mother.

Whenever I was sick, cool hands rested on my forehead. The alabaster hands, so unadorned by the usual rings or other vain ornamentation, stayed until all the fever was dissipated.

When, toward the end of her short life, Mom needed my care, I would often take her tiny hands into my own. I would try to ease her pain by emulating some of her own patterns of soothing speech and tender hand holding. When so doing, I studied her fingers, thin skin and the violet mole that was what always considered more a symbol of royalty than one of devaluation. (Mom had tried to remove it when taunted by other girls in convent school.)

Such beauty, such love. Only a mother's hand could be so. I was so lucky to have held hers, if only for a short span as lifetimes are measured.

Quite the opposite of my mother's hands were those of her father. Born a farmer. Worked for his family. Worked outdoors when mittens would have hindered his progress and were therefore put aside while skin thickened and cracked. Frigid weather conditions prevailed, comfort be damned.

Scarred hands. Some fingertips had been lost when the farming was put behind and the pulp and paper mills filled his life. Those were the days of fifty-six-hour shifts. When only injury was reason to lay one's work aside and recuperation made compulsory. Even then, those old hands (I only remember them as being old) always had something to keep them busy.

The wrist bone on his left side jutted far out at some grotesque angle because this man returned to work far before he should have after one terrible accident. There was no time allotted for proper healing or unproductive therapy in the early days of the twentieth century. A scar was part of one's education. A misplaced bone or joint that didn't bend properly were the diplomas that labeled such men either successes because of survival, or failures because of total disability.

Grandpa Bilton survived. But his deformed hands with the odd, misshapen joints and missing digits, rough skin and wounded ways were testaments to an era when hard work was expected and the accepted results were often painful, arthritic hands.

A grandchild doesn't realize why something is different. I always studied Grandpa's hands, though. There was something about them that was different than any others I'd encountered. So rough, so rugged, so crooked. The best back rubs in my life came from these hands. Once, at the age of nine, when I had a wart on my foot, these same hands rubbed it away. When I ever had a cut, the bleeding was soon stopped by these Neanderthal hands. These hands hung by Grandpa's sides as he heard about the passing of his own daughter. These hands wiped away his own tears and mine.

So when my children look at my hands—half soft (on top) like my mother's and half ruined (on the palms) like Grandpa's—I hold them up with pride. Oh, I'll never be the delicate flower that was my mother, nor will I be the working machine that was my grandfather. Yet, somewhere in my own hands lies a part of both. And my children, who will never know either person, might someday remember my hands and know that they can choose either side of these coins and know love.

This couple, dreaming their dreams, head to head and old rugged hand in old rugged hand, demanded that I look at them closely and press every image deeply into my memory bank. Why? Had my parental units lived a long and healthy life together, had they shared love instead of what they had, would they be before some other flight attendant on a flight back home and to me? Candlelight only lasts for as long as the fuel is available and the wick holds a flame.

Wax. Easily melted but giving off the fuel to keep the flame alight even as it allows its form to morph, melt, and vanish as vapor. Is this what love is? Yes, the warmth of a love light and two hands entwined now and forever. Blessed be.

BREAKING PATTERNS

September 2010

THE FLIGHT WAS to be only an hour, and there were less than 90 seats of the 150 in use. An easy flight with three of us working, I thought. The importance of having a great crew isn't always obvious. We'd get through service with no rushing. We'd have time to kibitz with customers. We'd have time to do a lot of trips up and down the aisle to pick up "unwanted service items." We were a team of three and loved our job. However, we sure were delighted that this flight was light because it was the third day of a four-day trip, and we were feeling it. East Coast to West Coast, up and down, in and out. The night before, as I stood in the shower at a California hotel, I felt as though the tub was heaving and I was being tossed on stormy seas. Sea legs for air travel. Swollen, throbbing legs and some circles under my eyes were in evidence. Not that I'm complaining! The trip was going well, and the full flights were full of characters that only a flight attendant could understand and appreciate. All three of us were happy, simpatico, and working hand in glove.

Just finishing the drink deliveries and heading to the back to get my basket of snacks, a distinguished man in his late forties asked me to sit beside him. He'd boarded the flight last and was terribly out of breath. He'd asked me, "Mind if I sit anywhere I want to?" There was something about him that looked like a combination of "I've had a terrible day" and "You're the only one who can grant me absolution," so I said of course, and I took him to an exit row. I wasn't going to charge him and told him, "This is an extra-leg-room seat, but you sure need a bit of alone time, so make yourself at home, and I'll give you the safety briefing." He accepted and plunked himself down. Nobody else was in that row, so he really could unwind and have peace. Good, I thought, he sure seemed to need it.

"Have you had a rough day?"

"Yes. A rough week, actually. A girl who works for me asked to go help a friend who is being abused. She would have needed to take a couple of buses through two towns, so I said I'd take her. Fast forward: the girl had a huge bruise on her arm and she was in bad shape. I told the woman who works for me that I wanted her to take care of this abused woman. Both spent time in the office during the week in hopes that the victim would stay away from the abuser."—I just listened and then it was close the door, safety demo, and takeoff time. I did have a chance to deliver the latest issue of my newspaper, the *Optimist*, which had a lot of stories about physical and emotional abuse within its eight pages. For the past twenty-one years, I've published a little eight-page, subtle counter-suicide newspaper for teens. *The Optimist* newspaper is a Vermont Domestic Non-Profit Corporation and is distributed around the United States and Canada. Psychological, emotional, and physical aspects of adolescents are defined and tools to survive the pain of these years are published.

"Here, sir. This might have something that will help you deal with that friend of your employee. "

Because I had an amazing crew that saw and understood the pain in this man's mannerisms, it was possible for me to give him my full attention when he asked me to join him. I told him, "This is against the rules, but you need to talk, don't you?" And talk he did. Imploringly. With the pain and hurt and honesty of someone who had controlled tears, frustrations, anguish, and grief over the past twenty-five years of his life. The enormity of this man's collected miseries could never be measured by mortal man.

"Your paper is about preventing suicide? I have to tell you about my experiences." He'd lost two nephews to this blight, but there was something worse in store for him. His very own sister, who depended on him during her own times of crisis, had finally succeeded in killing herself. The horrible consequence of an abusive, controlling spouse? Yes, but not her own. The man's own wife, knowing that his sister was in the depths of despair, had intercepted all of the suicidal woman's calls for days. The brother never knew his sister was trying desperately to reach him for the hours of talk she needed to pull her out of the abyss of depression.

"My wife just told me, 'Your sister would just talk to you for hours so I never told you about the calls.'" Cold. Calculating.

Controlling. Tragic. "If I'd only been able to talk to my sister, like always. . . ."

Tears welled up in his eyes as he shared this. The floodgates were opened, and the vitriol that had been destroying him for the two and a half decades of emotional, physical, and spiritual abuse poured out of him. He spilled the toxins with no less force than someone experiencing projectile vomiting. He was purging the resentments, hatred, fears, the frustrations of lost years trying to "prove himself worthy" to the one who'd never be satisfied. The castrating bitch of a wife whom he'd provided for, impregnated twice, and put up with had been instrumental in the death of his sister and the almost complete destruction of his being.

Then he had the opportunity to help another victim of the same sort of calculated torture that he'd suffered. This new person in his life, this broken and battered woman, had managed to laugh out loud with him a few times during the past week of angst and indecision. He'd been a savior to her, or he tried to be. He'd been a gallant knight in shining armor (my words, not his!). She'd been grateful, gracious, and a bit of what she must have been before the tarnishing of her personality, destruction of her sanity, and beating of her body became the goals of her terrible lover. The man, who had been sharing both his past week and past twenty-five years with me, discovered that he was still a man inside. He always will be, too. He saw himself and the pattern of his behavior in technicolor as it was mirrored by the woman who, a week before, had been unknown to him. Perhaps he was a complete stranger to himself until he met her? It's easy to deny our own patterns as we repeat them. It's easier still to see it in others and not apply our own sage advice to ourselves. It's not difficult to believe that someone else is right in their negative judgment of us.

"I decided this week to divorce my wife."

But the woman has been bouncing back and forth to her alcoholic abuser since the time she first tried to escape. She's with him at the time of this writing, in fact. She "loves" him. He "needs" her, said her would be savior. Yet, he's hopeful for her. For himself. For themselves.

How incredible it is when one life touches another. The seeds he planted in this shadow woman need time to germinate within her. Maybe it will be a short growing season. More than likely it will be a faraway harvest.

He'd tried so very hard to counsel her and advise her of the reality of this domestic abuse, and he fell for her at the same time. His words and chivalrous actions won't be forgotten. In fact, he will put them to his own use immediately. Blessed be.

ONE NIGHT, ONE FLIGHT

NOBODY CAN EVER predict what will happen from point A to point B on a flight. The magical mix of personalities can offer up the most optimistic, thrilling look into the future, a vivid picture of times past, or put the spotlight on a soul stunted by a harsh and paralyzed existence.

She was standing in the departure gate area, and looked stunning. I whispered to her, "I remember when all women dressed for flights." I thought her bearing was one of complete confidence. Hungarian, I thought. Wrong on two counts already.

He was the epitome of happiness from the moment he boarded. As I offered a smiley-face sticker, I was laughingly directed to give it to the woman following him. Both laughed out loud as they headed down the aisle. Newlyweds, I thought. Not too far off was I on this guess.

A man alone in the first row. Very easy of manner but with a sinewy build born of intense forward thrust. A lean and hungry look without giving away intent. His profession and specialty are usually defined by a linear view of all. Taxonomy in action for all people, places, and things. Yet his approach to life seemed open to all things. All ideas. All peoples. He answered each of my questions without hesitation and seemed proud of his accomplishments but not at all conceited. Omniscience usually breeds arrogance. None noted. Was he lean because of an overly active basal metabolism rate married to ambition? Such an easy smile, but inner workings forged in the fires of curiosity. Maybe I was right about this one.

The flight and the stories of its inhabitants unfolded between New York and Chicago. Time, distance, rarified air, and humanity. Always a recipe for sharing of self because of the circumstance and a deadline. Now or never. Tell all to the flight attendant because everyone knows that the chances of seeing her again are zero to none. All secrets are shared because, at thirty-five thousand feet above Mother Earth, there's a bond among strangers.

"How did you meet?" I asked the happy couple from some former Eastern-bloc country.

"It's a long story. . . ."

"It's a short flight, so abbreviate."

"We met in first grade. Then we didn't see each other for years. I came to this country. We found each other."

Together for two years and it only took half a lifetime for them to rekindle a love that began before either understood escape from behind the Iron Curtain. Love will win out, and this couple, so joyous and full of all passions, is proof of just this.

And the story told by the stunning well-groomed woman I'd met before boarding the flight: "We had an arranged marriage. You know what that is? In Armenia. We were so young. I think he was just seventeen or eighteen when we married. That's forty-four years ago. We got married. The children came. After very few years it went down, down, down."

"Does he run you down? Insult you?"

Her face contorted and her eyes closed as she forced "Yes" from between pursed lips.

"I'll tell you," she continued, "a while ago he took me to the drug store for my prescriptions. He started to yell and yell and yell that I was taking too long inside that store. I went to the sidewalk where he was and said, 'Calm yourself. Calm down, please.' He yelled and I thought he would tear down that building. He started round and round the car. I took my cell phone and dialed 911. He could see the police car coming down the street, and he drove away, his foot to the floor. I answered all questions, gave his cell phone number, our address. They called him and the policeman said, 'You left your wife outside of the pharmacy. She was just getting her pills. We have your number. We have your address. This is a warning. If you do anything to her again we will come after you!' My husband didn't even talk to me for a month."

"When did this happen?"

"Three months ago." This was punctuated by a tiny, tight-lipped, knowing smile.

"If he does this again, will you call 911?"

"Yes!"

I wondered why she didn't leave him altogether, but that was the all-American woman's voice hollowly bouncing an idea off the hardened walls of my heart. What do I know of the Armenian woman's vulnerabilities and pride? Nothing.

And the understated, dapper man in the first row seemed so open and willing to hear me as well as reveal the ins and outs of his professional life. He was on his way to another high point in his medical career, but he didn't seem too thrilled about the possibility of another feather in his cap. There seemed just one compartment of his inner being that was a tad empty, and maybe for the first time, he'd figured out what was missing. Maybe he'd always known, but the vibe on the plane offered two views of life and love. Knowingly or unwittingly, he'd been touched as much as I because he'd had a front-row seat to love at its best and worst. The full spectrum of have and have not may have given him pause to ask himself, "Where am I, and where do I want to be?"

The couple found each other. The woman's finding herself. The man? Now he knows what he wants. Maybe he'll look back across the few decades of his life and remember a girl in his first grade class. Maybe he'll look her up? Maybe she's been waiting for his call. Love will win out.

Everyone deserves this intangible commodity, be they separated by years and continents, imprisoned in an arranged marriage, or educated out of the vast pool of available love interests. It's finding it and making it work as best you can that's the hard part. Knowing love happens is what keeps most of us going, isn't it?

IT'S A MATCH!

JFK to Long Beach, September 2008

TO LOVE. TO CHERISH. To nurture. To protect. To honor. Is that a match? It's a match!

Personally, I waited too many decades just imagining what it might be like to have someone look at me the way Josh looked at Rachel. Here were two Orthodox Jews—he in the slightly wrinkled white shirt, black everything else, yarmulke, prayer shawl mostly submerged beneath his soft paunch, and probably no more than a few inches over five feet tall. Not a handsome man by anyone's standards. She, dressed in black from head to toe and not at all winsome to the average eye. So why did they catch and hold my attention from the time they boarded at JFK until we landed in Burbank?

The twinkle in their eyes and what caused it to be so all encompassing.

While boarding, I often pass out smiley-face stickers to

help break the ice and give everyone some sort of common denominator on board. Believe it or not, this little gesture really cuts down on the usual tendency of individuals to ignore one another because they've no baseline for a conversational opening gambit. These little stickers inform visually, and everyone has to admit that they've submitted to the "attack of the smiley."

Yet rarely has the reaction to being blessed with a sticker given me so much satisfaction as that of Josh and Rachel. Josh was first to accept and did so with one of the most jubilant laughs on record. I can't remember his words, but they were directed at the woman in his wake, and she cracked up too. When she drew up along side of me she said, "Well, I'd like two smiley faces!" She accompanied the demand with a very uninhibited chuckle, and then as her husband looked on and laughed some more, I noticed people all around begin to laugh. It was obvious by the epidemic of giggles that this couple had something magical surrounding them. What could it have been? Whatever it was, everyone was catching it, and I knew that this flight was about to be one of the best ever.

Over the hours and hours from the East Coast to the West Coast, many conversations are available for the plucking. When I kneel down beside someone just to check how they're doing, I can usually get an entire life history if I play my cards right. Sometimes just a quick, "How's this trip going for you so far?" and a touch on an arm or quick hand squeeze can elicit heretofore untold secrets or opinions. Hey, they think they'll never see me again, so I'm the perfect sounding board, right? God, I'm so lucky! Sometimes, folks head into a galley to stretch when what they're really looking for is an ear. Chats with flight attendants often are really dress rehearsals for some performance before a critical audience in wait at their final destination.

Josh and Rachel sat across the aisle from each other and, from my vantage point in the galley, I could see their heads like two plants growing toward life-giving sunshine, bending one to the other time and again. And every time I passed them, they were laughing. Now remember, JFK to California represents a very long time in the air, and that equates to a marathon of merriment. While others slept, this duo seemed more and more awake with every air mile. I managed a question or two every time my body passed between them, and they didn't disappoint. They were equally witty and totally into each other. When one gave a quick response to one of my inane queries, the other would let out a whoop, and we'd all collapse over it.

The inevitable visit to the galley was first made by Rachel. I looked at her perfect skin and into her bright eyes, shapeless clothing, and obvious youth but only asked, "How long have you been married?" Her response was instant, "We got married last July!" Ah, I thought, doing the math, July, August, September—three months max, I estimated. But I'd met multiple couples who didn't glow after two days of marriage, and this Orthodox couple was apparently totally in sync and without the inhibition usually exhibited in their conservative society.

"Were you matched by a yenta?" I asked, hoping it wasn't a rude question. "Well, of course!" was the smiling answer.

"And it's working out for you?" was my maternal inquiry. And here's where everything came together. It wasn't so much this youngster's answer, but everything that was put into it.

Close your eyes and picture the scene. It was nothing short of everything cliché. I mean the cliché that every woman wishes she was a part of when asked if a relationship is working out. The hands instantly moved to her heart and made a tight fist, her eyes narrowed and she sent them upward, and I thought for a minute she was going to succumb to the proverbial swoon of a Southern belle! And there was a bit o' the devil in those dark and sparkling orbs when she squeezed out an "Oh yes!" that barely got by the lump in her throat, which must have been forged in the fires of passion and contained all the surprises and mysteries only revealed to the luckiest of satisfied women. I could only smile and think, "Ah yes, she's enjoying all the perks of a great romantic love!" It gave me the warmest sensation, and I was very proud of that newlywed, not only for getting the relationship thing, but for unabashedly beaming her multiple joys to a stranger, in fact, to the world.

Not long after my visit from Rachel, her groom came forth. His cheeks glowed and were rosy. I know there's no Santa Claus in his culture, but if there were, Josh could be the poster boy. He defined joy with his body language. The short, heavy arms were flung away from his portly core, and his covered, colorless, patchy beard was aimed at the ceiling every time he threw his head backward to let out a laugh. I told him how happy just seeing him and his bride together made me feel. He became, not altogether serious, but he toned down his amusement barometer just long enough to lean forward and gush, "Tomorrow we'll be married two months! Exactly two months tomorrow!" It was as though this man, so completely lusted after by his young bride, knew he might be the only man alive that had the secret to life all figured out. Love and nothing short of awe poured out of that ever-so-young fellow. And he seemed so surprised to find himself blissfully married to such a woman. "Oh. Such a woman!" he said no less than three times. That seems to have been his answer.

Like I said, some of us go all the way through life without feeling what this beautiful couple found out through the luck of the draw, the wisdom of a matchmaker, and a religion that might have the answers after all. It might not always be obvious to outsiders, but what does anyone know of love in America today? That it's temporary and fits into the box of convenience and quid pro quo expectations? That it's based on external beauty, the fashion police, and appropriate behavior? That it has to be complicated?

When we see a couple that falls into a category of its own creation, it should give us pause. Why should relationships be complicated? If a man shares all with his girl and she with him, could they be anything less than best friends? When you surround open communication with uniformity of culture, unabashed senses of humor, mutual awe, a youthful lust, and time to fly across the country for adventure—that blessed time alone and away from the overseers or chaperones of any stripe—what could be better? Like I said at the beginning of this story, some of us wait almost a lifetime to feel what this twosome might have for the next seventy-plus years. But if theirs is the gold standard for happiness, then let's aim for it without the hang-ups we've brought upon ourselves. If some of us have it already, a resounding mazel tov!

LOVE UNDER A LIGHT BULB

Somewhere around 1975: Mexican culture, marvelous family!

IT ALWAYS BEGAN the same way for me. Meeting people was never difficult to begin with, but without exception, after I'd availed myself of rented time on a water ski, the driver and observer would want me to spend the rest of my vacation behind or in their boat. Why? I guess I was an uninhibited skier and not at all the typical tourist.

This was Acapulco, and I was a casual observer standing on some enormous dock. The usual coin divers were the only aquatic performers as tourists chucked their fool's gold off the cruise ship into the bay. The boat, outboard motor spitting, came to the mooring, and the two skinny brown men inside began their optimistic solicitation by holding up an old laminated wooden slalom ski. It looked like it may never have seen better days, even when new. The front binding, torn. The rear one on the verge of complete disintegration. The ski itself, colorless with the layered wood showing marked signs of delamination.

I looked into the boat. On the floor, a loose gas tank, a couple of precarious seats each tied with old, thinning rope to a cleat; a broken paddle; and a torn life jacket made up the inventory. There was a tangled mass of ski rope ending in what looked like a simple double knot somewhere on the transom dangerously close to the propeller.

"I'll go," I said to the smaller of the two young men.

"Five dollars," came the response from the laughing fellow holding up the ski.

Into the boat I jumped, aided by a hand that had been quickly extended, not for the money but to help me into the mess.

"I'm Raul and this is my cuzzing Jesús."

"I'm Heather."

"You know how to ski?"

"Yes. I'd like a slalom run, if that works for you."

We pushed off, and the engine snorted us away from other traffic and jumped in. Raul tossed me the ski and the rope with a handle. That handle was greasy from being towed in water populated by large vessels and I wondered if I could get a true grip. Ah, that poor excuse for a ski was the biggest threat to a safe run. The forward binding couldn't be made to fit my foot. No problem, the general attitude that infused our little trio was so friendly and laughter-ridden that to do this run, just for the challenge of overcoming equipment failings, was fine with me.

When the rope had no more slack and I was ready, I yelled, "Hit it." I wondered if the rope, frayed as it was and poorly attached to the leaky boat, would snap as it tried to get me up. It held, and off we went. It takes a great driver to make any run good for the skier, and the last thing I expected from the happy duo in the derelict boat was a good run. I figured they'd hit every corner wide and have me struggling to overcome the interwoven wakes created by our own boat. Maybe they'd just take me in a large circle, I thought, thereby making it impossible to cut back and forth even if that old ski held up to that sort of stress. Not on your life. Jesús was expert, and that fifteen minutes on Acapulco Bay was a great time. I felt terrific, and that ski, loosely fitted to one foot while the other fought for survival in a flapping rear binding, withstood just about every test, from deep cutting to wake jumping with pretty dramatic landings. Then it was finished. The contract had been fulfilled. And with those strong, sinew-ridden arms pulling a completely out-of-breath skier over the port side of that poor excuse for a boat, a bond that still warms me, some three and a half decades later, was forged.

Raul, excited to have met a fellow skier, announced, "I want to show you the real Acapulco. You come with me all day today? You come with me tomorrow, and I will show you the market. You come with me in two days, and I'll show you a beach where the sand squeaks. You come?"

And so it was that a hyperkinetic Mexican of my own age adopted me. And I, him.

In those days, as today, I enjoyed traveling by myself because others slow me down, and no native of any country deigns to embrace somebody already in another's company.

On this particular trip, however, I had joined a group of others from Montreal. I didn't drink. I got up early. I didn't sit by a hotel pool tanning. I was weird for my age and the times. Sharing a room with one of the girls on that trip was stressful because of my boring persona in the face of "real fun." Because of my own interests, I was boring to all. Downright antisocial, in fact, and my roommate was very vocal in her chastisement of my chosen native activities, I can tell you.

"They're dirty, Heather. They're common. They're uneducated. They're beggars. They're after only one thing. They're dangerous for God's sake, Heather."

Well, Raul wasn't. No native I met during that week fit any of the descriptions or warnings given me by my Canadian fellow travelers. I was having the time of my life and being educated by an expansive young man with no ulterior motives whatsoever. We really enjoyed each other's company, and it was a real treat to be taken all over the place, in public transportation, to markets and communities where I was the only non-Mexican.

One day, Raul met me at preordained spot and guided me to an outdoor market.

"Have you ever tasted carrot juice?"

I couldn't remember if ever I had, actually, but the taste of that nectar, as it was prepared in the market on that day, is with me still. God, it was so delicious. It went down like velvet. The market was congested and overstuffed with fruit and vegetable hawkers of every sort. It was very loud. Raul led me through the maze of colors, textures, people of all ages, punctuated by the comments, in-jokes, and banter permitted by a shared culture. Everywhere there was laughter. And flies.

Great black swarms of flies all over the place, but nobody paid them any mind so I tried to do the same.

Somewhere, deep in the thick of the sweaty populace and the cloud of insects, we arrived at a table holding a blender thick with carrot pulp and the ever-present flock of flies. The heavy, dark man behind the table was so happy to see Raul, and my friend was equally thrilled with the reunion. I was introduced to the jovial man, unshaven and sweating because of the heat and the physical exertions that accompanied his every verbal exchange. He'd throw those meaty arms up, then out, then he'd slap his thighs as he bent over to laugh and cough. He'd arch backward, thick hands slapping his fat stomach, which showed buttons unceremoniously distanced from completely ignored buttonholes. Think of Sergeant Garcia in the old *Zorro* television show, and you've got this fellow's appearance pegged. Happiness personified. Joy shared. He threw the carrots into that blender and turned it on. It sounded stronger than the ski boat's outboard and probably got better speed. When the drink was ready, I got the first taste. It was beyond the best thing ever to touch my taste buds and slide down my throat. Then Raul had a swig, and so it went until the blender was empty. A shared drink with high spirits, good humor, and flies. I don't know how many of those bugs got into that drink, but it didn't matter because the end product was nothing short of divine.

When I told my roommate what I'd experienced at that market, she was shocked.

"My God, Heather. What's the matter with you? Are you crazy? You're going to get Montezuma's revenge. I can't believe how stupid you are. And you're probably going to get gang raped. You are, you know. The Mexicans are known for that. I'm never going anywhere with you again. None of us are."

With that, our friendship ended, and the next day, Raul took me to a beach where the white sand squeaked when we walked upon it. That day, my roommate and everyone else in that group, none of whom had ventured out of the hotel for dining pleasures, contracted the worst case of Montezuma's revenge in that hotel's long history of serving tourists "sanitized for your protection" edibles. They're condemnation of my fraternization with natives and warnings about the pitfalls of enjoying local food and drink proved ironic.

At the end of the week, Raul took me to the outside of his church. "Here's where my sister's getting married tomorrow. I have many sisters and brothers. Will you meet me here after the marriage and come to her party with me and my family?"

The reason I wasn't to attend the nuptials was plain to me. It was a holy service in the most Catholic of ways, and only the family, some one hundred relatives, would be in attendance.

I wore a summer dress and pretty shoes for the reception. Simple, respectful garb that hinted at feminine but didn't flirt. As the congregation descended from the church, I was nearly knocked over by a wave of pure joy. Always joy. Everything I'd felt since meeting Raul had been joy, delight, wonder, happiness, and easy, warm friendship. The openness of that man was like none other before or since because of its innocence and simplicity, respect and pride. Now here came a bride and her groom and a tsunami of laughing people of every age, in the widest spectrum of colors, ribbons in the young ones' hair, and smiles on every face—the best makeup in the world. And I was looking at them all by myself and wondering, "How could I be so lucky, me, a stranger no more, to have been invited into this huge bubble of family excitement and love? Why me? Why am I so lucky?"

The happy couple, surrounded by a throng of children, passed me. The wedding guests, a mass of colorful laughter, were as one. They seemed joined by something concrete, and it struck me as so amazing. Unlike the formalities and not-to-be-crossed lines of demarcation formed by who's who on the ladder of family hierarchy where I'm from, this gaggle of humanity was completely without delineation. The elders, the middle-aged, the men, the women, and the children distributed themselves equally behind the newlyweds. No line of marching automatons were they; no, it was a sea of happy humanity weaving in and out among themselves without self-importance or any preordained order. Raul was at my side and laughing. He took me by the arm, and we joined that throng. There was no special treatment from anyone as I melted into the crowd. I was with their Raul, so I was instantly one of them as we marched through the failing light of day into an evening that would be filled with music, dancing, laughter, love, and the story of my partner's family ties. I was to be shown a prime example of nonjudgmental, totally accepting, unconditional love that all families, everywhere, should know—could know if survival and love, faith and acceptance, mutual respect and simplicity were to replace judgment.

As we made our way to the reception, many children, probably curious about this blonde woman but too polite to ask directly, sent shy looks my way. I smiled back and before long, Raul and I were separated by a dozen little girls, each one trying to hold my hand. The laughter was our shared language. The warm little hands in mine were the stories. I'd never been the girl who cooed over the babies in strangers' carriages. Nor did I particularly enjoy my babysitting jobs during my teen years. Yet for the first time in my life, from this group of little ones ignited a firestorm of maternal instinct that has been mine ever since.

The open courtyard was lit by one bare light bulb suspended on a wire that ran from one building to another. Chairs were set up in a square bordering the walls of tenement housing. The first order of the evening was the feeding of the guests, and this was undertaken by the bride and her groom. Someone ladled one scoop of runny black beans onto the thinnest of paper plates, and the couple delivered each individually. Guest after seated guest was fed in turn along each wall. When presented my serving, it amazed me that the leaking vessel hadn't ruined this buoyant bride's gorgeous white gown. Handing the soppy meal to me, we locked eyes as her new husband laughed with everyone in my immediate vicinity. They were black and warm, those eyes, and proud of her situation and of her family. Those eyes laid bare any doubt about my being the luckiest person in the world to have been asked to join the party. A beautiful bride's honest eyes and her happy man in tow gave me such a rush of gratitude that I would have hugged them both very hard if my meal wasn't dripping all over the place already.

As the music began, I was surrounded and pulled up by hordes of children. Raul smiled and told me to dance with his little sisters. How many sisters did he have, I wondered. The answer came soon enough. During a lull in the dancing, I was taken by my date to be introduced to his aunts, uncles, more brothers and sisters, cousins, and finally to his mother. She took me in her arms and said, "Raul, he told me about you. Are you liking it, this party?" Her body was full and welcoming. Her embrace strong but gentle. She was goodness and the Madonna incarnate to me. My own mother had been long dead, and as most left motherless in life do, I searched her face for something that I could make my own and keep forever. I found love there and will never forget it. For a nanosecond, I was another daughter to her, if only in my imagination. After the briefest of chats, her son took me to the outskirts of the dancing crowd. For once, the little ones weren't all around me; I guess they'd found another point of interest after finding out I wasn't an exotic being, but just a typical girl from away. I guess, after close scrutiny, I was judged acceptable "as is, where is," even though I was the only nonfamily member in attendance. To have been accepted to the point of invisibility meant an awful lot to me.

Pointing up at a certain apartment, Raul stated, "That's where I live. I sleep on the fire escape most of the time because there's not room inside and I'm the oldest son."

I can't remember if he had ten or fourteen siblings, but it amazed me that his little mother had produced so many and looked so great.

In a completely matter of fact way, he said, "We all have different fathers. My mother is a prostitute." In fact, I detected a bit of pride as he told me. Yes I did. You see, she supported her family, loved them, raised them as devout Catholics. Each child who'd shared the dance floor with me was polite, clean, happy, healthy, and loving. That mother herself had nothing but respect from her son and made an absolutely wonderful mother of the bride.

It was her profession that would have caused her social castigation by a judgmental population made up of others like my Canadian roommate, who was suffering and terribly sick back in our four-star hotel.

Travel broadens the mind if we take the road less traveled. If we trust. Otherwise, why leave our own backyards? Why go anywhere if not to test the waters of other cultures and hope that the natives adopt us and show us their ways? Their lives. Their way of surviving. It's so humbling to be in the presence of any native population and sad that tourists so often judge natives to be substandard. Preconceived notions perpetuated by narrow-minded visitors to a foreign country don't leave much room for education and growth, do they? I think that any different way of life that threatens to change a North American's status quo could actually be superior. Sadly, anyone who thrives on material gain and forgets the simplicity of unconditional acceptance, forgiveness of sins, and the sharing of a plain meal or a family history that hasn't been revised to suit the expectations of present company misses much. How comfortable I felt under that bare light bulb with Raul and his loving relatives.

Every person had exposed a different beauty. The eyes, the hair, the smile, the hands, or the skin were individually committed to my mind's photo gallery. Everyone so giving and warm. The Mexican people my roommate would never allow herself to meet, let alone know, were nesting in my heart that night. Blessed. So blessed was I by every one of them at that plain reception where only one scoop out of a vat of watery black beans was offered. Yet, immeasurable amounts of love were shared. All this under one bare 40-watt lightbulb. In daylight this would be classified as a slum by tourists. To me, it will always symbolize family and all that one might be. Ever.

THE WIND BENEATH HIS WINGS

San Francisco to JFK, a timeless love in 2008

HE WAS WEARING a leather jacket and matching western hat when I met him sitting at the boarding gate at SFO (San Francisco International Airport). There was a brace on his right hand and wrist to help his newly injected-with-cortisone carpal tunnel syndrome. I could tell he was tall and handsome even as he sat, busily working on his laptop. There was a genuine warmth about him, and I sat down to his right when I found out he was on my flight to JFK, just to know him a bit more. I took his forearm and hand to check out that horrible condition and asked if he was a writer.

"Yes. I had to write a lot last year to finish a book."

In answer to further questioning, I learned that the gentle fellow was a professor with a PhD in history, Stanford being the institution mentioned. He spoke of the average education turning out graduates whose only discernable goal was to earn enormous amounts of money. I agreed, saying that education should better prepare graduates to make positive contributions to a sustainable society; to counter the individualism so prevalent today, studies should include environmental consciousness, social awareness, and spiritual depth. It seemed impossible to just chat with this man because his entire persona radiated a knowing. An omniscience without egocentric accompaniment. In his presence I felt overwhelming waves of knowledge, understanding, and acceptance lapping against my being. Yes, he was emanating a rhythmic series of ripples from his core, and they were constant. That's how the gifted who are totally secure within themselves, know who they are, why they are, and need no applause share themselves. They just let what they know escape the inner sanctums of their mind at equally spaced intervals for the rest of us to either grasp or ignore. No pressure, but a lot of opportunity for the surrounding minions to absorb the offerings.

While boarding, the woman who preceded the dapper professor was sporting round spectacles softly tinted blue. Something she said left me with the new knowledge that this was a powerful duo. Fact duly noted, ma'am. An impression of pride and protectiveness was tangible as the woman slipped by me, followed by the author.

The flight, with a ratio of three seats to one customer, wasn't making a lot of revenue, but it sure was nice to invite the customers to spread out and make themselves at home. The woman took window, aircraft left. The erudite man occupied window, aircraft right. An aisle and four seats came between them, but there was some invisible filament that rendered those few feet moot. The invisible link seemed composed of respect, comfort, familiarity, and a strength of wills. I could feel it.

Almost right after takeoff he fell asleep. With those long legs drawn up so that not so much of the soles of his shoes protruded into the aisle, the man slumbered. It takes some sort of subconscious effort on the part of any sleeping flyer to configure himself to the exact size and shape of airplane seats, I thought. And an innate consideration for others, too!

On the other side of the sleeping man, the bespectacled, avant-garde woman relaxed. I leaned over, saying, "I interviewed your beloved before boarding, ma'am, but you and I didn't have a chance to chat. What is it that you do when you're not flying around?"

"I'm a decorator."

We talked about this and that, and it wasn't but a few moments before this woman, probably about my age, some time short of sixty, started giving me the real story of her life. And of her love.

You see, this woman, although accomplished in her own right as a decorator and someone who has stepped into the world of antiques onto a plateau firm enough to have "run a couple of galleries in New York," had chosen to speak of that sleeping man opposite her.

The discussion became focused on her love's life work. You see, the husband's name is Clarence B. Jones, PhD, Scholar in Residence at Stanford University's Martin Luther King, Jr., Research and Education Institute.

Why was this man chosen for this auspicious position? Well

to start with, he was an attorney and frequent speechwriter for Martin Luther King, Jr. That book he spoke of writing, *What Would Martin Say?* (2008), is one that brings the great civil rights activist back to life. How? With integrity.

Having intimate knowledge of the man and his thought processes, ethics, spirit, and inner workings, Dr. Jones has asked questions relevant to the present and answered them in Dr. King's voice. That book, which in no small part caused the author's carpal tunnel syndrome, came from other internal pains as well. What great strength it must have taken to lay selected difficult issues at the feet of someone dead more than four decades. To even believe that answers might be intuited from beyond the boundaries of life as we know it smacks of fraud. Yet not in this case. Not at all. Remember, I used the word *integrity*.

In his book, Dr. Jones suffered more than a cliché physical reaction to contemporary ergonomic misuse. He had to go back in time and access the man who *was*, enter into a mind that was thought lost forever at the time of his assassination, and come up with estimated verbal projections that would begin with the mind-set of an activist in the sixties and, using the fifty years of social evolution, speak the words that Dr. King would utter today. Yes, not *might* speak, but *would*. There's a chemical reaction when pureness of intent marries integrity, when ego is left on the shelf, and honesty, based on a trust built during the most difficult years of struggle for equality in this country, is figured into the extrapolation formula.

Like I said before, individuals who share without guile or a personal agenda know that their works are for the future of man. The good might come long after the teacher has passed from this mortal coil, but this doesn't matter to the true teacher, that true conduit of knowledge and wisdom to the masses. Dr. Jones is just that: a man extending one hand back to hold his friend's, the other, with palm open, giving the words to all who would hear them today. I'd venture that the injured one was the hand holding fast to the beliefs of Martin Luther King, Jr. Yes, it would be that one; the vast amount of information and work to catch every nuance for a book that held on to the dead man's ideas and might again get this country going in the right direction must have been terribly hard on that appendage as it stretched through a vacuum of years. This strenuous effort caused a tenacious man to overuse a limb. Professionals say that carpal tunnel syndrome results from poor body mechanics, but in this case, could it not be from that long reach into the past to pick up every single sentence given in response to today's burning questions? I think so. I do.

Now picture this relaxed, self-confident, incredibly open woman sharing her innermost self with me. It wasn't conspiratorial at all, but each word was accompanied with a leaning forward or back, and always the eyes reached into mine with such a pleading pull. You see, this lovely lady wanted me to feel how deeply her affections flowed and just how fabulous her life is with her mate. She needn't have added the postures or eye contact for emphasis. Why? Because, when a woman loves a man deeply, it's so obvious. It shows in the cocked head and silent smile when a woman just looks across an aisle at him. It shows when, if she thinks nobody's watching her, she glances at her man and lets her eyes wonder from the top of his head to the tips of his shiny shoes as a memory of passions enjoyed dances behind her glasses. Ah, yes, Ms. Walters gave many signs that her love was the real thing. And it's a warm and adoring love, at that. And it's an exciting and mind-expanding experience for both parties, most definitely. Satisfying in every way, I'd wager; artistically, scientifically, intellectually, spiritually, historically, and every other which way.

"Look at him. He's tired. We travel all the time. He lectures. So brilliant. He's in Mensa. It's scary sometimes, what he knows. We'll be discussing the Renaissance, and he'll just know every date, every event from that time. He just knows such an incredible amount, but he'd never flaunt it. He'll just let it out slowly."

Now, that's exactly what I felt when sitting with him at SFO! Continuing her discourse on the new book, she went on.

"He'll be doing a lot of TV interviews when the book comes out. It's taken him the last two years to finish it, and he did it with Joel Engler, a fellow from California. They just seemed to gel and worked so well together from their first conversation. Engler is younger than him. Do you know Clarence is seventy-seven? He looks younger, doesn't he? His daughter's turning eighteen tomorrow, February seventh. That's why we're going to New York, actually. For his daughter's eighteenth birthday."

After sharing so much of her pride and admiration regarding the sleeping man in the row across the aisle, this obviously free spirit of a woman opened the next door to me. Over that threshold were the rooms holding her life experiences.

"I dated many men during a fourteen-year period. Many men. Some brilliant. And they're still my friends. I learned something from each one." We discussed this because I believe that there are so many ways to become educated about life, love, the world, and all it holds, and I was so glad to meet another woman who has gleaned political, environmental, social, and much more awareness from opening herself up to love on all levels without fearing stigma or negative ramifications from any bourgeoisie mind-set. Relationships offer great opportunities to learn, not only about the other party, but about the vast array of subjects that haven't entered one's atmosphere until a new liaison comes into play. College degrees, however adequate by today's measure of success, are still fairly linear. If they teach a student to be forever curious, lifelong learning will ensue, but not always in a classroom, from books, or other usual sources. Living life, saying yes, and taking risks have yielded some incredible knowledge for those who get up every morning excited to jump into a new day with an open mind! It was obvious that Ms. Walters was a student of many professors, and I'm sure they benefited from exposure to her generous spirit, clarifying vocabulary on all levels, and her flair for living life to the fullest!

Another door opened, and I was shown into the warmest room in her artist's mind. It was beautiful and contained another couple, one she held up as the epitome of romantic love, cherishing, and all the glories that only one special high priest of passion, patience, and appreciation can bestow. Her eyes, partially shadowed behind those blue lenses, had already shown expressiveness usually kept for punctuation marks after secrets between best friends. But now I saw tears caused from a memory that could be acted out on a Broadway stage with nothing more than a dark, propless set, two main characters, a spotlight, and music.

"I told you I was a decorator, but I crossed over into antiques at one point and ran a couple of galleries in New York. Well, every once in a while, a couple would come into the gallery. First the man would ask if his wife could sit down. I'd say, 'Of course,' and he'd help her into a chair, and then he'd walk around and look in the cases. He'd stop in front of certain cases and ask to see a piece; I'd remove it and pass it to him. He'd feel it." At this juncture, the storyteller looked into her own hands, and I could visualize a smooth work of art held in her palms. Still staring at her hands she ran first one and then the other over the imaginary item. "Then he'd take it over to his wife and place it in her hands, and she'd feel it all over, too. They collected ivory, you see. Now this woman was absolutely gorgeous. Her blonde hair was always in a French twist. Her clothes, immaculate. Her entire manner was perfect, and so was her husband's. He was a complete gentleman. Oh, I thought they made just the best of couples." With this, her tears began. Not flowing, just brimming around her eyes.

"Then, one day I went to the Rainbow Room. Do you know it?" I nodded. "Well, it was there that I saw the couple from the gallery. They were dancing in perfect step. And that's when I noticed—she was blind! I asked the maître d', and he told me that the man did her makeup and everything else. She was always just perfect. She always wore dark glasses, you see, so I never knew. Now, that's love. The devotion. Such devotion!"

Her fingers wiped away tears that fell behind her glasses, and then, in pantomime, she struck a man's dancing pose and demonstrated as she said, "He just guided her and they just danced. The maître d' told me they came three times a week just to dance." One hand positioned itself in the air again and she said, "He just guided her. . . ."

She glanced wistfully at her beau, still sound asleep in his row. "He's so amazing to me."

I said, "You deserve it. You're giving him a great deal of encouragement and motivation, aren't you? It's obvious that you cherish him, too. You're the wind beneath his wings."

In a disbelieving way she quietly said, "We heard that song last year, the one with those words and he looked at me and said, 'That's you. You're the wind beneath my wings.'"

I think, in her life as in mine, the loves we've lost were never wasted times. No, they were the stepping stones to what we agreed we both have now, that perfect partner who, for whatever reasons, is devoted to us just as we are. Sometimes it takes half a lifetime to figure out what works in the long term. Sometimes it takes seeing one other couple who are getting it right even as they struggle through circumstances that would prove too difficult if there was no love. However happy endings are reached, it doesn't matter. Just as Dr. Jones has reached back in time to pull answers from his long-lost friend, who preached what universal love could be like in our country, so do we all reach into what was once seen, in some distant past time, to be the perfect example of what love might be between two grown people.

It all starts with example and need never end with death.

GATE 10, TERMINAL 6

Before working for SkyNation, I was a weekly commuter between Burlington, Vermont and JFK New York and back again on this airline...I'd also sworn never to date again. I was healing from the empty-nest syndrome and my cat had died, I was enjoying a great partnership at the Muscular Therapy Center of New York and I was actually happier than I'd been in a decade....
JFK to Burlington

I STATIONED MYSELF against a partition between security and gate ten. I'd never felt better because my absolute decision to continue to experience all new things—like I'd done before becoming a wife and mother—was irrefutable. Irreversible. The rest of my free life lay ahead of me, and I was on top of the world with no more emotional encumbrances. I hadn't felt so good since before I'd dated the father of my children. I was back, and I knew it! As I awaited boarding, I read all about our feckless president's decision to go to war with Iraq should Saddam Hussein not come forward, hat in hand and throw himself on the mercy of the world court. We were going to war. I was so glad I'd spoken my heart and mind the night before when being interviewed by three European and four Asian television stations plus one Catholic magazine published in Paris. However, I wondered if some huge hand might come down upon my honed-in-Vermont outspoken persona. The specter of Guantanamo Bay's holding tanks hadn't entered the American collective mentality. Yet.

"Rows twenty to twenty-six may now board."

I folded the paper and started a slow mosey to join the dovetailing streams of people heading for the check-in counter. Suddenly I was on the ground, and two large men, shoulder-to-shoulder, were moving away from the strike zone. I was up in a flash and said in the most dramatic-comedic way, "Well, I guess *they* want to get to Burlington before I do!"

A man bent at the waist by my side, swept his left arm outward, and said, "After you."

"Chivalry is not dead," was my response, and I began a diva-like prance in the direction of the gate. When I reached the jetway, I sensed him behind me. "Hmm. I think I'll tighten my buttock muscles and swing my hips," I thought. I swear to God, I'd never consciously done anything so overtly flirtatious in my life. And I haven't since. Something made me hope that the man who'd been so quick-witted and funny back in the terminal was watching my bottom! I guess I figured there was nothing to fear because, as of that very day, I'd sworn off romantic entanglements for all time.

Near the aircraft door, the human traffic had come to a complete halt. I knew the man was behind me and thought

I should acknowledge him, after all, he diffused what might have been an embarrassing situation for me back there. I turned and held up my *USA Today* with Bush's threat in large print. "What did you think of Bush's speech last night?"

"I can't say I agree with everything he said."

Good answer I thought. This guy heard the speech and thought about it. Hmm. He's not a stupid man.

I reached my aisle seat knowing he was still close. Why was I aware? Why did I feel this? Why did I even care? He took the middle seat beside me.

"Oh, would you like me to sit in the middle? I'm small."

"I'm small."

We shared our first audible chuckle. Hmm . . . he's quick, I thought.

"Where have you been?" I asked, just to be a tiny bit sociable.

"Tampa."

"Did you do any fishing?"

"No. I walked."

"Swimming or snorkeling?"

"I just walked."

I thought, well, there you go. What did you expect, an exciting man? There aren't any, so why continue this chat?

"Why Tampa?"

"I went to visit my mother."

Great. A boring man who's probably a mama's boy. Seriously, that characterization crossed my mind. The guy was alone, had visited his mother, and admitted to doing nothing but solitary walking. Wow, thrills for him!

I caught a glimpse of his wrists and a bit of brown forearm

sometime during the first few minutes, and I heard a bit of his genuine laughter. And he definitely had a sense of humor. Ha, just my luck, a nice man, and the door had shut on such opportunities for me, because, as I said before, I'd sworn off men forever and ever. Amen

"What do you do besides walk?" I was feeling there must be something I should know about him. Why?

"I build bridges."

"Civil engineer?"

"No. I suppose I should have been." At this declaration and admission I saw a faraway look behind both eyes. How many "should haves" in this man's life? It was our first noncomedic exchange. Hmm . . . a man with a few regrets, I thought. Maybe he's just had some sort of epiphany, too. And there was a very attractive, wistful vulnerability about him at that point.

The window seat was empty, and to keep the conversation flowing, we chose to profile the oncoming humanity wondering who'd fill that void. The boarding horde offered a wide array of types. Old and young, tanned and pale, smiling and somber. Each gave us a chance to exhibit our profiling acumen to one another. He really made me laugh! The man was just plain funny! He had beautiful hands. Although I'd decided on a lifetime of celibacy and noninvolvement, I couldn't help thinking that this man's hands would be wonderful as lover's hands. And those muscular, tawny, perfect wrists and forearms were so indicative of strength! I was allowing myself to feel something electric and didn't want to.

A man started down the aisle, his curly black hair nearly touching the roof of the plane. He carried a large pizza in one hand and an extra large container of Coke in the other.

His movement toward us was clumsy because he was just a mountain of a man with an unwieldy two-fisted load of spillable food and drink.

"If he's got the window seat, I'm jumping over you!" I said with exaggerated fear in widened eyes.

He laughed. I was openly flirting with him for the second time, if you count my fanny wiggling on the jet bridge. There was a fleeting fantasy in the farthest reaches of my mind that put me eye-to-eye on top of this witty man in the middle seat. I was allowed to think that! After all, it would not, could not, ever happen in reality.

The monolithic man came closer. We anticipated his inevitable arrival at our row with bated breath. After he passed us by, I turned to my row mate and said, "Well, maybe he's only delivering for Domino's!" That's when we first shared a real, out-of-the-belly laugh. It felt so natural. We could have been the only ones on that entire plane during the time we were laughing. It felt just great and so openly natural for both of us. I'm not projecting into the man's psyche by assuming mutual "natural" feelings. His self-confident, always-alive manner invited mutual gleefulness, and it was something I wasn't used to anymore, but he sure was! Laughing alone was how I usually carried on when things tickled my funny bone. Very few share my view of the world and its constantly changing parade of situational comedies. This man did and then some. Why not? We'd never see each other again, so why not join in an outrageous definition of what most folks don't appreciate as just plain funny?

Then a middle-aged woman turned and kissed the man behind her. He then sat across the aisle, one row ahead of ours. Her eyes turned to us and she bent down saying, "Excuse me but I'm by the window."

"Are you traveling with that man or are you just in the habit of kissing strangers before you sit down on planes?" I asked.

"No. No. We're together."

"Oh. Then I'll sit in his seat, and he can come back here and sit with you!" I offered.

Her eyes passed from me to the man beside me and back to me, "Well, what about you? Aren't you two together?"

Unbuckling my seatbelt and standing up, very ready to change seats, I said, "We're just having a wild affair, passionate but meaningless."

She looked a bit shocked. Apparently, the man beside me had said yes to her inquiry, but I hadn't heard him.

All the seats were swapped. I took the man's aisle seat. The funny, chivalrous, mother-loving walker took the window as the couple filled the row.

I thought, even as I crossed the narrow aisle, "You just blew your chance with a very nice man, Heather." Somehow, I couldn't console myself by tricking my mind into thinking I'd dodged a bullet. I had regrets right away. He'd been so funny. He seemed so quick and smart. His arms were my fantasy arms, and those hands—I wanted them to hold me. Forget it, Heather, remember your new life awaits! So why didn't I feel very lucky right at that moment?

There was a kerfuffle in their row just before the safety demonstration, and the flight attendant got flustered. They were still swapping seats! The man had moved from window to aisle and made me aware throughout the flight that he was watching my every move.

A tap on my arm. "What's your name?"

"Heather McKeown."

I couldn't concentrate on any of the inane television shows. One on horses took up a few minutes, but the rest blurred. The laughter from their row was loud and bordered on obnoxious, but I couldn't escape the feeling that this guy's humor was contagious.

Tap. "Are you still married?"

I felt my face totally redden, "My divorce was very recent, but we're still friends. Here, read my paper," I countered and thrust my USA Today into his hands. Maybe that will shut him up I thought. Why had his inquiry so embarrassed me? Their laughter continued.

Tap. Tap. "May I call you?"

"No."

We landed. Deplaned. After the baggage carousel returned our bags, I slowly walked away, knowing yet again that an opportunity was being wasted. He either caught up with me or turned around and waited, but he was suddenly facing me, green eyes looking straight into mine. He was small! "Janice says we'd make a nice couple."

Somehow he told me he traveled about a thousand miles to work and back every day but he loved it. In a final desperate pitch to sell me on himself he said, "I love kids!" I'd told him about the *Optimist* newspaper I guess.

Hmm. A man happy in his work who didn't mind going the extra mile. Refreshing attitude!

He spoke to a young boy and his aunt who were just back from Orlando and the world of Mickey Mouse. That boy wasn't forthcoming or happy at all. Nor was his aunt.

Hmm, he's not shy. That's good.

In the bus to the parking lot he made sure the driver knew that Heather McKeown was aboard so my car would be made ready. Such a gentleman, I thought as I thanked him.

We went in to pay our parking fees, and he allowed me to go first. "You go ahead. I don't have to be anywhere." I snuck a peek at his parking stub; it looked like Richard R. Bushey was his name. (The following day I used this information to have his background checked by a detective friend of mine. He came up clean.)

He offered to load my heavy knapsack into my car. He hefted it into my back seat. Some very visceral, knee-jerk reaction made me offer him a copy of my paper. I said, "My e-mail's in there . . . if ever you want to tell me what you think of the paper." I simultaneously kicked and applauded myself for opening a door to this forward, but not desperate, man.

I drove off and checked my rearview mirror from the starting point until the exit for the ferry to New York State was behind me. Why? I was hoping that he'd follow me anywhere. Find me. Find me. Hold me. Kiss me. Make love to me. I wanted to know him better but knew I never would. And that was mostly *my* choice, right? Men slow me down!

I salivated and marinated in my own juices as I thought of that man. That Richard R. Bushey of Plattsburgh, New York. That man with arms to die for, hands that I craved to touch me, and a laugh that was so real that I couldn't help share it.

By the time two weeks had passed, I'd had him vetted by law enforcement and written him a letter of admission; even though I'd addressed an envelope, I knew I'd never actually send it. Too risky! There were two R. R. Bushey's in his mailing area, so what if it went to the wrong one? Oh well. It wasn't meant to be.

His first e-mail reached me after two weeks filled with thoughts of him—I hadn't cooled off at all but wanted him—terribly. Even just once.

That's our story. The first chapter anyway. We're still writing the book, but this first meeting wasn't by chance at all, was it? Those two burly men who knocked us over should have been in front of us as we boarded the flight to Burlington. We never saw them after the original impact, and now we both know that they were angels, no different than Clarence of *It's a Wonderful Life*, who came to Earth to help George Bailey realize what was truly important in life: love itself. They were sent to save us from a total divorce from romance and unconditional adult loving we had both accepted as our due. Well, I never gave up hope, but I felt I'd be better off without any couple-instigated complications for the rest of this incarnation, that's for sure.

Stranger things have happened, I'm sure. Life's miracles continue to unfold, and I'm so glad I have you to share them with me, Rick.

Thanks for your persistence.

Thanks for your consistency.

Thanks for proving that I could trust a relationship.

Thanks for making me laugh.

Thanks for your patience.

Thanks for loving me so much that I've grown to depend on that wonderful thing.

Your love.

And, before I forget, thanks for saying "Go for it!" when I wanted to apply for a job at SkyNation!

LOOK UP AND WAIT

San Francisco Bay upon approach of first A-380 into SFO

ON THE EVENING my parents burned the mortgage on our suburban Montreal home, something else happened that was more important than property acquisition in the vast scheme of things. My brother, Mom, Grandpa James, and yours truly were in the back yard to watch Dad gleefully and ceremoniously set fire to papers. I wasn't yet ten years old and realized that the house we'd occupied for five years was now ours. I'd always assumed it to be, so the fact that the burden of some sort of cash outlay was a thing of the past didn't make me feel any more secure. It was great to see everyone so happy though. I think my father had been promoted to sales manager around that time as well. Maybe even that week actually. Nothing about ownership or professional prestige meant much to me. Still doesn't, really. But celebrating adult achievement on that night, something did happen to impress.

Sputnik. The first satellite launched into outer space would be visible from our tiny, now-owned spot on the globe. I remember my grandfather saying, "That's the future, Heather." We just had to look up and wait. My eyes followed the ascending burnt, blackened paper as it was carried upward by some invisible means, and standing alone in the crowd, I saw Sputnik and thought my own abstract thoughts.

Aviation has always played a huge role in my life. Dad flew Cessnas, and so did I. Of course it had been a father's wish to have his only son sit in the copilot's seat, but my poor brother was a victim of motion sickness in every vehicle, from a station wagon to a plane flying straight and level on a calm day. Give us a seat on a ride at the local fair and we'd be sick for days. Once, at the drive-in, we saw *The Bonneville Salt Flats*, and we didn't even make it through the first auto race across that barren landscape before my sibling collapsed into a terrible fit of nausea. Oh dear. Anyway, the controls fell to me, and I became the official family copilot before I could even drive a car. I still think altimeters should be on every Toyota, just to make me feel comfortable.

My friends and I used to park at the end of runways, recline comfortably on the hood of the car and watch aircraft approach. We tried to guess what they were by their engine harmonies or the position of their lights. Well a girl has to have fun, right? Looking up is what we did best, that and wishing we were up there ourselves.

All this was decades ago. So many years have separated me from my old hometown in Quebec, yet the fascination with all things airborne hasn't diminished. The old Viscounts and Super Constellations, DC-3s, and even the Concordes have gone by the boards, but there's always something about to take off that takes our minds off the old birds, eh? And always, there are skeptics, naysayers, or positive backers of invention ready to dismiss or applaud new technology or styles. I've never been on the side of the skeptics, but that may have changed today. Today might be the line of demarcation between the youthful and aged, open- to closed-minded, optimistic to pessimistic persona of the girl who was always trying to "slip the surly bonds of Earth and touch the face of God." Again, I quote from the poem, "High Flight" by John Gillespie Magee, Jr.

Today, as I began my jog along the flight path of so many planes aiming for the San Francisco Airport, I felt pretty darn happy. A great path, fabulous climate, and racing beside me over the water was plane after plane. Coooooool! I had it all and knew it. Life was proceeding as it should this fine California morning. In front of me was a portly man in a white shirt, suit coat flung easily over a shoulder and a rather large leather duffle bag under an arm. His white hair was blown into a single, well-brushed wave by the wind. I just knew he'd look sparkly from a frontal view, and as I passed, we exchanged greetings. He was so buoyant that I turned and jogged backward to pass on a few more words. His Irish accent was no surprise because the man was just as bubbly as any Fenian I'd ever met. He asked if I was on the path to witness the landing of the A-380. I couldn't believe my luck! My timing is far from perfect most of the time, but the fact that this gargantuan Airbus creation was due to come into view within the next five minutes blew me away!

I started to walk with the man, looking back to the approaching traffic with that same sense of wonder from bygone years at the end of a Montreal International runway with my flying pal, Brent Sutherland. "Is that it?" "Is that it?" we asked each other time and again as the moments passed and the inevitability of seeing the largest passenger aircraft known to man lodged itself into our collective reality. We were coming upon more and more people, all carrying cameras and watching the parade of scheduled flights as they landed. Anticipation personified!

I was looking for what? A big plane. And then, as we all stood in front of a cement fish cleaning station on a bank of San Francisco Bay, there it was. I felt like I was watching *Jaws* and I was about to hear, "We're going to need a bigger runway." It was a monster. A plane so large, so incredibly out of place in the line of previous aircraft, that I stopped breathing. I think we all did. Suddenly, among this crowd of respectful onlookers, I saw a man sitting on a cement wall and I felt drawn to his side. I wanted to sit beside someone looking through eyes like mine, without the imposition of any manufactured lens. We shared those moments, shoulder to shoulder, because we both knew that we were witnessing something that might or might not be *our* future in aviation. It was frightening and thrilling. What were we really looking at? A white elephant? The best thing to hit the sky since, what, Sputnik? A moving target? A monument to the memory of the *Titanic* or *Hindenburg*? All of the above?

Like the naysayers of yore who bemoaned our invasion of outer space and its drain on the national bank account, today marked my first hesitation point. Is the march toward a supersizing of aircraft customer-load capabilities the way to go? Somewhere at the gut level I feel it's not viable. Somehow, it's not safe, not necessary. I'm sure that the air-mile and load-factor ratio has been worked out to suit certain routes and demands, but reticence has replaced my open-armed welcome of new ideas. Just today. Just for this monster aircraft. This was a shock to my system. Will this resistance to something new forever be the line of demarcation between my accepting self and one who is a doddering old cuss with one foot in the past and the other on the cusp of obscurity?

Not being able to predict the future of aviation, but wanting to take the temperature of a microcosm of obviously rapt individuals, I interviewed men and women along that jogging path. "What do you think of the A-380?"

"I won't fly it until it's been around a few years."

"I can't see the point in it. Where the hell will anyone take that thing? Are there enough airports able to handle it?"

"I'll bet it's a fuel hound. A real gas guzzler!"

"You can't get two hundred people to agree on a the perfect airline food; how ya' gonna' get eight hundred to go in the same direction?"

"I think the market from here to Europe won't pay off. Maybe from here to Asia we could fill that plane and make it efficient."

"I'm going back to Fiji soon, and I won't get in anything as big as that."

Back at my hotel, on the elevator back to my floor, I asked a Louisiana native what he thought of this new, enormous A-380. He said, "I don't know anything about it and I don't care, but a lot of people laughed at the Wright Brothers, so what do I know?"

Fair enough. Humanity's march to the future has always

been marked by those who dream and others who hold back their support. Today I fell into the latter category for the first time in my life. I pray this doesn't become one of my many character flaws on a permanent basis.

So, I was moved. Moved and exhilarated, awestruck and, quite frankly, frightened when I watched that soundless approach and graceful descent as this monumental experiment skimmed the waters of San Francisco Bay. As others snapped photos, I leaned into that stranger, and we held our breaths as she landed with no less than perfection of style on a cool Thursday morning. I guess I might never fly on a plane like her, but I won't deny the beauty displayed. The sheer elegance of her presence. A grande dame making an entrance not to be forgotten. Ever. Like Sputnik oh so many decades ago, the image will stay with me. Why?

Is this the future? Was that satellite, so far in the past, once the future? I'm still looking up, and I highly recommend you do the same. Why not?

As long as we keep looking up and patiently wait for the next surprise to come into view there'll be avionic evolution. As I write this, I'm thirty-six thousand feet above sea level on an Airbus A-320. That little girl in her backyard looked up and saw a new thing. Sputnik seems so far back in time that I can't believe it even happened during my life! Perhaps some child looked at that A-380 this morning and somewhere ages and ages hence will be writing about some aviation conveyance yet unknown to me. Why? Because that youngster might keep looking up and waiting for that very chance. This worked for me. In fact, as much as I enjoy my life high above the clouds, there was something about just looking up that kept me grounded.

PART SIX
LANDING

RALEIGH, MY SPIRITUAL MECCA

THE AIRPORT GATES don't spark the imagination at all. They're all gray and plain, walls unadorned with the usual prideful displays of local talent and historical accomplishments seen at other terminals around the country. But the van service to the downtown hotel is always manned by one sort of personality or another willing to share all that one driver can possibly vocalize within a twenty-five-minute commute. Be the monologue about the historical points of interest, overcoming of a thirty-year drinking problem, or tales of what New Orleans and Biloxi were really like for the four months following Hurricane Katrina, each mile is guaranteed to be filled with words of passion, honesty, grace, and faith. That's what this story's about: faith, and how it feels when an infusion of sincere belief is delivered by a community of devout yet human entities.

In the recent past I was spiritually eviscerated. I encountered some folks who were elevated by mortal law onto a man-made high peak of self-congratulatory righteousness. Nature abhors a vacuum, thank heavens, so the void in my being was destined to be replenished by another.

There exists a purity in the air of Raleigh, North Carolina, a clarity that seems to give no protection from direct light. The atmosphere seems to have less molecular density, so the resistance felt in other places doesn't work against a soul in this modern city.

One night I arrived in the hotel lobby to find it jam packed with Shaw University alumni. Black and proud. Decked out and comfortable. Success on every tailored shoulder and poise on every shimmering dress. So much laughter and joy in the connection of old friends. Judging by the average age, the classmates must have been students just as the civil rights movement took shape on their campus, with the first sit-ins staged right there.

That hotel lobby, teaming with Shaw alumni, gave off a contagious vibrancy that only familiarity could evoke, and I fairly slid through it on my way to the elevator. I could feel myself inhaling the great vibes, but I wasn't exhaling so it felt like I was swelling. A needed outlet presented itself in the shape of an older black man standing by himself, sporting a nylon jacket and baseball cap. We locked eyes and I was drawn into his absolutely buoyant energy field. He said, "God bless you!" Feeling like I'd known and loved this entity in a past life and wanting more than a passing verbal touch, I went to him and we extended all four of our hands at the same time as though welcoming one another back into a warm, shared nest.

"Bless you, too. Are you here celebrating the Shaw homecoming tonight?" I asked.

"No, ahm jest heah in God's name trusting in a man who I drove heah. He left me heah to go get his money so's he could pay me that twelve dollah and a half he owe me. See? And if it be God's will, I be seein' him raht back heah with that twelve dollahs and fitty cents he owe me. I believe he'll be back very soon now."

Feeling at once skeptical, I asked this ancient how long his fare had been gone. "He bin gone quite some time, God bless him, but a'hl wait knowin' he'll do the right thing. I trust in God and Jesus and believe he'll be heah with my twelve dollahs and fitty cents." We still held hands, and my grip firmed up as I drew him closer to me and put my eyes into his, "You know, if he doesn't come back, you've still blessed him. He'll never forget you and your trust. If you don't get that money, he'll be paying it forward because he took some of you away with him, maybe the best part of him so far in his life!"

With an amazingly strong hug and a round of "God bless yous," we ended our chance meeting. I felt the molecules of this elder rubbing off on me and felt his gift come into me. Before the elevator doors closed I saw him standing alone in this place surrounded by so many, and thought he was the light that radiated all that could be good and true and divine in the world.

In Raleigh, getting personal and loving completely seems perfectly right. Unconditional love is rarely felt outside of a grandmother's kitchen these days, but once in a while, if you're ready, willing, and able to open yourself up to a society that lives and gives love just as naturally as the rest of us breathe air, then you'll probably be somewhere in North Carolina. Specifically, Raleigh.

I run. Having no sense of direction but a lot of endurance is the perfect combination if you want to meet people off the beaten paths in American cities. Hey, if I'm lost, I'm in extrovert heaven. So in every new place, I leave the hotel and just trot along with no particular place to go and usually a few hours to have mini-adventures and chance meetings with natives.

This day, cool and clear, I found myself on the sidelines of the Shaw homecoming parade, and it was great! The marching bands had more bounce and zip than any other I'd ever seen. The music, the beat, the fancy footwork inspired me to keep up the pace. The beauty queens of all ages were just that, beautiful and regal but without the cool arrogance of ladies I've seen in other open cars in other sorts of celebrations. These women seemed to know all the folks on the sidelines personally. Not in the literal sense, but with the commonality of race, pride, humor, and warmth exchanged in passing and felt by each side. Because I was overtaking the parade from the rear, I was catching up to these bands, banner-carrying children, marching local organizations, and the other participants. To be respectful, I went behind the crowds who watched from sidewalks around town. It wasn't long before I realized I was the only white person watching this, the best of the best parades I'd ever seen. Lucky me! This was the second time I'd felt so blessed since my arrival late the night before. I was enjoying the passing view so much that I reversed my direction to see it all over again, this time from beginning to end!

The very last group was one composed of young men and women who not only had fabulous marching and dancing music, but bodies that could dance. The costumes were rich magenta in color, and hems of bright yellow frills skirted the upper thighs of the girls who moved in ways that would throw my back into spasm if ever I tried to duplicate their gyrations. The result was my first set of tears that day. I stopped and just let the crying begin. The music, the movement, the pure, unadulterated joyous energy streaming out of that last group went through me and stopped at my backbone, then bounced back to reverberate from each of my ribs smack-dab into my heart! To feel such a tremendous surge of youthful bliss was my third blessing, and the day was yet so young!

As I jogged past Tupper Memorial Baptist Mission, an elderly lady turned around and smiled. I said, "This is the best parade I've ever seen!" She replied, "You've got that right," and extended two hands, which I took as I stopped in front of her. Her eyes were small and her face a map of tiny creases. She was so beautiful, and I felt that overflow of warmth again. Complete, perfect acceptance had come once again to me. I told her that Shaw graduated some wonderful people. She said, "They did, and you're wonderful, too." Why? Why this blanket of love for a stranger in their midst. I didn't have time to question before arms wrapped around me, and mine around this lady I'd probably never see again. "God bless you, girl," and with a warm chuckle she released me. "God bless you, too." Geez, I felt so good here in a town of missions, and churches, blessings, and the kindness of strangers. I felt no ulterior motives or evangelical pushing. I felt a purity of souls who share all with anyone just because.

The finale was a single horseman on a tall dappled animal. The cowboy's handsome nobility as he and his mount performed dressage steps up the street pushed my tear ducts into action again. The tall-in-the-saddle equestrian wore a perfectly tilted cowboy hat but rode English-style. So perfectly executed out of the competition ring, it sent a definite message. Class. Perfection under pressure. Cooperation. Control of self and the living thing beneath the rider. I thought, "Who was that cowboy in Michener's book *Centennial*? This fellow reminds me so much of him. That smart bearing that exudes confidence and complete knowledge of one's own innate power and intelligence. . . . what *was* that character's name? Then I looked up and saw the street name I was on: Person Street. The character in *Centennial* who had so impressed me was Nate Person. Okay, I accepted that answers to many things would come to me in this place. This town of open love was placed in my path to prove that I cynically lacked respect for organized religions because they've never provided me with answers, only dogma. There has never been an answer without a caveat attached to my mortal soul from the houses of faith I've tried. Raleigh seemed like the place where I could keep falling to a soft landing even as my spirit ascended to the heavens. How comfortable a seduction I was enjoying that morning.

As runners without destinations know, way leads onto way, but many a time we find ourselves passing the same landmarks again and again. I passed the same people as I made my way around town. They were on the move, and so was I, but we kept bumping into each other and our recognition bred a jocular relationship of sorts.

"You still runnin', girl?"

"I sure am, it feels super today!"

We sensed each other's feelings as we passed. I was in their heads and souls, and they came into mine. It was social intercourse of the highest order, a touching of souls at an intimate level. The natives of Raleigh have this every day, but I had it only that day, so I was compelled to hold onto each shock wave of sharing for all time. To make it a memory that I could draw upon when I needed or wanted to in my life. After being touched so, one must never forget the feelings of these encounters. Ever.

Coming to a stop light, there stood a tall man who reminded me of Bob Marley. I told him that I'd cried several times already that morning because of the music, hugs, and joy shared by the folks of Raleigh. "You like it here, then?" "No. I love it here! I love the people!" I didn't start running again because, as we walked across the road together, I felt like this man was holding a door open for me into his own personal world and inviting me to cross the threshold into his life. It felt that genuine and comfortable. Can anyone really be related that instantly? Most assuredly. We stopped where a crowd gathered in a line leading to something about 150 feet up ahead of us. He joined the queue, and we said our goodbyes. My curiosity got the better of me as I got to the front of the line and I asked someone what was going on. "This is the Brown Bag Ministry organization. We feed the homeless." I looked back down the long line of people and said, "All these people are homeless?" I felt that, for all the open, shared love and warmth I'd digested this day, that many of the people who'd given of themselves had donated love to my cause. My hunger for a tangible faith. My need for spiritual sustenance in a lonely, chilly world of impersonal meetings had been assuaged in a couple of hours of jogging. Now, I could see the trade-off. Hunger, be it of the physical or ethereal sort, isn't the end game. Each appetite is uncomfortable, undesirable, unrelenting in its quest for satisfaction. There are givers and takers in this world on both sides. We obviously need each other no matter what the vacuum of our existence craves. The eternal balance of life on Earth demands inequality of one sort or another. The miracle is when one needy soul meets the one from the other side, and both are whole beings during these chance encounters as long as eye contact can be endured. Raleigh is my mecca for life's tottering balance.

To mull over these amazing meetings and sensory stimulations, my footfalls took me back to the parade route that had caused me to think, feel, love, laugh, cry, and *believe* that there are those who walk the walk and not just talk the talk. I turned off Martin Luther King, Jr., Boulevard at yet another corner of the Shaw campus, the bells of the chapel chimed out "Amazing Grace," and I aimed toward the sound. By the time I saw the actual church, another hymn, unfamiliar to me, played. Then my late mother's favorite hymn came over the loudspeakers. "Rock of ages cleft for me, let me hide myself in Thee; Let the water and the blood from Thy wounded side which flowed, be of sin the double-cure; Save from wrath and make me pure."

I slowed and let a man of Shaw catch up to me, and I leaned my right arm against his left, sharing, "This was my mother's favorite hymn," and he said, "I was just singin' it to mahself." We walked side by side until the last note, then we just reached and gave each other's dangling hands a squeeze before parting for all time.

I came to Raleigh without any preconceived notion or expectation. The chance that my bitterness at the hypocrisy of a population living in a vacuum of dictated parameters would be erased by the simple humanity of another set of Americans never entered my consciousness as a possibility. Yet there it was. A concentration of healing that seemed to pour out of every single person I met. From the cabbie awaiting payment to the celebrants outside a mission, a lone cowboy, or those who spoke affably to a single jogger on a parade route of joyousness, one who shared my long-dead mother's favorite hymn, or that hungry, homeless, lovely man—all touched me and jump-started the wounded spiritual battery to my soul. Those who touch, share, love, open up, lock eyes, and trust one another unconditionally will never be hungry again. Raleigh, North Carolina, is where I'll go henceforth to renew my faith in that universal energy that binds us all. I don't think I need travel physically to this place of true divinity. No, I'll just close my eyes and remember the tender, unselfish, unself-conscious generosity of the inhabitants. Now ingrained for all time in my psyche, Raleigh will hereafter be my internal destination for the reaffirmation of my love for all of mankind. What the native there needs, I might have in abundance. What I lack for sustenance, they have waiting for me. Thank God—or the universal energy that binds us all—for such miracles.

HIGHBROW TO HOEDOWN IN VERMONT

July 10, 2010

"MEDICAL TEAM NEEDED here." Marybeth was first to answer the call. Erik came second. Heather B followed. We were tending to a seventy-two-year old woman on the cool floor of a bathroom stall of the Enosburg Opera house. There was nothing but cooperative effort. The situation was being handled properly, so I went out to monitor the departing population with Darryl, Carlton, and Dee. This audience had just enjoyed four hours of music and comedy. None in this mass exodus realized that we were in flight-attendant mode awaiting an ambulance as they hugged us and laughed their way out the door.

Picture this: a tiny Vermont town on a hot July evening, a stage set with hay bales, flowers, an antique chair, a wagon wheel, and a dozen tall potted trees. Flesh it out with a program that included everything from a safety demo to a carry-on baggage skit, opera to blue grass, rock 'n' roll to show tunes and a TSA (Transportation Security Administration) skit. With twenty-six individual acts, this show did go on (and on).

For over twenty years, Highbrow to Hoedown has entertained and raised thousands of dollars annually at the Enosburg Opera House in Enosburg Falls, Vermont, for various community needs. These extravaganzas began in 1987 on the deck over my backyard septic tank so that my children could experience acting, singing, dancing, comedy, and a sense of community up close and personal. It has evolved into "flights of fancy" for another generation's education.

Since 2009, Darryl has emceed, and the SkyNation crew members listed above now fly in, stay at my house, perform their hearts out, and blow the audience away with their multiple talents. Being flight attendants, we're all performers anyway, right?

This year offered another surprise. Marc, formerly with SkyNation at the Burlington Airport and now a veteran of another department, led us all to the stage to begin the four-hour, televised show. To his surprise, he was presented with cake in the shape of an A-320 built to scale. Created with seven boxes of Rice Krispies, twelve bags of marshmallows, and two pounds of butter, it took five of us to walk it up the aisle to Marc, who was on stage. Last year, Darryl received the A-320 because it was his birthday weekend, and he'd given it up to emcee the show. Marc took the cake this year because his attitude is so terribly positive no matter where he is.

Thousands of dollars were raised and divided among the

Missisquoi Union High School music and drama department, Future Farmers of America, the Benjamin J. Quattlebaum Fund, Rural Partnerships, and the Bellows Free Academy leadership course. The people of Vermont are generous and so in love with music and comedy that these shows make fund-raising easy. Two Positive Space Passes, usable to any SkyNation destination, were donated.

The entire night was set up as though the audience was on a jet. Sound effects, our uniforms, the announcements, and our individual performances were constant references to flight. The atmosphere was like a jovial, cohesive, super-amazing, fun flight where every crew member was having and giving everything we had to the customers and to each other. Each of us, from Marybeth's amazing acrobatics, Darryl's winning personality, Carlton's and Erik's incredible voices, Heather B's and Dee's classy and beautiful stage presence, and my ability to be a shameless fool thrilled the crowd time and again. We're full of surprises.

Yet as I zipped into the washroom to splash water on my face in preparation for the hugs we'd receive as we bid all a fond "Thanks for flying with us," I stopped being a comic when a faint "Could you help me, please?" came from a large bathroom stall. No, that's all it took to snap us into the SkyNation flight-attendant mode. The woman was cared for by some while the others maintained their stage presence and continued the "evacuation" process, thereby clearing the way for the medics who were to arrive.

I called the patient the next morning, and she said, "Heather, I can't believe how wonderful all of your friends were. They just dropped everything and helped me so very much. Who were they? How did they know what to do? Who was that man who made me feel so much better? Everyone was great, so kind, so wonderful."

My answer? "My friends. My SkyNation brothers and sisters." They sing, they dance, they act, they tumble, they help, they share. They *are* the best.

'TWAS THE NIGHT BEFORE CHRISTMAS (AT JFK)

'Twas the night before Christmas,
all the customers fussed.
Nobody was smiling at any of us.
Our uniforms hung, and we'd all fixed our hair,
In hopes that we'd see St. Nick way up there.
Most of us wanted to be home in our beds
While visions of *pay protect* danced in our heads.
And guys in their nice ties, girls in neat skirts
Had just settled our brains for a long night of work.
When out at gate ten there arose such a clatter,
That we all left the lounge to see what was the matter.
Away past the food court we flew in blurred flashes,
Hoping to God we'd not fall on our asses.

The crowd was atwitter as we reached all the noise;
Apparently none felt the season's great joys.
So we figured the problem must be ground delay,
And we fell to the task we were charged with that day.
The baritones started, the tenors jumped in;
Mezzos and sopranos began their begin.
The crowd settled down, some smiled, some teared up,
But mostly they listened and that was enough.

The crew members sang with voices so merry;
The folks now delayed forgot to be wary.
Instead they chimed in with their multiple tones;
I think most turned off their cellular phones.
After awhile the ground hold was lifted;
The people departed with moods very shifted.
It doesn't take much to turn 'em around
Once music is added and harmony found.

And I heard them declare as they walked out of sight:
It's great that we're flying on this blessed night.
As for us who were working these trips that were
    boarded,
A sparkle was added as each plane was loaded.
And we all declared, though connections were tight,
Merry Christmas to all
And have a great flight.

ACKNOWLEDGMENTS

Every person I've ever met in my life is a part of this book. Why? Each has left their own indelible impression on my heart and taught me how it feels to be treated well or the opposite. Formal academe aside, there's nothing like attending the school of this world's population to set one's life on its serendipitous path. If you're not on the following list, believe me, it's not because you've been forgotten. Love, Heather

A great editor/publisher, Joseph Pittman of Vantage Point Books. Of course, I met him on one of my flights and his amazing, dancing, devilish eyes inspired a conversation about his writing and, subsequently, mine. Kathy Brock, our amazing copy editor, who slapped me on the wrist when I sounded preachy and showed the patience of Job as she made great suggestions for improvement.

My daughter, Holly, for announcing, "We're selling the restaurant. We're selling the house. We're moving from Vermont to Florida...and, we're having a baby." These words were the kick in the pants I needed to think about getting a job that offered free travel for my family as a perk. (OH, they're still in Vermont running another local business.) I love you very much!

My son, Dave, who knows how to love unconditionally and has the heart of a lion and the soul of a very kind angel. You've become a great man, Dave. I love you bunches!

My grandson, Shea, because he's loved and just had such a blast whenever we'd fly to New York together! He loved the crews, the planes and helped me prepare the cabin for the next flight every time we landed. He wore cleaning gloves and was a super seat belt folder, even at three, four and five years of age! And I'll never forget how he stood up in the front row and said, "Good-bye, thanks for flying with us!" to over a hundred folks as they deplaned. You're a natural, Shea!

My Grandmother, Winifred Mae Bilton, who taught me the joy and rewards of writing and the absolutely natural way to greet every stranger as someone worthy of love and an invitation "home" for a good meal.

My Grandfather, Leonard Vivian James, Sr. who wrote memoirs. I read them when I was very young and learned that the written word, if honest, can guide someone's steps along Life's path.

Marc, who, while working all my departing flights, when I was commuting to my job in Manhattan, made SkyNation seem like the most amazingly fun place to work. It IS!

Lucinda, the SkyNation flight attendant who encouraged me to apply when she heard that I'd always wanted to be a "stewardess." I was flying from JFK to Burlington after a party in Manhattan and this great woman, without a catty quality in her soul, even gave me her crewmember identification number to put on my application. The rest is history.

My brothers and sisters in Sky. Words can't convey how proud I am to call you friends, confidants, wise counselors, hilarious, brilliant, responsible, diverse and ever-so-terrific fellow crewmembers. I've learned so much from all of you and, like the song says, "You're simply the BEST!" I love you.

Every person who's ever told me their stories during short or long flights. Thanks also to all the people who just give me a hug as they deplane. I'M SO LUCKY!

Leonard Cohen, my muse, the poet who feels everything as deeply as do I. Maybe more? I once traveled to Greece in search of this man, hoping to commune with his mind. We're both from Montreal and maybe that's why our hearts are exposed nerves. Someday, someday, I really hope to ask this, my favorite writer, if this is true.

My beloved, Rick Bushey. Two years before getting hired by SkyNation, I met this patient, funny, intelligent, warm, supportive and kind man. Where? On a SkyNation plane when both of us were just flying to Burlington out of JFK. I'm the luckiest woman in the world. Yes, I am.